The language of mental health

The language of mental health

WILLIAM E. FANN, M.D.

Professor of Psychiatry, Associate Professor of
Pharmacology, Baylor College of Medicine; Chief,
Psychiatry Service, Veterans Administration Hospital,
Houston, Texas

CHARLES E. GOSHEN, M.D.

Professor of Psychiatry, Department of Psychiatry,
Vanderbilt University, Nashville, Tennessee

Second edition

598146

THE C. V. MOSBY COMPANY

Saint Louis   1977

Second edition

Copyright © 1977 by The C. V. Mosby Company

All rights reserved. No part of this book may be reproduced
in any manner without written permission of the publisher.

Previous edition copyrighted 1973

Printed in the United States of America

Distributed in Great Britain by Henry Kimpton, London

The C. V. Mosby Company
11830 Westline Industrial Drive, St. Louis, Missouri 63141

Library of Congress Cataloging in Publication Data

Fann, William E
    The language of mental health.

    Includes index.
    1. Psychiatry—Terminology. 2. Psychiatry—
Dictionaries. I. Goshen, Charles E., joint author.
II. Title. [DNLM: 1. Mental health—Dictionary.
WM13 F213L]
RC454.4.F36 1977   616.8′9′0014   76-40210
ISBN 0-8016-1548-8

GW/VH/VH 9 8 7 6 5 4 3 2 1

To

Eddie, Patsy, and **Alice**

PREFACE

The study of human behavior has emerged only relatively recently from the appellation of "fledgling science" and been recognized as the highly developed, highly complex, medical discipline that it is. With the continuing growth of the mental health and behavioral sciences, there has been a predictable expansion of technical vocabulary within the affected disciplines. Several good dictionaries and glossaries specialize in psychiatry, psychology, and related areas of thought and practice. Hinsie, Campbell, and Shatzky's *Psychiatric Dictionary,* now in its 4th edition, remains an important reference volume. Benjamin Wolman's *Dictionary of Behavioral Science* attempts a comprehensive and authoritative treatment of terminology within the field and approaches its goal admirably. The twenty-fifth edition of Dorland's *Illustrated Medical Dictionary* is an outstanding contribution to medical communication and scholarship, in the behavioral sciences as well as in the other medical disciplines. Less ambitious but nevertheless useful and carefully compiled behavioral science glossaries include the American Psychiatric Association's paperback *Psychiatric Glossary* and Owen White's *Glossary of Behavioral Terminology,* which specializes in investigatory aspects of psychiatry and psychology.

The compilers of each of these dictionaries and glossaries agree that proper and carefully considered standardization of vocabulary is vital to communication and advancement in any field of endeavor. They also agree that the rapid growth and reassessment of data and knowledge in the mental health and behavioral sciences imposes unique difficulties on their efforts to develop precise and complete definitions for terms that often mean different things to different well-informed people. Mutability is the only immutable thing about language at home and in the grocery store, as well as in the context of science. These changes are not unwelcome, though they do engender some confusion during transitional periods. There is a strong sense, particularly in science, that we benefit from a sort of Darwinism of terminology, that in an age of large-scale scientific experimentation we tend to drop from usage terms that expanding knowledge has proven obsolete or imprecise, and sharpen our definitions and understanding of terms that endure under closer scrutiny.

In this second edition, we have attempted to act on the recognition that the connotations and definitions of words can change rapidly. Since the first edition of this volume, much material has required reconsideration, with consequent expansions, deletions, or additional clarifications. The introductory remarks in each chapter have been revised, and many definitions have been altered on the basis of scientific work conducted during the intervening years by our colleagues in the field of mental health. In the first edition, for example, we indicated in the definition of alphagenics some skepticism about the legitimacy of this modality and referred to a paucity of carefully compiled data on the subject. In the years since this was written, a considerable amount of additional research has been done in alphagenics, and there is now every indication that it is a potentially important treatment technique for a variety of disturbances including vascular headache and severe epilepsy. The definition has accordingly been brought into conformity with the best current information. These remarks are also intended to provide some sense of the mental health and behavioral science disciplines to individuals in legal, governmental, and other professions that are coming into increasing contact with the issues of psychiatry, psychology, and social dynamics.

Although this volume falls generally within the genre of the glossary, that is, a list of unfamiliar terms and definitions, it differs in several important respects. The first of these is that the book is intended to be read as a text rather than as a reference work to be consulted only in response to specific questions. We hope to provide the reader with an introduction to the professional realm of mental health, mental illness, and behavioral science through instruction in the daily terminology of these professions.

As a text, it is not within the purview of this volume to provide the reader with a complete compilation of behavioral science terminology. We would refer any professional who requires this sort of comprehensiveness to Hinsie, Campbell, and Shatzky or to Wolman. The choice of terms has been determined most significantly by the prominence of a word in general mental health and behavioral science usage. The words chosen for definition will provide the undergraduate, intern, first-year resident, nursing or social work student with a basic working vocabulary with which to enter the study of mental disturbance and its treatment.

As in the first edition, we have attempted to avoid compounding bewilderment through definition of one technical term with another. Lay terms have been used in the discussions and definitions whenever possible, and cross-referencing has been minimized. For those who choose to use the book as a conventional glossary, an index with which to locate a term in response to a specific question has been added to this edition. Otherwise, we have maintained the format of arranging seven separately alphabetized vocabulary lists, each relating to the individual chapter subjects and intended to provide a representative sampling of issues and concerns germane to the subject.

Mrs. Nancy Berry patiently and carefully prepared the manuscript for the second edition and Bruce Richman of Baylor College of Medicine and the Houston Veterans Administration Hospital Research Service served as special editorial assistant; we are grateful for their assistance.

William E. Fann

Charles E. Goshen

CONTENTS

Appendixes

Introduction

Mental health professionals conduct their work in psychiatric hospitals, psychiatric units of general hospitals, state government departments of mental hygiene, counseling centers, schools for the retarded, community mental health centers, and private practice. The principal disciplines in which these professionals work include psychiatry and neurology, nursing, social work, psychology, pharmacology, sociology, rehabilitative medicine, and medical administration. As social and medical issues continue to converge around matters of mental health and mental illness, professionals from a variety of other fields are now being called on to participate in the process of providing and maintaining services for individuals suffering from emotional and mental disturbances. Individuals entering the mental health professions through the traditional disciplines, as well as those whose involvement emerges from other areas of expertise, must be suitably grounded in a common professional terminology. Our intention in preparing a volume of this type is to provide an introduction to the essential matters of mental health and mental disorder and to elucidate a basic vocabulary for students and practitioners entering the field from various training backgrounds. As the requirements and functions of mental health practice increase, the requirements of terminology necessarily increase, and words and concepts once considered in the exclusive province of law or statistics are now found to have important applications in psychiatry, psychology, and social work.

To a large extent, the language used in the mental health professions is the language of the behavioral sciences. In addition, the literature in the field reveals a rather extensive use of language taken from other fields, such as law and statistics. In general, the latter examples are used in communicating information about social problems or about research.

In addition to the professionals working in the mental health field who are directly concerned with patient or client contacts, there are other, usually administrative, personnel. These people are especially in need of information about the technical language used by the professionals, since their training is not so likely to have included a familiarity with it. In addition, the students who are either seeking general background knowledge in the field or planning to specialize in some phase of it will find valuable a collection of the various glossaries used.

Since the concept of behavioral science is currently unstandardized, differing definitions emanating from different sources will be encountered. In general, however, the concept has come into use only recently to mean a group of sciences that have in common the study of human behavior, rather than a particular science. In the typical university, these separate sciences are not collected together under any unifying organization, but tend to operate and evolve quite independently of each other. Nevertheless, each one tends to find access to and to make use of the knowledge, research, and other developments originating in the

1

others. Also, it is becoming increasingly common, although not yet very widespread, for people trained in one of these disciplines to work, teach, study, or do research in a department primarily devoted to one of the others in the group. A department of psychiatry in a medical school, for instance, may have on its faculty one or more psychologists, social workers, and, more rarely, anthropologists or sociologists. Each one of the various behavioral sciences, in turn, is often found to be subdivided or subdepartmentalized into specialty areas that may appear to be almost identical to a subspecialty in another. For instance, social psychology may appear to be much the same as certain types of sociology. In such cases the similarities are indeed considerable in respect to the content of the body of knowledge studied. However, there is likely to be a much greater difference in how the knowledge is used in each subspecialty. It is usually valid to conclude that the similarities among the behavioral sciences are manifested mostly by the body of information in use, whereas the differences are manifested by the kind of professional activities in which the members of each discipline engage.

The fact that a great deal of overlapping of the knowledge or information used in the various behavioral sciences does exist makes this book relevant, for the terminology used in any one behavioral science tends to be used in the others also. Nevertheless, there is also likely to be a tendency for one discipline to attach a different meaning to a particular concept from that given in another discipline. In other words, the commonality of language does not, unfortunately, coincide with a commonality of definition. Historically, these differences in meaning probably occurred because a given scientific discipline became familiar with the older, rather than the newer, literature in another related discipline and adopted the definitions implied or stated in the past. Meanwhile the discipline in which the terminology had originated might have developed in new directions, thereby giving old terms new meanings.

Some of the various fields of study or work

that can be considered as sharing in the body of knowledge of the behavioral sciences include:

1. Psychiatry
   a. Psychoanalysis
   b. Child psychiatry
   c. Forensic psychiatry
   d. Community psychiatry
2. Psychology
   a. Educational psychology
   b. Clinical psychology
   c. Experimental psychology
   d. Human factors
   e. Social psychology
3. Sociology
4. Anthropology
5. Social work
   a. Medical social work
   b. Psychiatric social work
6. Psychiatric nursing

Psychiatry is one of the specialties of clinical medicine comparable to internal medicine, surgery, pediatrics, and obstetrics. Psychiatrists undergo the same medical school training as the other specialists and receive an MD degree. After internship (usually 1 year), they then spend varying numbers of years training in the specialty. There are 17,000 to 20,000 physicians in the United States who call themselves psychiatrists. Those who undergo a rather rigorous, prescribed course of training and then, after 5 years, take a series of competitive examinations may succeed in becoming recognized by the American Board of Psychiatry and Neurology as certified specialists. Less than half of those physicians calling themselves psychiatrists have gone through this process to become "Diplomates" of the American Boards. In this specialty, patients with psychiatric problems are, of course, the focus of attention, and their treatment and disposition constitute the practice of psychiatry.

There are some people who have undergone certain kinds of training, but are not physicians, and who call themselves psychoanalysts. For the most part, however, a psychoanalyst is first a psychiatrist (therefore a physician) and then a psychoanalyst. There are no legal or licensing regulations to standardize the qualifications; hence the differences. In general, the typical psychoanalyst completes his training first as a psychiatrist; then he enters one of the 23 or so psychoanalytic training centers in the country for 3 to 5 years of additional training in the theory and practice of psychoanalysis. In other words, the psychoanalyst differs from the psychiatrist who is not one of this group principally in having had several additional years of training. In the past there tended to be a fairly marked difference between what a psychoanalyst did (almost always in private practice, and treating individual patients in relatively small numbers but over relatively long periods of time) and what other psychiatrists did. In recent years, however, the differences have become less marked. Psychoanalysts may now be found in teaching, research, and administrative positions, or working in hospitals; nonpsychoanalytic psychiatrists may be found working in private practice, treating patients in much the same way as the psychoanalysts do.

When a psychiatrist confines his training and practice (seldom completely, however) to the treatment of children instead of adults, he becomes known as a child (pediatric) psychiatrist. This is now a recognized subspecialty of psychiatry.

Forensic psychiatrists confine all or a large part of their practice either to the management of criminals who have psychiatric problems or to various kinds of courtroom work associated with making psychiatric evaluations of offenders brought to the attention of the court. Recently, special kinds of training have been developed to facilitate the development of this small subspecialty. In the past, it was not so likely that the forensic psychiatrist had a special kind of training. Formerly, the psychiatrist engaged in this kind of work was often referred to as an alienist.

Community psychiatry specifies where a psychiatrist (and other professionals such as social workers and psychologists) might work rather than a specific kind of work or training. Recently there has been a fairly rapid increase in comprehensive centers for community psychiatry as a result of a federal program that provides subsidies. These are all-purpose centers that seek to provide a wide spectrum of psychiatric or mental health services to a community. These centers are almost always supported by public agencies.

Psychology is a diverse field, with a rather large number of members. The field is typically represented in the liberal arts division of a university as a department comparable to departments such as English, geology, or history. In a university department, courses in introductory and more advanced types of psychology are offered to the general student body; these courses are very widely attended in almost all universities. Students seeking certification as teachers typically take one or more courses in psychology. Those who become specialists in psychology usually do so by working toward a graduate degree (master's or doctor's) in the field, and then most often concentrate on one of the several specialized fields. The various categories of psychological subjects studied are expressed in the list of courses offered by a department of psychology in a typical university: Learning and Motivation, Industrial Psychology, Abnormal Psychology, Statistics and Research Design, Personality Theory, Experimental Psychology, Sensory and Perceptual Psychology, Advertising Psychology, Psychology of Disadvantaged Children, Social Psychology, and Engineering Psychology.

The specialist in educational psychology usually works in a school's guidance department. He will have been trained in the administration and interpretation of achievement and placement tests and may work either in the general design of curricula and instruction or in the individual study of children having special learning problems.

The clinical psychologist is trained in the administration and interpretation of personality evaluation tests and intelligence tests, and is likely to work with psychiatrists and social workers in a mental hygiene clinic or in the counseling center of a college. He is involved either directly or indirectly in the evaluation and treatment of psychologically maladjusted people.

The experimental, or research, psychologist

generally works in a psychological laboratory (most often in a university), where he engages in research that may range from studies of animal behavior to computerized or statistical analyses of data.

The social psychologist is usually a researcher, and he may work in a university or in private business, especially in market-survey types of enterprises. His studies are concerned with the behavior of groups (for example, people's voting or buying habits), and thus he often appears to be doing work very similar to that of a sociologist.

Like psychology, the field of sociology is usually a separate liberal arts department in universities. It is not to be confused with social service. Much of what is true about psychology can be applied to sociology, with the difference that the former tends to focus attention on the behavior (such as learning and thinking) of individuals, whereas sociology directs its attention to the behavior of a society as a whole or to its subcultures. It is common for college students to take courses in sociology even when they do not intend to specialize in the field, and those who do specialize are most likely to do so at the graduate level (master's or doctor's degree level). The subspecialties of sociology are not as well demarcated as they are in psychology. It is becoming increasingly common for sociologists, psychologists, and anthropologists to either work together or to make similar kinds of studies. An index of the scope of interest in the field is evident in a typical list of courses offered by a university's sociology department: American Social Problems, Social Stratification, American Ethnic Groups, Social Change, Collective Behavior, Bureaucratic Organization, Criminology, Urban and Political Change, Family, Industrial Sociology, Community Structure, and Sociology of Religion.

The social worker is a professional who has been trained in a school of social work. This training typically is a graduate-level program leading to the degree of MSW (Master of Social Work). Social workers usually work for service organizations, either tax-supported or nonprofit private organizations; only rarely do they work with profit-making organizations. Their work is usually directed toward helping guide and advise individual clients or families who have social problems. Many of them work in public welfare agencies and deal directly with the welfare clients, assisting them in managing their resources and planning their lives. Smaller numbers of social workers are employed in school systems, where they assist students and their families with social problems. Still others work in specialized kinds of counseling agencies that are concerned with clients having problems related to birth control, adoption, foster homes, and so on.

Medical social work is a subspecialty of social work requiring special training that leads to the worker's qualifying for positions in hospitals. These workers assist patients in coping with family problems, financial problems, or various problems associated with physical disabilities and helping patients gain access to other community services or qualify for various kinds of benefits (such as insurance).

Closely related to medical social work, and properly regarded as another subdivision of this specialty, psychiatric social workers are likely to be found in a mental health clinic. The psychiatric social worker works with psychiatrists and psychologists. In the subdivision of responsibility often taking place in such multidisciplinary settings, the psychiatric social worker often has the task of working with the families of clients.

Psychiatric nursing is related to general nursing as psychiatry is to general medicine. In a comprehensive nursing school, all students probably receive a course in this specialty. Others go on to specialize in it exclusively. Psychiatric nurses are typically less involved with the actual physical care than nurses working in medical or surgical hospital units, but are much more involved in personally interacting with patients. The psychiatric nurse is usually trained in group therapy and in daily management of individuals whose mental illness is of such magnitude that hospitalization is required. The nurse and nurse's aide customarily have more direct contact with psychiatric patients than any other members of the treatment team, and their careful observations and reports of an individual's behavior and progress are critical to the process of therapy.

Psychiatric nurses and nurse's aides are highly trained in providing patients with interpersonal therapeutic experiences. Most mental health professionals agree that verbal exchange between the mentally ill individual and a sympathetic mentally healthy individual is an effective therapeutic technique in helping the patient to reestablish nonpathological communication with the world at large. Although all members of the hospital treatment team contribute to this process, registered nurses, licensed vocational or practical nurses, and nurse's aides invariably make the greatest contribution. In almost every psychiatric hospital or general hospital psychiatry service, the nursing staff spends more time in direct contact with patients than any other member of the treatment team.

CHAPTER 1

Mental disorder

The development of knowledge in the mental health professions during this century has been marked most prominently by the development of a standard diagnostic scheme and by large-scale research involving the causes, natures, and cures of mental disorders. Before the twentieth century, there was little distinction understood between the variety of mental disorders and virtually no standardization of terminology. General agreement concerning diagnostic terms and characteristics provides professionals with the ability to exchange information and to consider information with greater precision. The American Psychiatric Association publishes the second edition of the Diagnostic and Statistical Manual (DSM II), including names and descriptions of all recognized psychiatric pathology. A third edition of the manual, which will reflect adjustments in some psychiatric concepts since 1969, is in preparation.

In the early days of psychiatry, people with disturbances of thought or mood were conveniently classified into two groups: those whose general level of activity and excitement was high and those whose level was low. The more active, excited individuals were referred to as manic and the more subdued group as melancholic. This schema was modified by the German psychiatrist Emil Kraepelin when he identified common characteristics in a number of previously unrelated diagnoses and applied the single term *dementia praecox* to major psychiatric disorders that displayed a consistent process of thought and personality deterioration. In the 1920s, Eugen Bleuler suggested that

the term *schizophrenia,* meaning "separated from reason," be substituted for dementia praecox. Schizophrenia remains the principal diagnostic term for the most commonly seen type of psychotic disturbance.

Important diagnostic distinctions to be made in an individual patient are: (1) whether the condition is organically determined, that is, whether the brain is injured or diseased, and (2) whether the disturbance is a product of psychodynamics, the disorganization of defense mechanisms normally employed. Organic and dynamic psychiatric disorders often manifest similar symptoms. The most prominent of the psychiatric diagnoses are neurosis, affective disorders, and psychosis.

The neuroses are subclassified as anxiety neurosis, hysterical neurosis, phobic neurosis, obsessive-compulsive neurosis, and several other types. The neuroses are emotional disorders generally characterized by unresolved conflicts and anxiety. Although their degree of psychopathology is considered to be of substantially less magnitude than that of the psychoses, the components of anxiety, fear, and feelings of helplessness, which are often seen as symptoms of neurosis, can be severely unpleasant and, at times, disabling. Although serious disorientation, delusional thinking, and personality disintegration are not common elements of neurosis, as they are of psychosis, these symptoms can occur transiently in some neurotic episodes.

The affective disorders include depression and manic depression. They are characterized by disturbances of mood of such seriousness that the individual is significantly limited in his ability to function. Manic depression is considered an affective psychosis, and is usually characterized by alternating periods of severe depression and inappropriate elation. The individual suffering from manic depression experiences delusions and other forms of unrealistic thinking, including feelings of omnipotence during periods of elation and feeling of utter worthlessness during periods of depression.

Psychosis is considered the most severe of the general psychiatric disorders. It is characterized primarily by delusional thinking, disorganized thinking, hallucinations, memory disturbance, and gross inability to respond appropriately to the regular requirements of daily life. The principal subcategory among the psychoses is schizophrenia, which is not, as often thought, the "split personality" syndrome associated with Dr. Jekyll and Mr. Hyde. Schizophrenia is itself subclassified into several distinct types, but generally characteristic of all the schizophrenias is severe disturbance of thought processes, behavior, conceptualization and mood. The schizophrenic will often display bizarre behavior, conversational patterns in which normal associations seem to be ignored, and a strangely withdrawn mood. Simple schizophrenia is primarily characterized by withdrawal, apathy, and diminished intellectual functioning. Hebephrenic schizophrenia is marked by severely disorganized thinking, giggling, unusual posturing, prolonged periods of gazing into mirrors, and many complaints about physical health. Paranoid schizophrenia is most notably characterized by frightening delusions that the individual is the intended victim of people or forces desiring his destruction. The paranoid schizophrenic may be hostile in his attempts to defend himself against imagined enemies, and his thinking is often religiously oriented. Hallucinations are a common component of paranoid schizophrenia. Catatonic schizophrenia is marked by either an unusual increase in motor activity, or, more commonly, by complete withdrawal, refusal to speak, and maintenance of a fixed posture for considerable lengths of time. Other diagnostic subcategories of schizophrenia and psychosis are referred to in the glossary section of this chapter.

Various organic brain syndromes associated with disease or injury can manifest themselves in disturbances of thought and behavior. We have, therefore, included in this section a selection of terms associated with organic brain and neurological deficits that manifest themselves, in whole or in part, in psychiatric symptoms.

The concept of differential diagnosis is used in the mental health professions in much the same way as in other branches of medicine. With a given list of facts from which to choose a diagnosis, it often happens that the choice is not easy or self-evident, and more than one possibility seems likely. The list of choices that most likely includes the correct one is called the differential diagnosis. Diagnosis by exclusion is the process of finding evidence that eliminates certain choices from the list, thus leaving a final diagnosis. Final diagnosis is a term used to distinguish a diagnostic label attached to a certain case at the end of a hospital stay, for instance, from the diagnostic label previously used, called either admission diagnosis or tentative diagnosis. In either of the latter examples, it is assumed that more information is needed before a final decision can be determined.

Sometimes a certain piece of evidence concerning a case is said to be diagnostic, or pathognomonic. The implication is that that particular piece of evidence is the conclusive one needed to make the final choice of diagnosis. Similarly, other pieces of evidence are said to be nondiagnostic if they support more than one possible diagnosis.

Another term used frequently in diagnosis is syndrome. A syndrome is a set of signs or symptoms that occur together but that have no discernible common cause. In other words, a given syndrome may be found in various patients for whom differing diagnoses have been made. For instance, the hyperventilation syndrome may be found both in a patient with a condition that has been diagnosed as psychoneurosis and in one with a condition diagnosed as schizophrenia.

The diagnostic nomenclature
LIST OF MENTAL DISORDERS AND
THEIR CODE NUMBERS*

I. *Mental retardation*

Mental retardation (310-315)
310 Borderline mental retardation
311 Mild mental retardation
312 Moderate mental retardation
313 Severe mental retardation
314 Profound mental retardation
315 Unspecified mental retardation

The fourth-digit sub-divisions cited below should be used with each of the above categories. The associated physical condition should be specified as an additional diagnosis when known.

.0 Following infection or intoxication
.1 Following trauma or physical agent
.2 With disorders of metabolism, growth or nutrition
.3 Associated with gross brain disease (postnatal)
.4 Associated with diseases and conditions due to (unknown) prenatal influence
.5 With chromosomal abnormality
.6 Associated with prematurity
.7 Following major psychiatric disorder
.8 With psycho-social (environmental) deprivation
.9 With other (and unspecified) condition

II. *Organic brain syndromes*

(Disorders caused by or associated with impairment of brain tissue function)

II-A. *Psychoses associated with organic brain syndromes (290-294)*

290 Senile and pre-senile dementia
.0 Senile dementia
.1 Pre-senile dementia
291 Alcoholic psychosis
.0 Delirium tremens
.1 Korsakov's psychosis (alcoholic)
.2 Other alcoholic hallucinosis

.3 Alcohol paranoid state (Alcoholic paranoia)
.4 Acute alcohol intoxication
.5 Alcoholic deterioration
.6 Pathological intoxication
.9 Other (and unspecified) alcoholic psychosis
292 Psychosis associated with intracranial infection
.0 Psychosis with general paralysis
.1 Psychosis with other syphilis of central nervous system
.2 Psychosis with epidemic encephalitis
.3 Psychosis with other and unspecified encephalitis
.9 Psychosis with other (and unspecified) intracranial infection
293 Psychosis associated with other cerebral condition
.0 Psychosis with cerebral arteriosclerosis
.1 Psychosis with other cerebrovascular disturbance
.2 Psychosis with epilepsy
.3 Psychosis with intracranial neoplasm
.4 Psychosis with degenerative disease of the central nervous system
.5 Psychosis with brain trauma
.9 Psychosis with other (and unspecified) cerebral condition
294 Psychosis associated with other physical condition
.0 Psychosis with endocrine disorder
.1 Psychosis with metabolic or nutritional disorder
.2 Psychosis with systemic infection
.3 Psychosis with drug or poison intoxication (other than alcohol)
.4 Psychosis with childbirth
.8 Psychosis with other and undiagnosed physical condition
.9 Psychosis with unspecified physical condition

II-B. *Non-psychotic organic brain syndromes (309)*

309 Non-psychotic organic brain syndromes (Mental disorders not specified as psychotic associated with physical conditions)
.0 Non-psychotic OBS with intracranial infection

*From Diagnostic and statistical manual of mental disorders, ed. 2, Washington, D.C., 1968, American Psychiatric Association.

.1 Non-psychotic OBS with drug, poison, or systemic intoxication
.13 Non-psychotic OBS with alcohol (simple drunkenness)
.14 Non-psychotic OBS with other drug, poison, or systemic intoxication
.2 Non-psychotic OBS with brain trauma
.3 Non-psychotic OBS with circulatory disturbance
.4 Non-psychotic OBS with epilepsy
.5 Non-psychotic OBS with disturbance of metabolism, growth or nutrition
.6 Non-psychotic OBS with intracranial neoplasm
.8 Non-psychotic OBS with degenerative disease of central nervous system
.9 Non-psychotic OBS with other (and unspecified) physical condition
.91 Acute brain syndrome, not otherwise specified
.92 Chronic brain syndrome, not otherwise specified

III. *Psychoses not attributed to physical conditions listed previously (295-298)*

295 Schizophrenia
.0 Schizophrenia, simple type
.1 Schizophrenia, hebephrenic type
.2 Schizophrenia, catatonic type
.23 Schizophrenia, catatonic type, excited
.24 Schizophrenia, catatonic type, withdrawn
.3 Schrizophrenia, paranoid type
.4 Acute schizophrenic episode
.5 Schizophrenia, latent type
.6 Schizophrenia, residual type
.7 Schrizophrenia, schizo-affective type
.73 Schrizophrenia, schizo-affective type, excited
.74 Schrizophrenia, schizo-affective type, depressed
.8 Schizophrenia, childhood type
.90 Schrizophrenia, chronic undifferentiated type
.99 Schizophrenia, other (and unspecified) types

296 Major affective disorders (Affective psychoses)
.0 Involutional melancholia
.1 Manic-depressive illness, manic type (Manic-depressive psychosis, manic type)
.2 Manic-depressive illness, depressed type (Manic-depressive psychosis, depressed type)
.3 Manic-depressive illness, circular type (Manic-depressive psychosis, circular type)
.33 Manic-depressive illness, circular type, manic
.34 Manic-depressive illness, circular type, depressed
.8 Other major affective disorder (Affective psychoses, other)
.9 Unspecified major affective disorder (Affective disorder not otherwise specified) (Manic-depressive illness not otherwise specified)

297 Paranoid states
.0 Paranoia
.1 Involutional paranoid state (Involutional paraphrenia)
.9 Other paranoid state

298 Other psychoses
.0 Psychotic depressive reaction (Reactive depressive psychosis)
.1 Reactive excitation
.2 Reactive confusion (Acute or subacute confusional state)
.3 Acute paranoid reaction
.9 Reactive psychosis, unspecified

299 Unspecified psychosis (Dementia, insanity or psychosis not otherwise specified)

IV. *Neuroses (300)*

300 Neuroses
.0 Anxiety neurosis
.1 Hysterical neurosis
.13 Hysterical neurosis, conversion type
.14 Hysterical neurosis, dissociative type
.2 Phobic neurosis
.3 Obsessive compulsive neurosis
.4 Depressive neurosis
.5 Neurasthenic neurosis (Neurasthenia)
.6 Depersonalization neurosis (Depersonalization syndrome)
.7 Hypochondriacal neurosis
.8 Other neurosis
.9 Unspecified neurosis

V. *Personality disorders and certain other non-psychotic mental disorders (301-304)*

301 Personality disorders
   .0 Paranoid personality
   .1 Cyclothymic personality (Affective personality)
   .2 Schizoid personality
   .3 Explosive personality
   .4 Obsessive compulsive personality (Anankastic personality)
   .5 Hysterical personality
   .6 Asthenic personality
   .7 Antisocial personality
   .81 Passive-aggressive personality
   .82 Inadequate personality
   .89 Other personality disorders of specified types
   .9 Unspecified personality disorder
302 Sexual deviations
   .0 Homosexuality
   .1 Fetishism
   .2 Pedophilia
   .3 Transvestitism
   .4 Exhibitionism
   .5 Voyeurism
   .6 Sadism
   .7 Masochism
   .8 Other sexual deviation
   .9 Unspecified sexual deviation
303 Alcoholism
   .0 Episodic excessive drinking
   .1 Habitual excessive drinking
   .2 Alcohol addiction
   .9 Other (and unspecified) alcoholism
304 Drug dependence
   .0 Drug dependence, opium, opium alkaloids and their derivatives
   .1 Drug dependence, synthetic analgesics with morphinelike effects
   .2 Drug dependence, barbiturates
   .3 Drug dependence, other hypnotics and sedatives or tranquilizers
   .4 Drug dependence, cocaine
   .5 Drug dependence, Cannabis sativa (hashish, marihuana)
   .6 Drug dependence, other psycho-stimulants
   .7 Drug dependence, hallucinogens
   .8 Other drug dependence
   .9 Unspecified drug dependence

VI. *Psychophysiologic disorders (305)*

305 Psychophysiologic disorders (Physical disorders of presumably psychogenic origin)
   .0 Psychophysiologic skin disorder
   .1 Psychophysiologic musculoskeletal disorder
   .2 Psychophysiologic respiratory disorder
   .3 Psychophysiologic cardiovascular disorder
   .4 Psychophysiologic hemic and lymphatic disorder
   .5 Psychophysiologic gastro-intestinal disorder
   .6 Psychophysiologic genito-urinary disorder
   .7 Psychophysiologic endocrine disorder
   .8 Psychophysiologic disorder of organ of special sense
   .9 Psychophysiologic disorder of other type

VII. *Special symptoms (306)*

306 Special symptoms not elsewhere classified
   .0 Speech disturbance
   .1 Specific learning disturbance
   .2 Tic
   .3 Other psychomotor disorder
   .4 Disorders of sleep
   .5 Feeding disturbance
   .6 Enuresis
   .7 Encopresis
   .8 Cephalalgia
   .9 Other special symptom

VIII. *Transient situational disturbances (307)*

307 Transient situational disturbances
   .0 Adjustment reaction of infancy
   .1 Adjustment reaction of childhood
   .2 Adjustment reaction of adolescence
   .3 Adjustment reaction of adult life
   .4 Adjustment reaction of late life

IX. *Behavior disorders of childhood and adolescence (308)*

308 Behavior disorders of childhood and adolescence (Behavior disorders of childhood)
   .0 Hyperkinetic reaction of childhood (or adolescence)

.1 Withdrawing reaction of childhood (or adolescence)
.2 Overanxious reaction of childhood (or adolescence)
.3 Runaway reaction of childhood (or adolescence)
.4 Unsocialized aggressive reaction of childhood (or adolescence)
.5 Group delinquent reaction of childhood (or adolescence)
.9 Other reaction of childhood (or adolescence)

X. *Conditions without manifest psychiatric disorder and non-specific conditions (316-318)*

316 Social maladjustments without manifest psychiatric disorder
.0 Marital maladjustment
.1 Social maladjustment
.2 Occupational maladjustment
.3 Dyssocial behavior
.9 Other social maladjustment
317 Non-specific conditions
318 No mental disorder

XI. *Non-diagnostic terms for administrative use (319)*

319 Non-diagnostic terms for administrative use
.0 Diagnosis deferred
.1 Boarder
.2 Experiment only
.9 Other

SYMPTOMS AND PSYCHOPATHOLOGY

In general medicine, a symptom is any sign in the patient of an unusual state of health that is perceived by the patient or by the physician. Ordinarily, it is assumed that a symptom indicates the presence of a disease, but any marked physiological sign (such as rapid heart rate) may be misinterpreted as a sign of disease by either the patient or the physician. Similarly, in psychiatry a symptom is a noticeable sign of an unusual state of mental health, ordinarily suspected to be indicative of a psychopathological condition. A psychopathological condition, in turn, is any piece of psychologically abnormal behavior, comparable to a pathological condition in general medicine, which is a manifestation of any disease or injury. Patients seeking help for mental health problems are likely to complain of rather ordinary events or sensations as if they were indicative of a serious disorder. Therefore, a frequently occurring debate among mental health professionals is concerned with the question of whether a patient's given complaint is psychopathological. In these cases, more distinctions are likely to be made in the mental health professions between a complaint and a symptom than is the rule in general medicine. In general medicine it is usually assumed that what the patient complains about is a symptom, and that if there is a symptom, then there is a disease (pathological condition). The same reasoning is not followed as closely in the mental health professions. Instead, patients seen by mental health professionals not infrequently have evident psychopathological conditions; that is, they have some kind of unusual or abnormal psychological condition, and they usually have complaints. But these complaints are not always symptoms; they may be mere fantasies or normal physiological events.

The difference, then, between a symptom and a psychopathological condition is that the latter is any abnormal psychological state or condition (such as panic or depression), whereas the former is what is noticed or perceived by the patient (such as rapid heart rate, dry mouth, and constricted feeling of the throat-anxiety).

Before deeper levels of understanding of mental health problems had been achieved, the few mental health professionals practicing were preoccupied with descriptions of what they observed in patients—usually the severely disturbed, hospitalized patients. This early period is sometimes referred to as the period of descriptive psychiatry. Consequently, the writings and the language of the field consisted primarily of psychopathology—its descriptions, its nomenclature, and its classification. The language of psychopathology became very extensive but was only poorly organized. It was fashionable, for instance, to invent new terms for unusual phenomena, implying that each phenomenon had its own set of determining characteristics. It was a long time before significant common denominators were discovered that led to the grouping of conditions into the diagnostic categories used today. Now the tendency is toward grouping related phenomena into single categories, with a more restricted list of terms. For instance, in the nineteenth century each observed example of fear of some specific situation (such as fear of closed spaces, heights, or open spaces) was given a separate name (such as claustrophobia). Today, on the other hand, the trend is to see all these examples as phobias and to attach less importance to their specific names. Likewise, there were many names given to what were called the manias, but the use of these special names has nearly vanished.

Both symptoms and psychopathological conditions must be distinguished from diagnosis. Simply stated, a diagnosis is a collection of symptoms that appear to have a common denominator.

The accompanying chart groups most of the commonly used psychopathological terms into

TERMS USED TO DESCRIBE PSYCHOLOGICALLY ABNORMAL CHARACTERISTICS

Mild	Moderate	Serious
Agitation	Amnesia	Alcoholism
Anxiety	Anhedonia	Anorexia nervosa
Broken sleep	Anorexia	Antisocial behavior
Circumstantiality	Asocial behavior	Apathy
Compulsive acts	Battle dreams	Auditory hallucination
Conflicts	Bulimia	Blocking of thought
Defensiveness	Compulsive rituals	Cerea flexibilitas
Déjà vu	Concrete thinking	Clang association
Dependency	Cyclic moods	Confabulation
Difficulty in concentration	Depression	Delirium
Fantasy	Enuresis	Delusion of alien control
Frigidity	Euphoria	Delusion of grandeur
Hostility	Exaggerated sense of guilt	Delusions of guilt
Hypnagogic hallucination	Exhibitionism	Delusion of reference
Impotence	Fetishism	Depersonalization
Impulsiveness	Homosexuality	Deterioration of habits
Inattentiveness	Hyperventilation syndrome	Disorientation
Indecision	Hypochondriacal	Drug addiction
Insomnia	Inhibition of aggression	Flight of ideas
Introversion	La belle indifference	Grimacing
Litigiousness	Magical thinking	Homicidal attempt
Nail biting	Malingering	Hypochondriacal delusions
Nightmares	Obsessional preoccupation	Loss of contact with reality
Obsessional thoughts	Pavor nocturnus	Manneristic posturing
Palpitations	Phobias	Mutism
Passivity	Retrospective falsification	Neologism
Rigidity	Suicidal thoughts	Nihilistic delusions
Separation fear	Suspiciousness	Panic
Sleepwalking (somnambulism)	Stuttering	Perseveration
Stubbornness	Temper tantrums	Psychomotor retardation
Tension	Transvestism	Stereotaxy
Tics	Voyeurism	Stereotypy
Vagueness	Withdrawal	Stupor
Worry		Suicidal attempt
		Visual hallucination

three sections, according to their degree of severity. The "mild" group includes the minor neurotic traits and minor character disorders of "normal" people. The "moderate" group includes the well-defined psychoneurotic (and psychophysiologic) disorders. The "serious" group includes the psychoses. In general, patients who exhibit only psychopathological manifestations of the mild type are considered nearly normal, although potentially psychoneurotic; whereas psychopathological manifestations falling into both mild and moderate groups indicate a fully developed psychoneurosis. Finally, if any of the psychopathological conditions observed is "serious," then psychosis should be considered in diagnosis.

PHOBIAS

Current usage tends to favor the practice of referring to the morbid fear a person might have as a "phobia of . . . ," with a simple, common English phrase to describe the phenomenon. In former times, however, it was fashionable to give special terms to each example, such as those in the following list:

Phobia	*means*	morbid fear of
acarophobia		insects
acetophobia		sourness
acousticophobia		sounds
acrophobia		height
aerophobia		air
agoraphobia		open spaces
agyiophobia		streets
aichmophobia		sharp objects
ailurophobia		cats
algophobia		pain
amaxophobia		vehicles
amychophobia		being scratched
androphobia		men
anemophobia		wind
anthophobia		flowers
anthrophobia		people
antlophobia		floods
apeirophobia		infinity
aphephobia		being touched
apiphobia		bees
aquaphobia		water

Phobia	*means*	morbid fear of
arachnephobia		spiders
asthenophobia		weakness
astraphobia		lightning
ataxophobia		staggering
atephobia		doom
aulophobia		flute
auroraphobia		the northern lights
automysophobia		odor, being unclean
autophobia		self
bacillophobia		germs
bacteriophobia		germs
barophobia		gravity
basophobia		walking
bathophobia		falling
batophobia		height
belonephobia		sharp objects
bromhidrosiphobia		personal odor
catoptrophobia		one's own reflected image
cenophobia		open spaces
cenotophobia		newness
cheimaphobia		cold
chionophobia		snow
chrematophobia		money
chromatophobia		colors
chromophobia		colors
coitophobia		sexual intercourse
coprophobia		feces
cremnophobia		precipices
cynophobia		dogs
cypridophobia		venereal disease
demonophobia		evil spirits
demophobia		crowds
dermatophobia		skin
dermatosiophobia		skin infection
domatophobia		being closed in
doraphobia		animal pelts
dysmorphophobia		being maimed
ecophobia		home
emetophobia		vomiting
entomophobia		insects
eosophobia		dawn
eremophobia		being alone
ergasiophobia		being active
erotophobia		sex
galeophobia		cats
gamophobia		marriage
gelophobia		laughter
genophobia		sexual intercourse
gephyrophobia		bridges
gerontophobia		elderly persons
gymnophobia		nakedness

Phobia	*means*	morbid fear of	Phobia	*means*	morbid fear of
gynephobia		women	ornithophobia		birds
hadephobia		hell	osmophobia		odors
hamartophobia		sin	panophobia		all things
haphephobia		being touched	pantophobia		all things
haptephobia		being touched	paralipophobia		failing in duty
harpaxophobia		thieves	parasitophobia		parasites
hedonophobia		pleasure	parthenophobia		virgins
heliophobia		sun	peccatiphobia		sinning
helminthophobia		worms	pediculophobia		parasites
hemophobia		blood	pedophobia		children
hodophobia		traveling	peniaphobia		poverty
hyalophobia		glass	phagophobia		eating
hydrophobia		water	phantasmophobia		ghosts
hygrophobia		dampness	pharmacophobia		medicines
hypengyophobia		responsibility	phasmophobia		spirits
hypnophobia		sleep	phobophobia		fear
hypsophobia		falling	phonophobia		sounds
ichthyophobia		fish	phronemophobia		thinking
ideophobia		ideas	phthiriophobia		lice
kainophobia		newness	pnigophobia		smothering
kakorrhaphiophobia		failure	poinephobia		punishment
kathisophobia		remaining still	ponophobia		work
kenophobia		open space	potamophobia		rivers
keraunophobia		lightning	proctophobia		anus
kinesophobia		movement	prosceniophobia		the stage
kleptophobia		stealing	psychophobia		the mind
kopophobia		fatigue	psychrophobia		cold
laliophobia		talking	pteronophobia		feathers
levophobia		left	pyrophobia		fire
linonophobia		string	scabiophobia		scabies
megalophobia		large things	scatophobia		feces
merinthophobia		being bound	selaphobia		flashing light
metallophobia		metal	siderodromophobia		stars
meteorophobia		meteors	spectrophobia		mirrors
microbiophobia		germs	spermatophobia		semen
molysmophobia		dirt	stasibasiphobia		standing or walking
monophobia		being alone	stasiphobia		standing
mysophobia		dirt	syphilophobia		syphilis
necrophobia		corpse	taphophobia		being buried alive
neophobia		novelty	thalassophobia		sea
noctiphobia		night	thanatophobia		death
nosophobia		illness	theophobia		God
nostophobia		home	thermophobia		heat
nyctophobia		night	tocophobia		pregnancy
ochlophobia		crowds	tonitrophobia		thunder
odontophobia		teeth	topophobia		a place
odynophobia		pain	toxicophobia		poison
oikophobia		home	tremophobia		trembling
ombrophobia		rain	trichopathophobia		hair
onomatophobia		words	tricophobia		hair
ophidiophobia		snakes	triskaidekaphobia		thirteen

Phobia	*means*	morbid fear of
uranophobia		heaven
vaccinophobia		vaccines
venereophobia		venereal disease
vermiphobia		worms
xenophobia		strangers
xylophobia		trees, wood
zelophobia		jealousy
zoophobia		animals

MANIAS

As is the case of the phobias, there was a period around the turn of the twentieth century when many apparently unusual phenomena were referred to as particular kinds of manias. The term mania itself, in contrast to phobia, is rarely used anymore except in the term hypomania or, more commonly, in the adjective hypomanic. The state referred to under this category is a general increase in the rate of activity or excitement, perhaps even within "normal limits." The special terms used in the past and having the suffix *mania* included:

> acute, chronic, or recurrent manias: applied according to the timing of the condition
> akinetic mania: psychotic states associated with immobile posturing
> Bell's mania (or mania gravis): delirium
> Caesar mania: grandiose delusion of being a king
> chattering mania: characterized by unintelligible gibberish
> collecting mania: uncontrolled desire to collect objects
> dipsomania (or mania à potu): alcoholism
> ephemeral mania: transient mildly excited state
> errabund (wandering) mania: aimless wandering
> grumbling mania: constant, pessimistic complaining
> histrionic mania: delusions of being a famous actor
> hypomania: milder form of excited, exalted states
> hysterical mania: excited states in hysterics
> mania mitis: mild psychosis
> mania de perfection: obsessive perfectionism
> mania de raissonante: psychotic disorder of the thinking process

> mania de rumination: obsessive preoccupation with memories
> mania senilis: excited psychosis of old age
> mania sine delirio: mania without delirium, mild type
> mania transitoria: transient excited state
> metaphysical mania: obsessive preoccupation with philosophical speculation
> postmenopausal mania: excited states following the menopause
> puerperal mania: psychosis following childbirth
> stuporous mania: similar to catatonia
> tropical mania: psychosis supposedly occurring in the tropics

More simply stated and defined, the so-called manias that can be called "abnormal obsessions with or desires for . . ." are included in the following list:

Mania	*means*	abnormal desire for or obsession with
ablutomania		handwashing
acoustomania		sounds
agoramania		open space
agromania		being alone
aichmomania		sharp objects
ailuromania		cats
algomania		pain
andromania		men
aphrodisiomania		erotic behavior
basomania		walking
bromhidrosimania		personal odor
cenomania		novelty
chionomania		snow
chrematomania		property
chromatomania		colors
coitomania		sexual intercourse
copromania		feces
cynomania		dogs
demomania		crowds
demonomania		evil spirits
dermatomania		skin
dromomania		wandering
ecomania		home
emetomania		vomiting
entomomania		insects
eosomania		dawn
eremomania		being alone
ergasiomania		activity
erotomania		sex
gamomania		marriage

Mania *means*	abnormal desire for or obsession with
gelomania	laughter
gephyromania	bridges
graphomania	writing
gymnomania	nakedness
gynemania	women
haphemania	being touched
hedonomania	pleasure
helminthomania	worms
hemomania	blood
hodomania	traveling
hyalomania	glass
hydromania	water
hypengyomania	responsibility
hypnomania	sleep
ichthyomania	fish
iconomania	idols
ideomania	ideas
kakorrhaphiomania	failure
kinesomania	movement
kleptomania	stealing
laliomania	talking
levomania	left
megalomania	grandiosity
metallomania	metals
nyctomania	night
ochlomania	crowds
ophidiomania	snakes
ornithomania	birds
osmomania	odors
phonomania	sounds
potamomania	rivers
pteronomania	feathers
pyromania	fire
scatomania	feces
spectromania	mirrors, reflections
stasimania	standing
thalassomania	sea
thanatomania	death
theomania	God
tocomania	pregnancy
toxicomania	poisons
trichotillomania	hair
uranomania	heaven
vaccinomania	vaccination
xylomania	trees
zoomania	animals

GLOSSARY

abderite. A mentally deficient person.

abdominal epilepsy. Dysrhythmic abdominal pain.

aberrant energy expression. Unorganized, abnormal modes of expression of psychic and motor energy seen in the symptom of neuroses and psychoses.

abiotrophic. An inherent constitutional weakness or a premature decay of affected parts of the nervous system. An example is found in Huntington's chorea.

aboiement. Production of abnormal or unusual sound, especially the uncontrollable and involuntary expressions seen in severely regressed schizophrenic patients; animalistic noise.

absence. Brief clouding of consciousness seen in petit mal epilepsy.

absent minded. A common term for someone who is forgetful; especially habitually so.

abstinence syndrome. A condition associated with complete withdrawal, usually sudden, from alcohol, barbiturates, stimulants, or opiates; characterized by dysphoric symptoms ranging from mild physical and mental discomfort to grand mal seizures.

abulia. Pronounced lack of energy, initiative.

abulic. Characterized by loss of willpower; showing abulia.

acalculia. Inability to do even simple arithmetic problems; a condition usually associated with organic brain disease.

acatalepsia. Impairment or lack of ability to understand or to reason.

acatamathesia. Inability to grasp the meaning of perceived objects or situations; inability to comprehend the meaning of spoken language.

acataphasia. Inability to carry out correct arrangement of words, phrasing, and sentence structure of common speech.

acathisia. Akathisia.

accident proneness. A trait ascribed to certain people who have frequent accidents. It is often listed under psychosomatic disorders, in which personality factors seem to contribute to organic conditions. Various theories have been advanced to explain the phenomenon; for example, inattentiveness resulting from daydreaming or the unconscious wish to punish oneself.

acoria. Bulimia.

acousma. An auditory hallucination of a simple nature such as hissing or buzzing.

acracia. Impotence; loss of power; inefficiency.

acrasia. Intemperance; profligacy; absence of self-control.

acrocyanosis. Bluish discoloration of lower legs and hands, found in schizophrenic patients; thought to be caused by autonomic disturbances until it was discovered to be secondary to circulatory stasis, resulting from the patient's prolonged, almost complete immobility. It is seldom seen now, because patients are kept active and given supervised therapy programs.

acro-esthesia. Pronounced sensitivity to stimulation of the extremities (for example, a touch may be felt as being extremely painful).

acroparesthesia. Tingling, burning sensation of the feet and hands.

actual neurosis. In the early days of the psychoanalytic movement, it was assumed that there existed both organic and functional neuroses, and this term applied to the organic type. Supposedly, the condition was caused by depletion or disturbances of central nervous system libido. Freud referred to the functional type as transference neurosis. The nomenclature is now obsolete, but the energy concept rooted here is still held valid by strict Freudian theorists.

acute brain syndrome. A variety of reversible organic states characteristically manifested by confusion, disorientation, and cloudy sensorium. Examples include drug or alcohol intoxication, mild head trauma, and mild anoxia; these are distinguished from chronic brain syndrome in that they are reversible.

acute situational neurosis. A diagnostic state precipitated by an extremely painful, frightening, or disappointing experience.

addiction. The effect of habitual ingestion of narcotic drugs in ever increasing proportions to the point of physical dependency. According to this theory, the condition is seen as the result of a metabolic abnormality requiring the addicting drug for sustenance, the true test being the appearance of withdrawal symptoms upon terminating drug consumption. Others have postulated this habituation as a mere search for comfort, and the withdrawal syndrome as an accumulation of toxic effects previously masked by the narcotic effect of the drugs. The World Health Organization now recommends that the term drug dependency be used, because of the lack of general agreement. The term is now becoming the word of choice to describe uncontrollable drug use.

adjustment reactions. Transient psychogenic reactions to stress. These are divided into those of infancy, childhood, adolescence, adulthood, and late life.

adualism. Lack of ability to distinguish between the two realities, that of the mind and that of the external world; a trait seen in schizophrenia. Analogous to the term lack of ego boundaries as used in orthodox psychoanalysis.

adult situational reaction. Superficial maladjustment to environmental factors; a transient disturbance. There is usually no evidence of serious or chronic underlying personality factors.

adynamia. Debility; weakness; loss of strength; asthenia.

aerophagia. The swallowing of air. In anxiety or hysterical conditions it can cause troublesome symptoms, such as chronic distension of the stomach, belching, and vomiting.

affect hunger. A term applied by Levy to the impoverishment of and need for positive feelings, such as recognition, security, affection, and sympathy, that is sometimes found in children of overprotective mothers.

affectionless child. A child unable to show or give warmth, closeness, love, or other emotional interaction with people, usually because of a pathological home environment. It is usually considered a form of sociopathy rather than a psychosis. It has been described as a cause of learning problems in children so affected.

affective disorders. Disorders characterized by a primary disturbance of mood. In the psychotic conditions there is accompanying derangement of thought and behavior. Such psychoses are manic-depressive reactions and psychotic-depressive reactions; milder disorders are cyclothymic personality disturbances and neurotic depression.

affective psychoses. Disorders in which either excitement or depression is prominent. This general diagnostic group includes manic-depressive psychosis, involutional psychosis, psychotic depression, and possibly schizoaffective reactions.

ageusia. Impairment of the sense of taste.

agitated depression. A depressed state that is accompanied by intense, repetitive, but essentially purposeless activity (such as pacing the floor or wringing the hands).

agitolalia. Excessively rapid, cluttered, slurred, distorted speech.

agitophasia. Agitolalia.

agnosia. Loss of the ability to recognize or comprehend familiar stimuli, persons, situations. Cerebral perceptual organization is impaired without disorder of the sense receptor organs.

agrammatism. Inability to use logical or grammatical sequence in speech; an aphasia.

agraphia. Inability to write; a form of aphasia, usually a symptom of cerebral malfunction.

agyria. Lissencephaly.

ahypnosia. Ahypnia. (See p. 115.)

akathisia. Acathisia; inability to remain still. In psychiatry it is usually seen as a complication of therapy with phenothiazines and other major tranquilizers, such as a butyrophenone. The acute cases are reversible when use of the offending drug is discontinued. However, in some cases the symptoms may persist, becoming chronic and irreversible.

akinesia. Absence or reduction of voluntary movement; a symptom of conditions ranging in severity from hysteria to catatonic schizophrenia.

akinetic mutism. A comalike state caused by localized brain damage as opposed to a coma state produced by widespread or diffuse brain damage. In this comalike state the patient may appear to be awake and may lie with his eyes open, but he fails to respond to light, noise, and objects, and he usually remains mute, but may produce unintelligible words and sounds. A patient in such a state may lack all spontaneous speech and movement. This syndrome is usually the result of injury to the brainstem or of cerebrovascular accidents. Synonym: coma vigil.

alalia. Inability to produce speech.

alcohol hallucinosis. A specific alcohol withdrawal state with vivid, threatening auditory and visual hallucinations, but without marked disorientation, clouding of consciousness, or restlessness as would be present in delirium tremens.

alcohol intolerance. A state of acute excitement, with clouding of consciousness upon even minimal ingestion of alcohol. This may be a type of pathologic intoxication.

alcoholic encephalopathy. A degenerative disease of the brain caused by chronic and usually heavy ingestion of alcohol.

alcoholic pseudoparesis. In chronic alcoholics a state of severe overall deterioration resembling general paresis and including pronounced changes in emotion, such as increased lability and aggressiveness.

alcoholic psychosis. A variety of chronic psychosis seen in patients with long histories of alcoholism, manifested by loss of memory and judgment. General atrophy of the brain is seen at autopsy. Recent studies indicate that the pathological condition is the result of a nutritional deficiency rather than alcohol toxicity and is, therefore, likely to be accompanied by other evidences of vitamin deficiency.

alcoholism. Dependency on alcohol, usually characterized by the imbibing of alcohol to an excessive degree over substantial periods of time. It is often regarded either as a medical problem with biochemical determinants or as a psychiatric prob-

lem occurring in people of certain personality structures. A useful criterion, though not generally accepted, of what constitutes alcoholism is the finding that the person frequently uses alcohol uncontrollably and for irrational purposes, in contrast to the use of controlled amounts for socially accepted purposes, which typifies social drinking.

alexia. Inability to read; a form of aphasia usually associated with cerebral dysfunction.

alienation. A condition of estrangement, feeling apart from one's environment, self, or feelings. May produce a feeling of strangeness or unreality. Seen in depersonalization phenomena, obsessional states, and more serious mental illnesses.

allochiria. A phenomenon in which a sensation is felt on the side of the body opposite from that stimulated; most often seen in hysterical conditions.

allolalia. Abnormal or unusual speech.

alpha alcoholism. A category of alcoholism proposed by E. M. Jellinek to refer to excessive and inappropriate drinking, without loss of control or loss of ability to abstain.

alpha rhythm. A type of tracing found on an EEG recording with a characteristic 8.5 to 12.5 waves per second. This rhythm is most pronounced when the individual is relaxed and has his eyes closed. It is reasonably constant from individual to individual and in the same individual from time to time. High production of alpha waves is often associated with a state of peak mental and physical performance, a relaxed yet extremely sensitive alertness.

alysm. Restlessness in the ill.

alysmus. Dysphoria, anguish, anxiety, depression accompanying an illness.

alysosis. Profound ennui; boredom.

Alverez's syndrome. Nongaseous abdominal bloating, which may superficially simulate pregnancy. Usually occurs without amenorrhea in middle-aged women who may have many accompanying hysterical features.

Alzheimer's disease. A progressive brain atrophy, usually fatal within a few years, described by the German neurologist Alois Alzheimer in 1906. With the progression of the pathological condition of the brain, there is likely to be a deterioration in memory and judgment, which may lead to psychosis. The cause is unknown, and the condition is quite rare.

amaurotic familial idiocy. A form of a rare condition, a lipoidosis, in which a ganglioside accumulates in the central nervous system. It is associated with blindness, mental deficiency, progressive physical deterioration, and early death. It is an inherited condition transmitted by a single recessive gene.

amentia. A term used by Meynert to designate the condition of acute confusional delirious reactions that sometimes accompany states of marked exhaustion. It is used by English and German psychiatrists for this condition. American psychiatrists occasionally use the word to mean mental deficiency or feeblemindedness.

amimia. Impairment of the use of gestures.

aminotoxicosis. The presence of abnormal amines or metabolites in the blood and urine of schizophrenics; these may play a causative role in the condition.

amnesia. The inability to recall past experience, often caused by physical or psychic trauma. An essential part of Freud's concept of the unconscious was based on the assumption that painful memories are obliterated from the memory; in this sense amnesia would be a part of normal forgetting of the past.

amnesic-confabulatory syndrome. A relatively common syndrome following head trauma. The outstanding feature is confabulation, which is accompanied by disorientation, disorder of perception, and poor retention of recently acquired information. This condition is similar to Korsakoff's syndrome except that it is of shorter duration and is not associated with polyneuropathy.

amok. A state of behavior seen in the Malays when a previously normal person suddenly becomes violent and rages through the village attacking people at random until he is overcome by exhaustion or force or until he is killed. The term now more broadly denotes any such wild behavior.

amorphosynthesis. A term used by Denny-Brown to denote the inability of a person with parietal lobe brain damage to synthesize information from one side of the brain to another. In damage to the right parietal lobe he may recognize his clothing but not be able to dress himself, because he cannot match the articles to the left side of his body.

anal character. See p. 77.

anal eroticism. See p. 77.

anal intercourse. See p. 53.

anal love. See p. 77.

anal phase. See p. 77.

anandria. Absence of male characteristics.

anaphia. Loss of deficiency of tactile sense.

anergy. Lack of energy, passivity; sometimes almost complete inactivity in schizophrenia.

anesthesia, hysterical. Loss of sensation, especially in localized body areas, not caused by organic nervous system disease. In each case there is an unconscious attempt to forget or to withdraw attention from traumatic external events.

anhedonia. The inability to obtain pleasure from acts formerly pleasurable.

anniversary reaction. An attack or recurrence of feelings and emotion, or even a psychotic state, occurring on the anniversary of a previously upsetting event.

anomia. Inability to associate persons and objects with their names; an aphasia.

anorexia nervosa. A condition found chiefly in young women; manifested by severe loss of appetite, food refusal, weight loss, and occasionally vomiting and amenorrhea. A patient qualifies for this diagnosis if the basis for the food refusal is psychogenic. This is not actually a discrete clinical entity, but a condition that may be found in association with several different conditions, such as schizophrenia, hysteria, and depression. As originally described by Gull in 1868, it was considered to be a manifestation of hysteria.

anosmia. Loss of the sense of smell.

anosognosia. Unconscious denial of the fact or loss of the ability to recognize that one has a disease or a bodily defect.

anxiety. See p. 54.

anxiety hysteria. A diagnostic term devised in the early days of the psychoanalytic school to mean what had been labeled a phobia before, but later had become known as conversion hysteria. Freud originally worked with persons in a diagnostic category referred to as hysteria (later on, conversion hysteria). After 1900 he also recognized obsessional or compulsive (later, obsessive-compulsive) neurosis. Still later, he used a category called anxiety hysteria to refer to a class of patients in which the presence of phobias was predominant. In current official nomenclature these phobias are classified as psychoneurotic disorders, phobic reactions.

anxiety neurosis. A term in common usage meaning a mild form of anxiety reaction, but is not listed in the official nomenclature.

anxiety reaction. A condition listed in the official nomenclature under psychoneurotic disorders. The main characteristic is a diffuse anxiety not restricted to special objects or situations; a severe anxious expectation, dread, apprehension that may also be associated with some somatic symptoms.

apandria. An aversion to males.

apastia. Refusing to eat food.

apathetic. Having the quality of apathy as a predominant personality feature, either transiently or chronically; a feature of many mild and severe psychiatric disorders.

apathy. Absence of emotion, indifference toward the environment or toward other individuals; in other words, the characteristic of directing one's attention inward (fantasy) rather than outward. When severe, this state is usually found to be a serious sign of psychologic disturbance and serves as an obstacle to therapy even in milder forms.

aphasia. Inability to talk coherently. Broadly, the term means impairment of expressive and communicative functions.

aphemia. Loss of speech caused by a central lesion.

aphonia. Loss of voice caused by a structural or functional impairment of the throat or larynx.

aphrasia. Agrammatism.

apraxia. Inability to conceive and carry out purposeful motor activity. It is a voluntary movement disorder, not paralysis.

arc de cercle. Behavior that resembles an exaggerated imitation of sexual intercourse; described by Charcot as occurring in hysterical fits. It is not seen in true epilepsy.

arieti effect. An automatic fragmentation of perceptual wholes followed by instantaneous reintegration according to primary process rather than secondary process principles of cognition. Seen in severely ill schizophrenics.

Army General Classification Test (A.G.C.T.). A general test of intelligence and aptitude developed as a screening and classification device and given to incoming servicemen. Scores can be used as a rough index of intelligence.

aromaturia. Excretion of higher than normal amounts of aromatic organic compounds in the urine. Found in certain schizophrenics.

asexual. See p. 54.

as if characters. See p. 54.

astasia abasia. The inability to stand or walk; likely to be found in hysteria and conversion reactions.

asthenia. Physical weakness, loss of strength. Neurasthenia is an old diagnostic term for chronic weakness or fatigue without physical cause. Neurocirculatory asthenia was a diagnostic term used in the past for conditions that appeared to be caused by cardiovascular insufficiency in the absence of organic lesions.

asymbolia. Inability to recognize or understand symbols; an aphasia.

asyndesis. A term used by Norman Cameron to describe the loss of connecting links in logical thinking; seen in schizophrenia and metanymy.

ataxia. Literally means without orderly arrangement, but is usually understood to mean unsteadiness, uncoordination, or irregularity of gait and associated body movements. It is found in certain diseases of the nervous system, alcohol and drug intoxication, and hysteria.

athetosis. Slow, irregular, and apparently purposeless movement of the extremities; associated with drug toxicity, especially from the major tranquilizers, and neurological disorders.

atonic seizure. A type of epilepsy in which there is little or no jerking or other movement and no tensing of the muscles.

atypical child. A term sometimes given to children who have a schizophreniclike condition.

auditory seizures. The hearing of sounds and noise during an epileptic seizure. It is rarely seen as the only manifestation of a seizure but is more likely to occur as part of a more generalized attack. They are thought to originate in the temporal lobe.

aura. A premonitory sign that warns the individual of an approaching crisis. It is usually used to refer to some sensory impression that precedes a convulsion in persons with epilepsy. An aura may be visual, auditory, tactile, or olfactory.

autism. Literally, living within oneself; a process of subjective, introspective thinking likely to be rich in fantasy. It is a prominent symptom in schizophrenia; it is part of normal psychological processes in varying degrees, especially in children.

autistic child. Children, described by Kanner, whose thinking is self-centered and fantastic, who develop a very private language, who relate extremely poorly to other persons but well to inanimate objects, and who become very withdrawn from reality. He suggests that this condition is a precursor to schizophrenia.

automatism. Undirected, sometimes symbolic behavior or movements carried out repeatedly and unconsciously in fugue states, schizophrenia, and some epileptic conditions.

autoplastic. See p. 78.

autoscopic syndrome. The delusion in which a person sees an exact double of himself (not another person who looks like himself, but the patient himself), often appearing as a mirror image.

averted schizophrenia. See p. 78.

awholism, primary. An abnormality of perception in acute schizophrenia, a spontaneous effort by the subject to reaggregate and reform wholes from fragmented and broken perceived aggregates. The reaggregation is loose or unrealistic.

bad me. See p. 78.

ballismus. Jerking and flailing movements of legs and arms; a manifestation of basal ganglia disease.

baragnosis. Inability to recognize weights of objects; usually indicates damage to certain areas of the brain, especially the parietal lobe.

barylalia. Slow, thick speech.

basic anxiety. See p. 79.

battarismus. Stuttering.

battered child. A severely mistreated child; a child bruised or beaten, often with multiple lacerations and bone fractures.

battle fatigue. Physical and emotional exhaustion secondary to stress of combat or other extreme conditions of war; a percipitating stress in a variety of behavior disorders. World War I synonym: shell shock.

behavior disorders. A broad range of conduct or action in an individual that brings him to treatment and causes him social, legal, or personal problems, but has no specific underlying psychological or organic cause.

Bender Gestalt Test. A psychological test used to assess visual-motor organization.

bestiality. Animallike behavior exhibited by human beings; sometimes refers to sexual relations between animals and human beings.

beta alcoholism. According to Jellinek's classification, advanced alcoholism in which cirrhosis, gastritis, and neuritis occur, but in which physical or psychological dependence on alcohol cannot be demonstrated.

beta rhythm. A finding on normal EEG tracings characterized by low-amplitude waves of 18 to 25 waves per second. A less frequent finding than alpha rhythm.

bigamy. Having more than one wife.

Binet-Simon Test. A widely used test of intelligence. With results from this test, the intelligence quotient (I.Q.) for the person can be determined.

Binswanger's disease. A diffuse demyelinating disease of the brain; rare.

bipolar depression. An affective disorder in which the patient experiences both mania (or hypomania) and depression. Thought to have a strong genetic causative component. See unipolar depression.

bipolar psychosis. An affective psychosis in which the patient experiences both manic and depressive

episodes of psychotic proportion; manic-depressive psychosis. Thought to have a strong genetic causative component.

birth trauma. See p. 79.

bisexual theory. See p. 79.

blackout. See p. 55.

blepharospasm. Intense closure of the eyelids, also rapid blinking of the eyelids.

blocking. See p. 131.

body protest. Ester L. Richards' term for physical illness (for example, ulcers, rash) that may serve as a vent for frustration, worry, or anger.

borderline personality. Melitta Schmideberg's term for that patient who remains essentially unstable and peculiar all of his life. She did not regard this condition as a prepsychotic state or necessarily leading to a more severe disorder but rather, as a defense against further decompensation (that is, into a psychosis). Included are the schizoid, depressive, paranoid, querulous, hypochondriac, and antisocial types.

boxer's encephalopathy. Posttraumatic psychosis, diffuse.

bradykinesia. Marked slowing of bodily movements; a component of naturally occurring and drug-induced neurological conditions (for example, Parkinson's disease).

bradylalia. Slowness of speech.

bradyphrenia. Slowness of thinking.

brain syndrome (acute or chronic). Official diagnosis with many subdivisions, in which organic brain damage is productive of mental as well as neurological manifestations. See list on p. 8.

brain wave. An electroencephalograph tracing.

breast envy. See p. 79.

breath holding. Episodes in the first 4 to 5 years of some children who, in the midst of violent crying, suddenly stop breathing for approximately 30 seconds. During this time the child may become cyanotic, flail the arms and legs, appear distressed, and even become unconscious. It is usually taken as a sign of a disturbed parent-child relationship.

Broca's aphasia. The inability to find correct verbal expressions for objects and an inability to repeat letters, words, or sentences. It is caused by impairment of functions of Broca's area of the brain.

bromidism. Intoxication with bromide compounds.

bromidrosis. Perspiration with a foul odor.

bromism. Bromide poisoning. Bromides are salts of sodium and potassium that are sometimes used in medicine as sedatives.

bromoderma. Acnelike lesions of the skin, caused by bromide intoxication.

bruxism. Grinding of the teeth during sleep.

bulimia. Insatiable hunger or appetite.

cachexia. Severe wasting of the body tissue caused by prolonged malnutrition; seen in anorexia nervosa, certain endocrine disorders, and malignancies.

cachinnation. Roisterous, inappropriate laughter often seen in hebephrenic schizophrenics.

cacogenic. Most severely physically and mentally defective.

camptocormia. Pronounced bending forward of the trunk seen in posttraumatic neuroses, psychoneuroses, and schizophrenia without definite organic cause.

cardiac neurosis. Morbid fear of coronary disease or that one has cardiac disease with no demonstrable heart disease present. Sometimes excessive worry about one's heart after experiencing real or imagined symptoms of cardiac disease.

cardiac psychosis. Psychotic state percipitated by a myocardial infarction.

cardiospasm. Difficulty in swallowing, pain in the upper abdomen, vomiting. It is secondary to physical disease of the lower esophagus or upper stomach. Emotional factors play a strong role in causing symptoms in many patients.

cardiovascular reaction, psychophysiologic. Any disorder of the heart or blood vessels in which emotional factors contribute to the condition.

carphology. Floccillation; picking or plucking movements; usually seen in delirium, organic brain conditions, and schizophrenia

carpopedal spasm. Cramping and spasms of the wrists and ankles sometimes seen in a hyperventilation syndrome attack.

castration anxiety. An exaggerated fear of punishment in the child, which is sometimes carried into adulthood. This psychoanalytic theory was based on the finding that the child wishes to possess the parent of the opposite sex, bringing about fear of retaliation by the parent of the same sex. Synonym: castration complex (see p. 79).

catalepsy. A state in which a rigid, unresponsive posture is maintained for long periods of time; characteristic of catatonic schizophrenia. It was once thought to be a form of epilepsy.

cataplexy. Temporary paralysis or weakness of the musculature following sudden emotional outbursts, especially laughter. It is sometimes thought to be a manifestation of epilepsy and is often associated with narcolepsy.

catastrophic reaction. Depersonalization, inability to speak, severe anxiety, rage reactions, and hallucinations, especially in children with damage to the temporal lobe of the brain. Typically it is a reaction to stress but may appear in sudden episodes without being provoked.

catathymic crisis. Werthaus' term for commission of crimes by schizophrenics in an attempt to overcome an oncoming or already existing psychosis.

catatonic schizophrenia. A type of schizophrenia typified by unusual posturing and mannerisms, often associated with mutism.

categorical demand. See p. 79.

central conflict. Karen Horney's term for the conflict between the real self and the idealized self.

cephalalgia. Headache.

cerea flexibilitas. Waxy flexibility.

character disorders. Personality disorders.

chorea. Literally, dance; a neurological disorder characterized by involuntary, spasmodic, and jerking movements of all or parts of the body. When severe, it gives the person a peculiar style of walking that appears to be a ludicrous dance.

choreiform movements. Body movements that resemble a true chorea.

chronic brain syndrome. Permanent, irreversible impairment of brain function; characterized by varying degrees of memory loss, inability to solve problems, disorientation, speech problems, visual changes, some increase or decrease of muscle tone, and paralysis.

chronic subdural hematoma. A mass that develops between the dura mater and brain from an acute subdural hematoma (blood clot) that expands over time. The clinical course is essentially that of a neoplasm. Surgical removal is required.

circumlocution. Inability to make a direct or concise statement; often seen in senile conditions.

circumstantiality. The process of including irrelevant, useless, or even bizarre information in communicating to another; seen in schizophrenia, mania, and organic brain syndrome.

cisvestitism. Wearing clothes inappropriate to age, social status, or acceptation, but appropriate to one's gender.

clang association. An associative disturbance in which the sound of a word, rather than its meaning, touches off a new train of thought (for example, song-wrong, seen-queen, or flew-blue). This is seen in manic patients and excited schizophrenic patients.

clavus. The feeling one has during a headache that a nail is being driven into the head; a symptom in hysterical patients.

clouding of consciousness. A partial loss of awareness, alertness, or attentiveness; sometimes associated with epilepsy, senility, and mental conditions such as a neurosis or psychosis.

cluster headaches. Recurrent headaches of several causes; may recur daily for a month or more. They can usually be distinguished from migraine headaches by the symptoms, location, onset, and pattern of occurrence.

color-form sorting test. A psychological instrument using items of various colors and forms to be sorted in order to test impairment of conceptual thinking. Patients with brain damage, for instance, would have difficulty sorting the items in a logical fashion.

coma. A deep state of unconsciousness during which the patient does not respond to strong stimuli.

coma vigil. Akinetic mutism.

combat fatigue. See battle fatigue.

combat neurosis. A traumatic neurosis induced by severe stress in battle.

compensation neurosis. Neurotic states that seem to be most prominent during periods of litigation, but that seem to subside once a favorable financial settlement is made. It is not an official diagnosis.

compulsion. The performance of an unreasonable act, usually repetitive, that seems contrary to the individual's better judgment and that he is unable to control. Examples are excessive hand washing and excessive orderliness in habits. It is usually seen in the type of person sometimes known as the compulsive personality or in the condition called obsessive-compulsive neurosis.

compulsive personality. A type of person given to excessive neatness, orderliness, obstinacy, and rituals, and likely to demonstrate neurotic or depressive states. This person may be rigid and usually unable to relax; he is overinhibited, overconscientious, and has an unusual compass for work. This is classified as a Personality Trait Disturbance.

compulsive ritual. In the compulsive personality, the compulsions often take the form of rituals (such as handwashing, stepping on cracks, repeating certain words) in which a certain precise form is followed in carrying out actions, the form being repeated in the same way each time.

concentration camp syndrome. A chronic stress reaction characterized by fatigability, apathy, restlessness, and sleep disturbances, found in survivors of concentration camps.

conceptual apraxia. Inability to perform a given act properly because of inability to formulate a course of action. It is seen in certain cases of brain damage.

concussion. A period of unconsciousness following a closed-head injury (that is, where the skull is not broken open).

concussion psychoses. A severe mental abnormality associated with head injury; a posttraumatic psychosis. Psychotic states are more likely to follow contusion or laceration of brain tissue than a simple concussion.

concussion syndrome. A short period of unconsciousness typically followed by diffuse headache, dizziness, nausea, vomiting, often including confusion and disorientation upon awakening.

conduct disorder. A disturbance of behavior in childhood, not a manifestation of an adjustment reaction or more severe mental condition.

confabulation. A ploy to conceal the memory defects. To do so the subject invents stories concerning his recent past. It is seen in conditions where there is marked memory loss resulting from organic brain pathology.

conversion hysteria. Synonymous with psychoneurotic disorder, conversion reaction.

conversion reaction. A psychological condition in which the anxiety-provoking impulse is converted into functional symptoms (such as anesthesia, paralysis, or dyskinesia). The symptoms are in organs under voluntary control, serve to meet the immediate needs of the patient, and are associated with a secondary gain. The term is classified under Psychoneurotic Disorders; Psychophysiological Disorders; la belle indifference.

convulsion. A violent, involuntary contraction or spasm of some or all of the muscles; associated with epilepsy, brain tumors, withdrawal of sedatives, some metabolic disorders, high fever, and electroshock therapy.

convulsive disorder. In psychiatry, a condition that is secondary to brain disease, that has a convulsion as a symptom, and that usually has some degree of mental or emotional problems associated with it.

coprolalia. The voluntary or involuntary use of obscene, vulgar, or filthy language.

coprophagia. Ingestion of feces; likely to be seen in regressed schizophrenics.

countercathexis. See p. 80.

counterphobic. The unconscious motivation to act against something of which one is afraid.

cretinism. A condition of general maldevelopment of a child, including mental retardation, brought about by inadequate thyroid hormone.

crucial phase of alcoholism. That time in the life history of the alcoholic during which he loses control of his drinking.

cruelty. See p. 57.

cryptomnesia. Recall of events not recognized by the subject as something he had previously experienced.

cultural conflict. See p. 57.

cunnilingus. See p. 57.

cycloid personality. An early or mild form of manic-depressive psychosis.

cyclothymic personality. A personality type that characteristically undergoes wide swings in mood and activity, from one extreme of elation or depression to the other. It is assumed by some to be a precursor to manic-depressive psychosis. It is listed in the official nomenclature under Personality Pattern Disturbance.

daymare. Psychological distress precipitated by fantasies while awake.

decentralization. A form of severe personality disintegration; severe regression; the loss of higher mental functions seen in some schizophrenics.

decerebrate rigidity. Marked rigidity and sustained contraction of all the extensor muscles, caused by cutting of certain nerve tracts from the cerebral cortex to lower motor nuclei in the brainstem.

decerebration. Loss of function of higher intellectual capacities of the brain; a state of unconsciousness with cessation of all sensory and motor activity of the brain cortex.

decompensation. The breakdown of mental and emotional function; regression to a less adequate state of function.

dedifferentiation. A reappearance of primitive psychological states (syncretism, synesthesia, paleologic thinking) in schizophrenia.

deficit reactions. Mental subnormality; pronounced inability to perform the mental function of problem solving. These reactions are divided into acute and chronic; those with and without associated organic brain disease and characterized by disorganization, regression, and desocialization.

déjà éntendu. A feeling, without basis in fact, that one has heard previously exactly what he is now hearing.

déjà vu. A phenomenon of human thinking in which, in the present, one has a sudden and apparently illogical feeling of having seen or heard the same thing in the past. Although this takes place occa-sionally in everybody's life, the schizophrenic is likely to report it with great frequency.

delirium. Confusion in thinking, often accompanied by fear. It is the result of a toxic state of the brain in which there is a disorder of the sensory inputs. False sensory images might be reported by the individual and the psychiatrist may misconstrue these to be hallucinations.

delirium tremens. A severe, abnormal state brought on by withdrawal after prolonged, heavy ingestion of sedative medication, most typically alcohol. The symptoms include intense fear, tremor, hallucinations, confusion, sleeplessness, and convulsions. It can be fatal if not treated.

delta alcoholism. E. M. Jellinek's term for those alcoholics who appear unable to abstain but who are able to control the amount ingested.

delta rhythm. A finding on EEG tracings characterized by 0.5 to 3.5 waves per second.

delusion. A false idea or belief that cannot be changed by logical reasoning or contrary evidence; a product of irrational thinking rather than mere ignorance. It is characteristic of psychosis.

dementia. An old term meaning psychosis; decrease in intellectual capacities, caused by organic brain disease.

dementia praecox. A diagnostic term adopted by Kraepelin for "psychosis of young people," including different types that previously had been regarded as distinct: paranoid, hebephrenic, and catatonic. The term was used in the standard nomenclature until the 1920s when Bleuler's term schizophrenia was adopted to replace it.

demyelinating diseases. A grouping of certain diseases of the nervous system characterized by loss of the myelin sheath that surrounds nerve cell axons.

denial of illness. A rejection of the fact that one is ill. It is usually of such a degree as to be a delusion. Such conditions as phantom limb phenomena, denial of blindness, and alcoholism are examples.

depersonalization. A state in which the person has distorted ideas of his own body or being. It is seen in a wide range of persons, from normal people to schizophrenics. It is often expressed as ideas of one's own body not belonging to oneself, that one is standing apart, observing himself in action, or that the body is changing in some bizarre way.

depression. A psychiatric condition in which there is a great reduction of activity, deep feelings of discouragement, sadness, hopelessness, a marked limitation of outside interests, and anorexia. The patient's communications usually consist of pessimistic predictions of failure, excuses for not making any effort, and a gloomy appraisal of the past, with emphasis on failures. The condition varies in degree and quality from mild to psychotic proportions. Depression is categorized variously as reactive versus endogenous, cyclic, involutional, senile, neurotic, psychoneurotic, or psychotic, according to severity, age of onset, and presence or absence of precipitating factors.

derealization. A feeling that the world is strange, different, and unreal. This feeling may occur in transient or mild degree in normal persons, but is felt intensely in certain pathological states.

dereistic. The quality of a thinking process that fails to follow the usual systems of logic; irrational thinking or fantasy.

dereistic thinking. Autism.

desocialization. See p. 104.

deterioration. Steady loss of resources in a psychiatric patient. Institutionalized patients in particular demonstrate a steady decline in their capabilities in connection with long periods of hospitalization, probably because of institutionalization and neglect.

deviant. Characterized by marked differences in behavior, morals, and attitudes from the usual social standards.

deviant sexual behavior. Any sexual act or behavior considered socially or culturally unacceptable. This includes such practices as sodomy, bestiality, and incest. Homosexuality, once included but no longer officially considered deviant, has been removed from psychopathology nomenclature.

diaschisis. Monakow's term denoting the dysfunction of one brain area caused by dysfunction of a related but sometimes distant brain area. Sudden shock to one area will cause shock in all connected areas.

disintegration. Psychological disorganization; inability to feel and think normally.

disorientation. The state of being unaware or uncertain of the correct time, place, or person. Disorientation is seen with brain injury or toxicity and in extreme panic states.

dissimilation. Jung's term for estrangement of the individual from the self as the individual adjusts to external forces.

dissimulation. Concealment of genuine feelings and emotions.

dissocial reaction. See p. 58.

Don Juan. A man who compulsively seduces women, not for the sexual pleasure as such, but to compensate (or even overcompensate) for his imagined deficiency in masculine sexuality.

double-bind. See p. 58.

dromolepsy. Epilepsy in which the person runs forward a few steps before falling.

drug dependency. A term suggested by the World Health Organization to replace such terms as addiction and habituation, which are often imprecise and do not have clear distinctions between them.

drug psychosis. A severe abnormal mental state that is manifested by hallucinations and induced by taking drugs. It is usually associated with drugs call psychomimetics; but it is occasionally seen as a complication of therapy using such medication as adrenal steroids, bromides, digitalis, atropine, alcohol, and amphetamines.

dynamic concepts. See p. 82.

dysarthria. Imperfect production of speech.

dysbasia. Difficulty in walking.

dysbulia. Pervasive indecision.

dysencephalization. Loss of or inability to use the higher intellectual functions; especially in reference to this phenomenon in schizophrenia. The shifting of brain function to lower centers with mediation of higher centers by lower centers.

dysesthesia. Disorder of tactile perception.

dyskinesia. A disorder of movement; used to denote disorder of muscle tone, secondary to nervous disease; it consists of involuntary movements such as chorea, athetosis, or slowing or impoverishment of movement.

dyslexia. Impairment of the ability to read.

dyslogia. Incoherent speech.

dysmegalopsia. A distortion of perception in psychosis, especially likely in schizophrenia, in which an object appears larger on one side than the other.

dysmetria. A disorder of ability to gauge one's own bodily movements.

dysmnesic syndrome. A condition, first described by Korsakoff, characterized by the inability to retain recently acquired information. Memory for events in the remote past is not usually affected. It is generally associated with organic brain disease.

dyspareunia. Painful sexual intercourse.

dysphagia. Painful or difficult swallowing.

dysphoria. Sadness, dejection, as opposed to euphoria.

dysplasia. Abnormal development of the body, its tissues, or organs.

dysplastic. See p. 82.

dysrhythmic abdominal pain. Paroxysmal abdominal pain associated with an abnormal EEG record and that responds to anticonvulsant medication. It is considered a form of epilepsy.

dysthymia. Morbid alteration of mood.

dystonia. Disturbance of muscle tone.

dystrophy. Disturbance of nutrition of a body part.

early infantile autism. Kanner's term for a condition in which the child as early as the first year of life shows marked tendencies to withdraw, becomes mute, desires sameness, relates to objects as people, and is oblivious to other people. Kanner thought this condition was possibly a precursor of schizophrenia.

ecdysiasm. Morbid tendency to disrobe in order to provoke and frustrate sexual desire in the opposite sex.

écho de la pensée. A psychotic person's feeling that others are pronouncing his thoughts. In other words, he is thinking the thoughts, but others are repeating them verbally.

echolalia. The repetition of words or sentences spoken by someone else; usually seen in schizophrenia.

echopraxia. Imitation of the body movements of another person; seen in schizophrenia.

ecnoia. Pronounced, prolonged fear reaction.

ecouteur. One who gains inordinate pleasure from listening to recounts of sexual matters.

edipism. Self-injury to the eyes.

effort syndrome. A group of symptoms of psychological origin, including shortness of breath, fast pulse, palpitation, chest pain, easy fatigue, and anxiety, that imitates cardiovascular disease. It is also called neurocirculatory asthenia and vegetative dystonia.

egersis. Prolonged or persistent wakefulness.

ego. See p. 82.

ego anxiety. Anxiety stemming from threats to the ego caused by conflicting demands of the id, the ego, and the super ego.

egodystonic. See p. 82.

ego splitting. See p. 82.

ejaculatio deficiens. Disorder of ejaculation, usually deficient semen production.

ejaculatio praecox. Ejaculation before intromission of completion of coitus.

electra complex. See p. 82.

electroencephalogram. The brain wave test in which wire leads are attached to the scalp and the minute electrical potentials generated by the brain cells are amplified and recorded. The test is useful in diagnosing organic brain diseases, epilepsy, brain tumors, and so on.

embololalia. Inclusion of irrelevant words or phrases in speech. It is associated with some schizophrenic and brain damage states.

emergency emotions. See p. 82.

encephalitis lethargica. A disturbance of sleep—mainly sleeping too much; a sequela of a certain type of encephalitis or infection of the brain. Synonym: von Economos' disease.

encopresis. Involuntary defecation: generally, defecation in bed.

enfant terrible. French term for a child or adolescent given to antisocial conduct.

enuresis. Bedwetting.

eonism. Female sexual behavior in a male.

epilepsy. A condition characterized by recurrent seizures with motor, sensory, and autonomic signs. Classification is based on symptoms, on anatomical site of origin, on EEG findings, and on etiologic factors, but none are completely satisfactory.

epileptic status. Seizures that occur in such rapid succession that the patient cannot recover from one before the next one begins.

epinosic gain. Benefits derived from being ill.

epsilon alcoholism. Problem drinking characterized by long binges that are without apparent cause, but in which there may be long periods of abstinence.

erethism. Morbid or pronounced excitability.

escape from reality. See p. 59.

euphoria. A pronounced feeling of well-being. The term is usually applied to the patient whose state of health or circumstance is not consistent with the feeling.

eviration. Distortion or morbid changes in male attitudes or behavior.

exhaustion psychoses. Abnormal psychological states brought on by prolonged exertion, sleeplessness, and starvation.

exhibitionism. The act of exposing the genitals to public view or to members of the opposite sex. The public usually associates exhibitionism, especially in males, with sexual perversion.

existential crisis. A period of psychological distress in which the person is concerned with finding meaning, new meaning, or new directions in his life.

expansiveness. A tendency toward exaggerated self-importance; euphoria. Horney's term for one solution to neurotic conflicts, in which the person is not in love with himself but with an irrational, glorified self-concept. Such a person may show strength, efficiency, aggression, domination, ambition, success, and insensitivity to the feelings of others. He mistrusts others and sees them as competitors. He views himself as confident, superior, and without limitations.

exploitative personality. Erich Fromm's term for a character orientation in which the person feels that the source of all good things (such as pleasure, knowledge, love, and affection) is external to himself, and that to meet his needs for those he must trick or force others into giving them to him.

externalization. Bringing intrapsychic conflict out into the open. It is also a mental mechanism in which the person unconsciously experiences his thoughts and feelings as occurring outside himself; it connotes a broader function than projection.

fabrication. Confabulation.

false confession. The tendency for severely depressed, masochistic, and psychotic persons to believe that they have committed criminal acts and to confess to them. For instance, schizophrenics will often appear for hospitalization following a widely publicized tragedy and claim to be the cause (for example, ''I caused the submarine Thresher to sink and was on it when it went down.'').

false pregnancy. Pseudocyesis.

false-self system. In the developing personality the temporary assumption of the personality of the most important person in the patient's life. Not identification (see p. 61).

feeblemindedness. An obsolete term for mental retardation.

fellatio. A variation of sexual activity (mouth to penis). It is often considered an example of sexual perversion.

feminine masochism. Freud's term referring to the trait of normal women to be passive, yielding, and longer suffering, and to take some pleasure from impositions in mothering and sexual activities.

festination. Tendency to involuntarily increase the speed in walking.

fetishism. The practice of attaching unusual or magical qualities to some object (for example, endowment of sexual interest in articles of clothing).

flagellantism. Obtaining pleasure from whipping or being whipped. Some psychoanalytic theorists claim that the pleasure derived is sexual.

flight into health. An occurrence in therapy in which the patient's becoming symptom-free prevents continued analysis of threatening and painful problems, leaving the underlying neurotic process unresolved.

flight of ideas. Thinking and speaking characterized by rapid and frequent changes in subject. It is characteristic of manic patients.

folie à deux. Two closely related people exhibiting nearly identical psychopathological conditions (for example, husband and wife, two siblings, or mother and son).

food grabbing. Actions of patients who, because of bulimia, are unable to control urges to take food from other patients. It is not considered to be the same as willful stealing.

formication. (Not to be confused with fornication.) The unusual sensation that insects are crawling on the skin; not infrequently found in delirium tremens.

free-floating anxiety. A state of fear described as having no attachment to any specific idea of danger. Freud stated that the presence of free-floating anxiety was characteristic of anxiety hysteria. A different point of view regards anxiety as the invariable response to any idea of imminent danger; therefore, the concept of free-floating anxiety would be invalid according to this view.

Fregoli illusion. Courbon's and Fail's term for a rare syndrome in which the patient identifies his persecutor successively in several persons (that is, the doctor, nursing attendant, neighbor, and so forth). The persecutor allegedly changes faces as the actor Fregoli once did on stage.

frottage. The act of pressing and rubbing the genitalia against a person of the opposite sex, done usually while fully clothed and while in a crowded, public place, and attempting to produce an orgasm in this manner.

frotteur. One who practices frottage.

fugue. A state in which the person appears to be rational and conscious, but of which he has no memory later on. The frequency with which alleged fugue states are associated with activities that could result in embarrassment or punishment makes them appear to be conscious falsifications rather than unconscious responses.

functional psychosis. A psychotic state without any demonstrable nervous system abnormality; without a physical, physiological, or biochemical abnormality.

gambling, impulsive. A behavior disorder in which the person gambles without consideration of the harm he is doing to himself and others. It is considered a behavior disorder, but in some cases there may be evidence or organic brain damage and mental deficiency.

gamma alcoholism. In E. M. Jellinek's classification, alcoholism characterized by a progressive course, physical dependence, acquired tolerance, and inability to control the drinking.

gammacism. A speech disorder in which the person

cannot pronounce the gutterals (g, k, x) so that he may say "doe" for "go."

gamma rhythm. EEG tracings characterized by more than 25 waves per second.

Ganser's syndrome. A simulation of a psychiatric problem. It is especially likely to be seen in prisoners who simulate a mental difficulty in order to gain a more satisfactory status. As originally described by Joseph Ganser, it is manifested by the device of giving approximate answers to questions with a deliberate attempt to create the impression of psychosis.

gargoylism. An inherited condition characterized by mental deficiency and marked deformity of the body and face, which gives the condition its name.

gelasmus. Hysterical, spasmodic laughter.

general paresis. Central nervous system syphilis.

geophagia. The act of eating dirt; a form of pica.

geriopsychosis. Senile psychosis.

Gesell scales. Tests that measure the general level of intelligence and maturity in children.

Gilles de la Tourette's syndrome. Severe facial expressions, choreo-athetoid movements of trunk and extremities, convulsions, and croprolalia. The cause is not certain. It is a rare condition seen almost exclusively in children.

globus hystericus. The sensation of a lump in the throat, usually associated with fear and often interfering with food intake. Fear is likely to be the basis for the symptom, which is probably mediated by a contraction of pharyngeal or laryngeal muscles. It is generally regarded as a hysterical symptom when no physical cause can be found.

glossodynia. Painful or unpleasant feeling of the tongue.

glossolalia. Unintelligible speech.

glue sniffing. Inhaling the volatile solvents of glue to produce an acute brain syndrome or toxic psychosis.

grandiosity. Unrealistic feeling of importance, worth, or of having unusual or magical powers. It may be seen as part of the delusion of certain psychoses.

grand mal epilepsy. Tonic-clonic seizures with loss of consciousness. Many of these seizures are preceded by significant signs and feelings called prodromata and by aura, which signal the onset of the seizure. During the tonic phase, all skeletal muscles of the body are in maximal contraction and rigidity. After this, follows the clonic phase of violent shaking and tremors, during which the patient may involuntarily bite his tongue, pass urine,

or defecate. At the end of the latter phase, the patient is in a deep coma from which he recovers slowly, usually in several hours.

grand mal seizures. Grand mal epilepsy.

graphology. See p. 84.

gratification. The meeting of a need; the satisfaction of a drive or an instinct.

grief. Ordinary sadness and disappointment resulting from the loss of a loved person or object. It is often contrasted with depression, which might be described as pathological grief.

grimace. A severe or exaggerated facial expression.

group perversion. Any sort of sexual activity involving the participation of more than two persons. One example of this is the orgy.

habit disorder. A diagnostic term for certain childhood psychiatric problems in which there is some unusual habit pattern evident (temper tantrums, thumb sucking at late ages, bedwetting, nail biting).

hair pulling. A tendency to pull one's own head hair or body hair. The practice may range from mild, habitual tugs to severe tugs in which large patches of scalp are denuded. Hair pulling usually indicates an emotional disturbance.

hallucinations. A false perception without an external stimulus (for example, the person may see or hear someone when there is no one there).

hallucinogen. See p. 84.

hallucinosis. The condition of experiencing hallucinations.

hallucinosis, alcohol. A state brought on by ingestion of alcohol in which the person hears and sometimes sees persons and things that are not there. These are usually threatening to him and disappear when sobriety returns. Alcohol hallucinosis is thought by many to be a latent psychotic state brought out by alcohol intoxication. In this state, the person is oriented to time and place, as contrasted to the lack of orientation in delirium tremens.

hangover. See p. 131.

haplology. Omission of syllables caused by rapidity or pressure of speech (for example, as seen in mania).

headache, psychogenic. Headaches produced by nonphysical causes. These are thought to be the most common types of headaches and are usually associated with repressed feeling and emotion (such as anger, range, or resentment).

hebephrenic. A type of schizophrenia manifested by an ineffectual, childlike silliness of behavior. No longer categorized as deviant or abnormal in official American Psychiatric Association nomenclature.

hebetic. Of puberty; specifically refers to mental illness during adolescence.

hebetude. Blunting of affect; dullness of emotion.

hemeraphonia. Inability to use the voice during the day; usually seen in hysterical states.

hemianesthesia, hysterical. Inability to feel anything over one half of the body. This condition can usually be differentiated from anesthesia produced by injury or disease of the nervous system by the anatomical distribution of the affected areas.

hemiballismus. Severe motor restlessness; flailing of arms and legs, on one side of the body only. It is caused by a lesion in the subthalamic nucleus of Lüys.

hemichorea. Having the characteristics of a chorea on only one side of the body.

heterolalia. Use of inappropriate or meaningless words instead of those intended.

heterophasia. Heterolalia.

hoarding personality. Erich Fromm's term for the person who feels that the outside world cannot be depended on and that he must keep and hoard his possessions, affections, love, and so on. Such a person tends to be remote, orderly, obsessive, and rigid.

homosexual. Engaging in sexual intercourse or having a sexual orientation toward persons of one's own sex; unconventional sex behavior between members of the same sex. Psychoanalytic theory places a great deal of emphasis on the importance of latent homosexuality. This concept presupposes the existence of unconscious homosexuality to which the subject reacts with characteristic behavior or with fear. Overt homosexuality is a term used to describe individuals who actually engage in homosexual practices. The content of schizophrenics' fantasies and hallucinations is often homosexual in character, and this observation has been used to support theories that ascribe etiological importance to latent homosexuality. A different theoretical approach sees homosexual manifestations as the result instead of the cause of some problem.

homosexual panic. An acute reaction in persons who are latent homosexuals and are exposed to life in barracks or dormitories for the first time or to closeness to men such as in a crowded bus. Fear of a breakdown may result in the person's becoming confused, hallucinated, and sometimes agitated to the point of becoming severely psychotic.

hospitalism. René Spitz's term for a lag in mental and physical development, apathy, immobility, frequent infections, physical wasting, withdrawal from strangers, and often death in infants institutionalized early and separated from their mothers.

Huntington's chorea. An inherited brain disorder in which there is progressive degeneration of brain tissue. There are both mental and physical symptoms; characteristically, these are jerking, twisting movements and grimaces. The usual age of onset is middle life.

Hurler's disease. Gargoylism.

hydrocephalus. A condition in which drainage of cerebrospinal fluid from within the brain is blocked, leading to distortion of the brain cavities, enlargement of the head, mental retardation, and possibly death. It can be congenital or acquired (for example, following an infection of the brain and its coverings).

hydrophobia. Rabies; an infectious disease of the brain, transmitted to man by infected animals and usually fatal when the fully developed condition is present.

hypalgesia. Reduced sensitivity to pain.

hyperacusia. Impairment of hearing.

hyperacusis. Hypersensitivity of hearing sense. There is an increased awareness of sound. Sounds are perceived as being unusually loud.

hyperhidrosis. Excessive sweating.

hyperkinesis. Excessive or exaggerated bodily movements.

hyperkinetic disorders. A condition in children that is characterized by poor impulse control, hyperactivity, difficulty in maintaining attention or shifting the subject of their thinking, and reduced ability to perform tasks requiring fine coordination.

hyperlogia. Loquacity.

hypermnesia. An increased ability to recall information not usually remembered. It is nearly always associated with an abnormal mental condition such as psychosis, head injury, and drug intoxication.

hyperopia. Farsightedness.

hyperosmia. Increased sensitivity to odors.

hyperpathia. An overreaction to stimuli; the experiencing of severe pain or marked discomfort in response to even light stimuli to the skin. Hyperpathia usually follows damage to the thalamus.

hyperponesis. Increased motor (muscle) activity not evident to visual examination but measurable by electromyograph.

hyperpragia. Pronounced increase in mental activity (in mania).

hypersexuality. Excessive sexual activity.

hypersomnia. Excessive sleeping or drowsiness.

hypertelorism. A deformity of the face characterized by excessive distance between the eyes. When pronounced it is often associated with mental deficiency.

hypervectorial. Wolman's term for a form of role reversal; in the family of a schizophrenic, the parents demand love, care, worry, parenting from the child who is terror stricken by this role and the abnormal mother-father-child relationship; the parents give little or no emotional nurturing to the child. Such a disturbance leads to schizophrenia in the child. See vectorial and vectoriasis praecox.

hyperventilation syndrome. Rapid, deep respiration that produces alkalosis, states of near unconsciousness, and tetany. It is often mistakenly diagnosed as epilepsy.

hypnagogic. Having the quality of inducing sleep.

hypnagogic hallucinations. In the drowsy state preceding sleep, the person vividly sees objects and persons and hears voices and sounds. They may be associated with a temporary state of paralysis but are not considered to be pathological.

hypnopompic. See p. 61.

hypobulia. Impairment of will.

hypochondria. An ancient diagnostic label applied to patients with frequent and manifold somatic complaints. Today, the term is used descriptively rather than diagnostically to refer to the patient who exhibits excessive complaints.

hypoesthesia. Reduced sensitivity to sensation, especially touch and pain.

hypokinesis. Reduction of bodily movements.

hypomanic. Behavior characterized by an abundance of activity and speech, but less extreme than that in a manic state. The term is used loosely sometimes to refer to relatively normal people who are unusually active, quick, and talkative.

hypophrasia. Slowness of speech.

hypothymia. Abnormally low intensity of emotional reactions; despair; depression.

hypsarrhythmia. Massive myoclonic seizures of infancy characterized by lapses of consciousness and abrupt flexion of head, trunk, or extremities; often associated with mental deficiency.

hysteria. Synonymous with conversion reaction. Hysteria is an ancient term, having many connotations throughout the ages; it was once attributed to the function of the uterus in women. By the end of the nineteenth century it had come to mean almost any kind of unusual behavior in women, especially when associated with dramatic disability in the absence of detectable physical pathological causes.

hysterical personality. A diagnostic term for persons who show lability, excitability, emotionality, exaggerated affects, suggestibility, histrionic gesturing, flashy dress, and conversion symptoms, without evidence of a psychosis. Sometimes it is used derogatorily.

idea of influence. Thinking that another person or an external power has control over one's thoughts, feeling, or behavior. It may be seen in paranoid states and schizophrenia.

ideas of reference. False ideas that other people are directing their attentions, thoughts, or activities upon oneself. It is often seen in schizophrenics and may be regarded as the precursor to a paranoic delusion (for example, the idea that strangers are talking about one).

ideational apraxia. Loss of the ability to use common objects; for example, the person may pick up a fork but may not be able to use it to pick up food.

idée fixe. A fixed, rigid idea; an obsession.

ideokinetic apraxia. Inability to plan and carry out simple skillful acts.

ideomotor apraxia. Inability to imitate or carry out hand movements.

ideoplastia. Suggestion, as in hypnosis.

idiogamy. See p. 61.

idiot savant. A person who, although apparently possessed of limited or deficient intelligence, shows an unusual aptitude for some particular kind of skill (such as music or memory).

imbecile. Obsolete term for a mentally retarded person.

impotence. See p. 61.

inadequate personality. A person who fails to carry out any physical, intellectual, emotional, or social duty adequately. This failure occurs even though the person has no severe mental or physical incapacity.

incest. Sexual relations between close blood relatives, especially between parent and child or between siblings.

incontinence. Inability to control the function of bladder or bowels. More broadly, it means the inability to control urges to unacceptable behavior.

induced psychosis. A severe mental abnormality brought on by events, personal influence, chemicals, trauma. Examples include folie à deux, drug psychosis, and posttraumatic psychosis.

infantile autism. A severe mental condition beginning in infancy that is characterized by the infant's failure to relate to his parents, complete indifference to the presence of adults, failure to develop speech and language, and obsessive repetition of behavior (such as head banging, shutting doors, and hair pulling).

infantile behavior. Conduct in adults who cannot delay or resist impulses, show temper tantrums, display sudden fits of anger, and express their erotic and sexual needs without sufficient regard for propriety. They are not necessarily neurotic or otherwise mentally ill, but because of their behavior, they often come into conflict with the law and other social agencies.

infantile cerebral lipoidosis. A group of inherited diseases manifested by mental retardation, in which there is an abnormal accumulation of lipids (fatty compounds) in the brain. These conditions are grouped variously by the type of lipids involved, the age of onset, and the area of brain affected. Symptoms may include blindness, paralysis, and death.

irrational. See p. 62.

insanity. An obsolete medical term for psychosis or mental illness; still used in legal terminology.

insomnia. Inability to fall asleep or to sleep long enough to secure adequate rest.

instrument. Any kind of measuring device used in psychological testing.

invalidism. Chronic ill health or prolongation of an illness or its symptoms that is caused by the desire for compensation from a pension, insurance payments, or other secondary gain.

involutional melancholia depressive. Involutional psychosis.

involutional psychosis. A psychotic state, typically depression, occurring in women at the time of menopause. In official nomenclature, involutional psychotic reaction occurs under the main heading of psychotic disorders (of psychogenic origin). It is called a late-age schizophrenia by some psychiatrists who include all psychogenic psychoses under the heading of schizophrenia.

ironed-out facies. Masklike facies.

irritability. The quality of anger mixed with oversensitivity and anxiety, especially in situations where the individual cannot resolve a conflict or otherwise effectively deal with reality situations. Irritability is seen often in manic states, brain diseases, and in some intoxication states.

irrumation. Fellatio.

jacksonian epilepsy. A focal or partial motor seizure, first described by Hughlings Jackson, that begins with twitching of a muscle group, often fingers, and progresses upward to the arm, neck, and head, often to become a generalized seizure.

jactation. Jactitation.

jactitation. Jumping and moving about restlessly.

Jakob-Creutzfeldt's disease. A relatively rare degenerative disease of the brain.

jamais vu. The false feeling of unfamiliarity with situations that have actually been experienced.

jealously, delusional. A condition found in schizophrenia and other disorders, in which there is no obvious provocation of the reactions. There are strongly ambivalent feelings, sustained anger and hostility, and no loss of interest in the loved person. It is often associated with sexual deviation.

jocasta complex. See p. 85.

juvenile paresis. Syphilis of the central nervous system acquired before birth or very soon afterwards. It is manifested by mental retardation, sight and hearing defects, and deformities of the nose and teeth.

kakidrosis. Perspiration with a foul odor.

katalepsy. Catalepsy.

katasexual. Necrophilic.

kinesalgia. Pain on movement.

kleptomania. The morbid irresistible urge to steal.

koro. A phobia reported among Chinese and Indonesians; the patient becomes fearful that his penis will disappear into his abdomen and he will die.

Krabbe's disease. Acute infantile, diffuse sclerosis of the brain leading to mental deficiency and organic brain disease.

kuru. An organic brain disease of uncertain cause that slowly progresses to death. The mental manifestations are mainly changes in mood and affect. This condition occurs mainly in the South Pacific area.

la belle indifference. A relative lack of concern shown toward a major disability. It is a quality exhibited by patients classified in the category of conversion hysteria.

labile. Rapid, unpredictable emotional change.

lability. The quality of making changes freely. Applied to a patient's emotional state when it changes easily and frequently.

lachschlag. Cataplexy.

lalopathy. Logopathy. (See p. 63.)

lambitus. See p. 62.

lapsus. See p. 85.

lata(h). A condition, found mainly in the Malays, in which the affected person shows a marked startle reaction, involuntary jumping and movements, and coprolalia.

Laurence-Moon-Biedl syndrome. Adiposogenital dystrophy. (See p. 114.)

lead pipe rigidity. Waxy flexibility.

learning defect. An inability, usually in children, to carry out the processes of acquiring and using information. It is most often found in children, but it can occur at any age and be caused by emotional disorder, habit, or organic disease.

learning disability. A disorder characterized by difficulty in learning to read (duplexia) write (dysgraphia) and calculate (dyscalculia). Affects school-age children of normal or above normal intelligence. May be related to slow progression of developing perceptual motor skills.

lesbian. A female homosexual.

lethal catatonia. A condition, probably a form of schizophrenia, in which the person remains in a state of severe psychomotor hyperexcitability until he is exhausted; formerly, some patients died of exhaustion. Now, with modern treatment, death is seldom the outcome.

lie detection test. The use of an instrument (polygraph) that records changes in physiological reactions, such as heart rate, respiration, blood pressure, and galvanic skin changes, that occur in response to emotions such as anxiety, anger, and tension. Supposedly, these responses differ when the person is truthful and when he is lying.

lie detector. Polygraph; an instrument that measures changes in a person's pulse rate, respiration, and skin resistance on a continuous sheet of paper. These changes may indicate whether or not a person is telling the truth if the record is taken during a period of questioning and if changes in response to various questions are noted.

limophoitas. Stress psychosis induced by starvation.

limophthisis. Emaciation secondary to starvation.

lissencephaly. A developmental defect in which the brain shows no convolutions. It is associated with severe mental deficiency. Synonym: agyria.

logamnesia. Moderate aphasia; forgetting of words.

logic-tight. A way of describing a person's resistance to accepting more logical explanations for his false beliefs. The term is usually applicable to delusions.

Lowe's disease. A disorder with mental deficiency associated with abnormal kidney function.

lucid interval. Clearness of thought between periods of confusion and irrational thinking. It may be associated with organic as well as nonorganic mental states.

lues. Syphilis.

luetic. Pertaining to syphilis.

lumbar puncture. A diagnostic procedure in which a hollow needle is inserted into the space surrounding the spinal cord to withdraw a sample of the cerebrospinal fluid in order to measure pressure of the fluid within the space; the needle insertion is made in the lumbar area of the spine.

lunacy. An obsolete term for psychosis; occasionally found today in legal terminology.

lust murder. Killing a person in an act of passion; murder to satisfy a sexual need; murder because of or involving sexual stimulation.

lycanthropy. The delusion that one is a wolf. Lycanthropy was a form of insanity reported during the middle ages.

lycorexia. Bulimia.

macropsia. An illusion that persons and objects are larger than they really are. This condition is seen in delirious, toxic, drug-induced states and in hysterical state.

mactation. Sacrificial murder.

magical thinking. Daydreaming; wishful thinking.

maladaptation. See p. 63.

malevolent transformation. See p. 86.

malignant identity diffusion. See p. 86.

malingering. Deliberate simulation of illness for the purpose of selfish gain. In the presence of physical complaints and in the absence of commensurate physical pathological conditions, the question of malingering is often raised, especially when there is a financial settlement at stake.

mania. A diagnostic term that refers to a psychotic state characterized by excitement and overactivity.

manic-depressive. A diagnostic term represented in the official nomenclature under Psychotic Disorders, as affective-reactions, manic-depressive reaction. Formerly, the psychotic states manifested by excitement and overactivity were known as manias and those demonstrated by underactivity and poverty of emotional expression as melancholias. Later, it was found that the same person might exhibit both of these at alternate periods of life; so the assumption grew that the two represented cycles in the same condition.

marasmus. Debility, atrophy, wasting. It is seen in anorexia nervosa and in emotionally neglected hospitalized children. It was first described by Rene Spitz.

Marchiafava's disease. Degeneration of the corpus callosum of the brain, associated mental deterioration, psychoticlike behavior, and neurological signs. It is a disease of unknown cause, but it is related to alcoholism.

marketing personality. Erich Fromm's term for the person who experiences himself as a commodity and his value as that of an exchange item.

masculine protest. The manifestation of a woman's wish to be like a man, such as wearing male attire and becoming aggressive and sadistic; from Alfred Adler's individual psychology.

masklike facies. Immobility of facial expressive movements; usually caused by increased muscle tone.

masochism. Obtaining pleasure from self-punishment. Psychoanalytic theory postulates that this pleasure is sexual in nature. The term is loosely used to denote willingly accepted hardship or sacrifice.

mass hysteria. An abnormality of group behavior in which members of the group carry out activity when together that might not be carried out by individuals (for example, streaking or rioting).

mass psychoses. Severe abnormal behavior of members of a group that none would carry out if alone (such as belief in witches and witch burning).

megalomania. Grandiosity.

melancholia. Obsolete diagnostic term for depression.

Meniere's disease. A condition of unknown origin, characterized by dizziness, noise in the ears, and deafness.

meningovascular lues. A form of syphilitic infection of the brain in which the main involvement is in the meninges and the blood vessels, with the nerve cell tissue being relatively uninvolved.

mental age. The level of achievement on a standard test as compared with averages for others of different ages.

mental defect. Obsolete term for mental retardation.

mental deficiency. The state of intellectual achievement that is substantially below that of others of the same age. The term is synonymous with mental retardation. Previously, the three levels of mental deficiency were termed moron (high), imbecile (middle), and idiot (low). Today the terms mild, moderate, and severe are used.

mental retardation. Mental deficiency.

mental subnormality. Mental deficiency.

mental tests. An early term for psychological tests.

merycism. Voluntary regurgitation and chewing of food. Rumination.

metalcoholic psychoses. A group of brain diseases and severe behavior disorders (for example, withdrawal states, such as delirium tremens and al-coholic hallucinosis, and such nonspecific states as the dysmnesic syndrome, paranoid reactions, and intellectual deterioration that accompany prolonged use of alcohol).

metanymy. Norman Cameron's term for the tendency of schizophrenics to use imprecise words (for example, "I have a happy house" to mean "I have a happy home").

methilepsia. Morbid desire for drugs.

meticulosity. Excessive neatness, punctiliousness, orderliness. It is seen in obsessive-compulsive disorders.

microgeny. The immediate unfolding of a phenomenon; the sequence of the necessary steps in the carrying out of a psychological process. The unconscious process of searching and association in developing a correct response to a stimulus.

micrographia. An impairment of handwriting in which the letters in the first part of a sentence are of normal size but become progressively smaller with each successive word. It is associated with Parkinson's disease.

microphonia. Weakness of voice.

micropsia. A condition in which persons and objects are perceived as being abnormally small. It is associated with toxic states, delirious conditions, and drug-induced states.

migraine. Headache characterized by recurrence in a definite pattern of preceding signs (for example, prodromal signs), such as nausea, vomiting, appearance of blind spots in the visual field, and other visceral symptoms. The pain is usually localized to one side of the head. It is thought to have multiple causes, but psychological factors are known to play a strong role.

Minnesota Multiphasic Personality Inventory (M.M.P.I.). A psychological test in which the subject answers a large number of "yes" or "no" questions; from these, estimates are made of personality configurations as compared to a statistical standard. The test is reported in the form of a profile.

misanthropy. See p. 64.

misidentification. The mistaken belief that a person or object is someone or something else. This may occur in normal persons, but it is seen to a pronounced degree as a feature of schizophrenic delusions.

misopedia. See p. 64.

mixoscopia. Voyeurism; especially of watching coitus.

mongolism. A complex of congenital deformities, including defective brain development and resultant mental deficiency, and especially characterized by an orientallike appearance of the face; Hurler's disease.

monophasia. Ability to utter only one word or phrase; an aphasia.

monoplegia. Paralysis of a single body part.

monosymptomatic schizophrenia. Schizophrenia manifest in only one delusion, with the remainder of the personality apparently intact.

mood swings. Variations in mood; usually denotes swings from elation to depression.

moral masochism. Freud's term for the attitudes of persons whose life styles show self-punitive behavior and who are overly strict and demanding of themselves.

moron. Obsolete term for a mentally retarded person.

morphinism. Morphine dependency.

mucous colitis. A severe condition of the colon characterized by pain, alternating periods of diarrhea and constipation, and passage of bloody fecal material. It is thought to have strong psychological factors in its causes.

multiple personality. A condition in which the person shows two or more kinds of behavior, as if he were two separate people.

nanism. Dwarfism.

narcissistic neurosis. Freud's term for what is now termed psychoneurosis (for example, anxiety reactions or obsessive-compulsive reactions).

narcolepsy. A condition characterized by attacks of overwhelming desire to sleep.

narcosis. Unconsciousness produced by drugs or anesthetics.

narcotism. Under the influence of or dependency produced by a narcotic.

necromimesis. Imitating death. The term is often used to mean the delusion that one is dead.

necrophilism. The morbid desire to be with or to have sexual intercourse with a dead body.

necrosadism. Erotic pleasure from mutilating a dead body.

negative therapeutic reaction. See p. 88.

negativism. The tendency to adopt a viewpoint opposite to that presented or a tendency to refuse all suggestions. It is seen in an exaggerated form in schizophrenia.

neography. Writing of neologisms.

neolalia. Speaking in neologisms.

neologism. A word coined by a person for which only he knows the meaning.

neomimism. Stereotyped senseless gestures.

neomism. Bobon's term for mannerisms, repetitions of movements, affectations, grimaces, and other nerve and unusual movements seen in schizophrenics. It is meant to indicate a relationship to neologisms and neoformisms.

neophasia. Neolalia.

neuralgia. Pain, usually recurrent in type, felt along the course of a nerve or cluster of nerves.

neurasthenia. An obsolete term denoting patients who complained of easy fatigability and helplessness. The presumption was that a state of nervous exhaustion was the basis.

neuritis. See p. 123.

neurocirculatory asthenia. Effort syndrome; also called vegetative dystonia.

neurodermatitis. An inflammatory rash of the skin thought to be primarily caused by psychological factors.

neurosis. An ill-defined term with no universal agreement about its definition. In general, it is now used to suggest a less serious psychiatric problem in which the person may experience moderate psychological pain, anxiety, and various bodily symptoms that are without physical cause. It is also used interchangeably with psychoneurosis.

neurotic. The state of having a neurosis or various symptoms of a neurosis. It is often used loosely as a mild epithet.

neurotic traits. See p. 64.

nictitation. Spasmodic blinking.

nightmare. See p. 64.

night terror. Pavor nocturnus.

nihilism. See p. 88.

nihilistic. Given to pessimistic ideas of worthlessness and aimlessness.

nihilistic delusions. The belief, likely to be found in schizophrenics and psychotically depressed persons, that the patient himself, other people, or even the world do not exist.

noctambulation. Somnambulism.

noesis. A condition of extreme elation seen in certain psychotic states in which the patient may feel that an immense revelation has occurred to him, that no mystery of the universe is unknown to him.

nomadism. Morbid tendency to wander.

noogenic neurosis. See p. 88.

nostomania. Intense homesickness.

not me. See p. 88.

nyctalopia. Night blindness.

nymphomania. An insatiable desire in women for sexual activity.

nystagmus. Involuntary side-to-side or up-and-down movements of the eyes. It is often associated with disease of the nervous system.

object-sorting test. A test to help determine organic brain disease.

obnubilation. Partial loss of consciousness.

obsession. A painful, unwelcome, persistent idea, emotion, or urge.

obsessive behavior. See p. 88.

obsessive character. A person who is orderly, obstinate, perfectionistic, overly meticulous and punctual, and frugal; given to marked ambivalence. Freud thought these traits were an outgrowth of conflict caused by excessive preoccupation with bowel training and designated them as examples of anal fixation.

obsessive-compulsive. A diagnostic term in the official nomenclature: Psychoneurotic Disorder, obsessive-compulsive reaction. It is a neurotic system characterized by an excessive preoccupation with orderliness, pessimistic thoughts, and rigid patterns of behavior.

obstruction. Blocking.

occupation neurosis. A condition, usually considered to be hysterical, in which the patient cannot execute a specialized movement required by his job, but can easily use these same movements and muscle groups in the performance of some other act.

oceanic feelings. Any feeling secondary to loss of distinction between the ego and the environment. They are thought to exist in earliest infancy prior to differentiation of the ego from external reality and are seen in states of pronounced regression (that is, schizophrenia) as all-encompassing dread, omnipotence.

oculogyric crisis. An acute dystonia involving the extrinsic muscles of the eyes, causing the eyes to involuntarily deviate. It is seen in hysterical states and secondary to treatment with neuroleptics.

odontoprisis. Bruxism.

oedipal complex. See p. 88.

olfactory seizure. The sensation of smelling something (usually an unpleasant odor), caused by abnormal brain activity. It is a form of epilepsy that rarely occurs alone; rather it occurs as part of a more generalized seizure.

oligophrenia. Mental deficiency.

omnipotence. Feeling all-powerful, all-knowing; seen in pronounced regression (that is, schizophrenia mania); megalomania.

onanism. Masturbation. Narrowly, it is coitus interruptus with ejaculation occurring outside the vagina.

oneiorphrenia. A rare disturbance, usually considered to be a borderline psychotic state, charac-terized by mild to severe dream-like states, confusion, and disorders of affect and thinking.

oneiroid. A dreamlike state.

onychophagy. Nail biting.

opiumism. Addiction to opium.

orality. See p. 89.

oral phase. See p. 89.

oral sadism. See p. 89.

organ eroticism. See p. 89.

organic brain disease. Mental or nervous morbidity caused by physical or physiological changes in the brain.

organic deficit reactions. Mental deficiency occurring in various degrees. They are usually divided into those secondary to structural or chemical changes in the brain and those that are not.

organicity. Indicative of organic changes in the brain (that is, errors of memory and judgment, loss of coordination).

organic psychosis. A psychotic state associated with a pathological condition of the brain.

organic tests. Tests used to detect brain damage.

orgone. See p. 89.

osmolagnia. Morbid attraction to certain odors.

osphresiolagnia. Morbid interest or attraction to odors.

overinclusive. Blurring of meanings by the attachment of the same definition to many objects, some of which are not related (for example, ''happy home'' used to refer to a house, a submarine, and trees, all at the same time).

overinhibited child. A conduct disorder in children characterized by traits of seclusiveness, shyness, and sensitiveness. In the overinhibited child, worrying, apathy, and undue submissiveness are also seen.

pain dependence. See p. 89.

paleologic thinking. A form of reasoning used by schizophrenics in which identical predicates rather than identical subjects are used to reach the conclusion. It differs from Aristotelian logic in which identical subjects are used to identify the conclusion. For instance, usually one might reason. ''To be President of the United States, one must be a citizen of this country. Carter is President, so he must, therefore, be a citizen.'' A schizophrenic might reason, ''To be President of the United States, one must be a citizen of this country. I am a citizen; therefore, I am President.''

palpitation. Awareness of one's own heart beat. It is a rapid and strong heart beat felt by the patient.

palsy. Paralysis.

pananxiety. Used in the description of pseudoneurotic schizophrenics to denote that the patient feels an all-pervading anxiety. The anxiety at first appears to be of neurotic intensity, but after a time in treatment the spread of the anxiety evolves and does not respond to treatment that would ordinarily be expected to produce improvement in most psychoneurotics. The anxiety is usually free floating and seldom subsides, even temporarily.

panneurosis. See p. 89.

pansexualism. See p. 89.

parageusia. Disorder of taste.

paraleresis. Mild delirium.

paralexia. A form of dyslexia in which the patient misreads printed words as words that are meaningless.

paralogia. Distortion of reason.

paralysis agitans. Parkinson's disease.

paralytic ileus. Paralysis of the ileal muscles; a rare complication of anticholinergic drug therapy.

paramimia. Inappropriate use of gestures; use of gestures that do not confirm current affect.

paramnesia. 1. A memory disorder in which the person confuses fantasies and dreams for real past events, and vice versa. It is pronounced in schizophrenics, but occurs to some degree in everyone. 2. Inability to remember exact meanings of words.

paranoia. A very rare form of psychosis, characterized by the gradual development of a complex paranoid system in which, most often, the patient becomes grandoise but may develop feelings of persecution. Characteristically, there are no hallucinations, and that portion of the personality that exists outside the paranoid system remains essentially intact despite the chronic course of the condition.

paranoid. The quality of falsely imagining others to be antagonistic; usually as a result of a massive use of projection.

paranoid personality. A diagnostic category that includes persons who show coldness, withdrawal, and extreme sensitivity in interpersonal relations. They utilize projection in dealing with anxiety, which makes them suspicious, serious, jealous, and stubborn. In official nomenclature it is listed under Personality Pattern Disturbance.

paranoid pseudocommunity. See p. 89.

paranoid schizophrenia. A reaction characterized by autistic, unrealistic thinking, mainly involving delusions of persecution or grandeur, ideas of influence, ideas of reference, and hallucinations. There is almost always an attitude of hostility and aggression and unpredictable behavior.

paranoid states. A subdivision of senile disorders manifested by hostility and extremely irrascible behavior, with the person involved having the marked feeling that everyone has turned against him.

paraphasia. Distortion of speech; an aphasia in which wrong or senseless combinations of words are used.

paraphilia. Practice of or habituation to sexual perversions.

paraphrasia. Paraphasia.

paraphrenia. Emil Kraepelin's term used to differentiate certain of the paranoid disorders from paranoid schizophrenia.

parataxic distortion. See p. 90.

parataxic messages. See p. 90.

parataxic mode. H. S. Sullivan's term for experiencing the world in an autistic interpretation of events and people and a subjective personal system of communication. Seen in young children and in mentally ill adults. (See prototaxic mode, p. 65, and syntaxic mode, p. 70.)

parathymia. Inappropriate mood.

paresis. Moderate or partial paralysis. It is sometimes used to denote dementia and paralysis such as would be found secondary to syphilitic infection of the nervous system.

paresthesia. An abnormal sensation; a perverted or morbid sensation (for example, a burning, crawling feeling).

parkinsonism. Parkinson's disease.

Parkinson's disease. Paralysis agitans. It is a condition characterized chiefly by masklike facial expression, coarse tremor, stooped posture, cogwheel rigidity of the muscles, slowness and reduction of movement, dysarthria, and abnormalities of gait and autonomic nervous system symptoms, caused by diffuse lesions in the basal ganglia. It may also be caused by organic brain disease. It is frequently seen, usually in a reversible form, secondary to treatment with major tranquilizers.

parorexia. Perversion of appetite.

parosmia. Distortion of olfaction.

partialism. A form of fetishism in which the person's sexual interest are fixated on a body part, such as feet, legs, or nose, to the exclusion of normal sexual interests.

passive aggression. A way of resisting the demands made by others with concealed inactive resistance such as procrastinating, pouting, stubbornness, and inefficiency. The practice of dawdling in children may be seen as an example of passive aggression.

passive-aggressive personality. A diagnostic term under personality trait disturbance, divided into three types: passive-dependent type, passive-aggressive type, and aggressive type, which is a persistent reaction type characterized by irritability, destructive behavior, and tantrums.

passive-dependent. See p. 65.

pathocure. The abatement of a neurotic condition with the appearance of an organic disease.

pathologic intoxication. A reaction to ingested alcohol, characterized by sudden severe excitation, symptoms and signs of drunkenness, and partial loss or clouding of consciousness, in addition to violent antisocial behavior. The person usually has no memory for the episodes, which terminate, usually, in sleep or when sobriety returns.

pavor diurnus. Attacks of terror, similar to pavor nocturnus, occurring during daytime.

pavor nocturnus. Nightmares, usually in children, manifested by excited activity, crying, and evidence of severe fright, often while seemingly still awake. Usually the child has no memory of the experience afterward. Night terror.

pederasty. A sexual deviation (intercourse per anus), usually with boys.

pedicatio. Originally meaning sexual desire for contact by an adult with a child, but that has now evolved generally to mean anal intercourse.

pellagra psychosis. A delirious state usually preceded by depression, anxiety, fatigability, and lack of energy secondary to prolonged deficiency of niacin (nicotinic acid). The mental symptoms exist in addition to skin changes, diarrhea, and mouth problems, which are characteristic of pellagra.

penis envy. See p. 90.

perfectionism. A character defense in which a person demands more of himself and of others than the situation requires. It is likely to be seen in a compulsive personality.

persecution complex. Used loosely to describe a person who feels that the world is against him; a person who feels ''sorry for himself.'' Also, it refers to the paranoid outlook of being malignantly mistreated.

perseveration. Frequent repetition of an activity, a verbal expression, or a mannerism. It is seen in schizophrenia where the repetition appears to be a type of ritual or in organic brain syndromes where memory defects might be the basis.

personal equation. Early psychologists' term for a measure of reaction time; the difference in time between an event and the person's reaction to it.

personality disorders. A category heading in the official diagnostic nomenclature that includes persons who exhibit unusual patterns of behavior, but who do not exhibit the distress and discomfort expected of the psychoneurotic or psychotic. Examples of this are alcoholism, drug addiction, schizoid personality. Synonym: character disorders.

personality pattern disturbance. A diagnostic category that includes persons with a deep-seated personality disturbance characterized by a pronounced inability to adapt to stress or change response patterns when needed. Often in the face of continued stress they regress to a psychotic state because of an inability to develop adult modes of expression and action.

personality trait disturbance. A diagnostic category that includes patients whose behavior is organized around a single, well-defined response tendency. Such tendencies are holdovers from early developmental periods that were useful and effective in those earlier periods but that are maladaptive and self-destructive when the person uses them in adult life.

perversio horribilis. Cannibalism when carried out as a sexual perversion.

perversion. Any one of the many unconventional types of sexual behavior. Examples of this are homosexuality, transvestism, and pederasty. Current studies suggest that unusual types of sexual practices may not be as pathological as they were once thought.

pervert. One given to practicing perversions.

petit mal epilepsy. A seizure disorder of childhood, rarely having onset after the age of twenty. It may be manifested by lapses of consciousness with twitching of facial muscles, lapses of consciousness with myoclonic twitches, and episodes of sudden loss of consciousness and muscle tone. It often disappears after adolescence but may persist into adulthood.

phallic woman. See p. 90.

phantom limb phenomenon. Vividly experiencing the existence of an amputated limb. The experience is usually one of pain that appears to come from the lost limb.

phobia. An intense fear of some situation not ordinarily associated with danger that results in attempts to avoid the situation. Examples are fear of small places, fear of open places, and fear of crossing the street.

phobic reaction. Phobia.

physical dependence. Physiological changes that

occur after prolonged drug use that apparently cause the organism to experience severe and unpleasant sensations if the intake of the drug is halted. These changes are not completely understood, but they are thought to be caused by changes in metabolic processes within the cells of the body.

piblokto. A mental disorder occurring in the Eskimo in which the person suddenly begins to scream, to run wildly, and to tear off his clothes. The person is usually calm and amnestic about the event afterward. It is usually considered to be a hysterical dissociative state.

pica. An appetite for or ingestion of unusual substances, such as dirt, hair, or feces. It is most likely to be seen in severely disturbed persons, although such practices also occur in normal young children and in chronically malnourished children.

Pick's disease. A progressive cerebral atrophy described by Arnold Pick (of Czechoslovakia). It is associated with a psychosis similar to that found in senility, and it is similar to Alzheimer's disease.

placing into mouth. Arieti's term for an advanced state of regression in schizophrenia; small objects are indiscriminately put in the mouth. Objects such as leaves, roaches, paper, pencils, and wood may also be chewed and swallowed with resulting injury to the patient.

pleniloquence. Garrulousness; excessive talking.

pleonexia. Morbid tendency for acquisition or gain.

pleurothotonus. Spastic lateral bending of the body.

plumbism. Lead poisoning.

pneumoencephalography. Injection of air into the ventricles of the brain as a contrast medium to better view the intracranial structures when x-ray films are made. This is carried out as a diagnostic procedure for brain disease.

polydipsia. Excessively frequent drinking or thirst.

polyuria. Excessively frequent urination.

pornographomania. The compulsive collection of erotic literature, art, movies, and so on, as opposed to the casual and occasional acquisition of such material by juveniles and other relatively normal persons.

pornolagnia. Morbid desire for prostitutes.

Porteus Maze Test. A psychological test used in the assessment of mental ability.

post-K2 syndrome. A form of concentration camp reaction that is, in turn, a form of a reaction to prolonged deprivation and abuse.

postoperative psychoses. Delirious, hallucinatory, or paranoid reactions to surgical procedures.

postpartum depression. Periods of depression seen in women after delivery of a child.

postpartum psychosis. Severe depression, paranoid states, or schizophrenia occurring in women in the puerperium (within the first few days) or as late as 3 to 12 months following childbirth. It may be caused by toxic, metabolic, or preexisting psychological factors.

posttraumatic encephalopathy, diffuse. Incoordination, staggering gait, coarse tremors, and intellectual deterioration secondary to multiple injuries of the brain. H. S. Martland described the condition as "punch drunk." It occurs mainly in professional prize fighters who have suffered many knockouts.

posttraumatic personality disorder. A behavior problem (for example, stealing, truancy, lying), usually secondary to brain damage caused by trauma, and where no evidence of a deeper psychological disorder exists.

posttraumatic psychoses, acute. Confusion, delirium, or excited maniclike states, or catatonic and depressive symptoms. These are frequently seen in association with tears and bruises of brain tissue and are often difficult to discern from other symptomatic psychoses. This state usually follows the coma and leads into a recovery period that might include a slowly resolving dysmnesic syndrome.

posttraumatic syndrome. Recurrent headache, insomnia, nightmares, easy fatigue, and weakness, plus many minor psychological symptoms, such as poor concentration, irritability, and lapses of memory; a complex long-lasting reaction following head injury. It may be mild or severe and disabling. The symptoms persist for weeks, months, and sometimes even years.

predeviate. Children who show traits of deviate sexuality from about the fourth or fifth year. In boys, these traits include idiopathic feminism, a history of exposure to homosexual seduction, and other conducive psychosocial factors. These traits, while even more difficult to detect in girls, probably include "tomboyishness." These traits, in the predeviate child become more evident as he approaches puberty. Not all true adult deviates show detectable behavior in childhood.

pregenital neuroses. Psychoanalytic term used for all psychosomatic conditions because the psychological conflicts involved apparently stem from adaptations made during developmental phases prior to the genital phase.

pregnancy psychosis. Paranoid, depressive, or confusional states occurring during pregnancy. If the condition persists or becomes chronic despite treatment, it is usually assumed that this condition represents exacerbation by pregnancy of a preexisting or latent psychotic state.

premature ejaculation. Partial impotence in which ejaculation occurs before or immediately after insertion of the penis. This is nearly always caused by psychological factors and is taken to indicate a disturbance of psychosexual function.

presbyophrenia. Literally "old mind"; a form of senile psychosis.

preschizophrenic personality. Personality types defined by Silvano Arieti as being the schizoid or the stormy personality.

pressure of speech. Voluble and copious verbal production that is difficult for the listener to interpret. It is most likely seen in psychoneurotic and manic states.

pretraumatic personality. The personality makeup of a person who suffers a head injury and undergoes changes characteristic of the posttraumatic syndrome. Such a factor is obviously important in determining the nature and severity of the posttraumatic condition.

priapism. Excessively frequent or prolonged erection of the penis, especially secondary to disease.

pride system. See p. 91.

primary awholism. See p. 20.

primary mental deficiency. A mental deficiency occurring where no cerebral impairment exists.

primary process thinking. Freud's term for that part of normal mental processes made up of wishful, imaginative thinking: darydreams, fantasy, dreams. This type of thinking or reasoning is not influenced by reality, time, or logic.

primary symptoms in schizophrenia. Disturbances of affect, associations, ambivalence, and autism. This is a contribution of Eugen Bleuler to the understanding of schizophrenia, in which he introduces a ranking of symptoms to replace mere description of clinical phenomena.

prison psychosis. A severe mental disorder induced by psychologically traumatic factors occurring in prison.

prodromal phase of alcoholism. E. M. Jellinek's term for the phase in which the alcoholic begins to experience blackouts.

prodromata. Any signs or symptoms that herald the approach of a disease.

prodrome. A sign or symptom that indicates the approach of a disease.

projective test. A type of psychological test in which the meaning of some stimulus is a product of the subject's imagination. Examples are the Rorschach Test and the Thematic Apperception Test. The opposite of a projective test is a structured test, in which each stimulus has a well-defined meaning or answer of its own.

propfschizophrenia. Schizophrenia in a mentally defective person.

pruritis. Itching, irritation of the skin. It can often be brought about or intensified by emotional factors such as anxiety. guilt, boredom, or sexual arousal, but exact psychophysiological mechanisms are not known.

pruritis ani. Excessive itching and irritation of the anal area.

pruritis vulvae. Excessive itching and irritation of the vulval area.

pseudocyesis. False pregnancy. It is a condition that sometimes can imitate true pregnancy almost exactly; cessation of menses, enlargement of the abdomen and breasts, and even labor pains. It is considered to be a hysterical phenomenon, but it is sometimes seen in psychotics.

pseudologia fantastica. Daydreaming differing from normal fantasy in that the person may believe that his fantasies are real and act on them. Such incorrect beliefs are dropped, however, when he is confronted with contradictory evidence. It is seen in sociopathic individuals and is different from confabulation and delusions.

pseudoneurotic schizophrenia. Hoche's and Pollatin's term for patients who are thought at first to be neurotic or psychoneurotic, but who do not respond to treatment as would be expected. After much treatment and time, the more severe and all-pervading personality picture of pananxiety, pansexualism, and panneurosis emerges, and the underlying diagnosis is made.

pseudoparesis, alcoholic. Severe deterioration of chronic alcoholics, resembling the clinical picture of general paresis.

pseudoreminiscence. Paramnesia that combines both confabulation and retrospective falsification.

psychalgia. See p. 65.

psychasthenia. Pierre Janet's term for one of two types of psychoneurosis, the other type being hysteria. The term is now rarely used.

psychic seizures. Episodic occurrence of behavioral acts and experiences such as forced thoughts, hallucinations, illusions, and delusions, accompanied by abnormalities in the patient's electroencephalogram.

psychological dependence. Craving for a drug, developing in a person after prolonged use of the drug.

psychometrics. Any kind of psychological test that measures something (for example, intelligence).

psychometric test. Psychological test that measures intelligence or other mental capacities.

psychomotor epilepsy. Episodes of increased muscle tone, automatic behavior, and lapses of consciousness, with strong muscle twitching and sudden loss of muscle tone, accompanied by changes in the electroencephalogram—usually 4 to 6 high-amplitude waves per second with superimposed high-frequency waves.

psychomotor retardation. Pronounced slowness of thought, speech, and action. It is seen in certain patients with depression, hypothyroidism, and some organic brain diseases.

psychoneurosis. A disorder characterized chiefly by directly expressed or felt anxiety that may be unconsciously controlled by various mental mechanisms (for example, introjection, conversion, displacement). Patients with this disorder do not show gross personality disorganization or distortion of reality (delusions, hallucinations, illusions). In the official diagnostic nomenclature it is listed under ''Disorders of psychogenic origin, or without clearly defined physical cause or structural change in the brain.'' It is one of the major groups of conditions that come under psychiatric care and the group that is usually regarded as less serious and less different from the normal than the psychoses.

psychoneurotic disorder. Psychoneurosis.

psychopathia sexualis. Kraft-Ebing's term for sexual perversion

psychopathic personality. A person whose characteristic behavior is unconventional or socially destructive (for example, a criminal). It is not an official term but is still used occasionally.

psychophysiologic reaction. Neurotic states accompanied by visceral expression of affect and physiological changes in some organ or system of the body (for example, psychophysiologic skin, respiratory, or cardiovascular reaction). It is different from conversion reaction in the following ways: (1) it fails to alleviate anxiety, (2) the origin of symptoms is physiologic rather than symbolic, (3) it produces structural changes in many cases, and (4) it involves organs and viscera innervated by the autonomic nervous system and therefore not under voluntary control.

psychosis (psychotic disorder). One of the major groups of psychiatric disorders in the official nomenclature, subdivided into the affective reactions, schizophrenia, involutional psychotic reactions, and paranoid reactions. It is considered the most serious and the greatest departure from normal. Euphemistic terms include insanity, lunacy, madness, and alienation.

psychosomatic. A diagnostic term replaced in the official nomenclature with psychophysiologic reactions. Conceptually, the term refers to a combined psychological and physiological study of human problems.

psychosomatic diseases. Psychophysiologic reactions.

psychotic-depressive reaction. Severe depression with evidence of a psychotic process such as hallucinations, delusions, or other distortions of perception or thinking. It includes cyclic, senile, toxic, and reactive types.

psychotic insight. See p. 92.

psychotoxic. See p. 92.

puerperal psychosis. Postpartum psychosis.

puerperium psychosis. Postpartum psychosis.

pyromania. The practice of gaining pleasure from setting fires.

pyknolepsy. Frequent petit mal seizures. The term refers to epilepsy that occurs in childhood and that has a benign prognosis.

queequeg phenomenon. Voodoo death (after the character in *Moby Dick*). (See p. 129.)

querulent. Overly suspicious, angry, litigious, complaining, dissatisfied, accusatory.

querulous personality. Melitta Schmideberg's term for a borderline personality possessing selfrighteous, angry, dissatisfied, oppositional, stubborn, and argumentative traits.

quiet delirium. Soft-spoken, incoherent speech and restlessness as only manifestation of a delirium. It is synonymous with delirium mite.

quietism. A state of calmness and passivity, inactivity, and nonparticipation. It is often associated with mysticism.

q-sort. A psychological test that helps identify personality variations.

rape. See p. 110.

raptus. Sudden, sometimes violent uncoordinated movement. It is especially associated with catatonia.

rating scale. A device for illustrating an individual's similarity to or difference from a group in respect to particular traits.

raw score. An unweighted or uncorrected score, as on a psychological test—uncorrected for age.

Raynaud's disease. Bilateral paroxysmal contraction of blood vessels of the digiti. These neurovascular attacks are precipitated by cold and emotion; the exact cause, however, is usually obscure.

reaction time. Time elapsing between stimulus and response; a measurement much used in assessing functioning of patients. Schizophrenics, especially chronically ill and hospitalized schizophrenics, show significant differences in these measurements as compared with normal people.

reactive depression. Depression in reaction to a real life disappointment or failure.

reading disability. Dyslexia.

receptive personality. Erich Fromm's term for the person who feels that the source of all pleasure, affection, love, knowledge, and so on is external to himself and that the only way to get his needs for these met is to receive them from this outside source.

recurrent catatonia. Episodes of catatonia and spontaneous remissions with symptom-free intervals. This is generally thought to have a metabolic or endocrine cause, but the exact cause is not known. It is a rare condition.

reify. See p. 67.

reliability. Consistency of scores obtained by an individual on a psychological test on different occasions.

repetition compulsion. See p. 93.

restless legs syndrome. Uncomfortable, peculiar, painful sensations in the muscles and bones of the legs. These sensations are partially relieved by almost continual movement of the legs. There is no known cause.

rest tremor. Tremor occurring while the extremity is at rest.

resymbolization. Unconscious conversion of inner conflicts and emotional experiences into somatic symptoms, phobias, changes in levels of consciousness (for example, amnesia, fugue states), and personality changes. It is a phenomenon seen in some hysterics.

retardation. Slowness of mentation.

retrograde amnesia. Loss of memory for events preceding brain injury. The degree of amnesia appears to be proportionate to the amount of brain damage.

retrogression. Regression. (See p. 67.)

retropulsion. A tendency to run backward. It is sometimes seen in basal ganglia disorders.

retrospective falsification. Recital of the past in which false details, meanings, and recollections of a real memory are distorted in response to psycho-

logical problems (for example, to support a neurotic symptom or to obtain sympathy).

return of the repressed. The breakdown of successful repression; recurrence of forgotten, painful memories, which are revived by a contemporary event. It often heralds the onset of a mental illness.

reversion. Synonymous with regression and retrogression.

Rorschach test. Use of ambiguous, unformed, unorganized material (for example, the "inkblots") that the patient organizes and interprets. In doing this, he projects his own inner feelings, thoughts, and behavior to the psychologist who can use these data to draw inferences about the patient's mental status. It is the most widely used projective test.

rut formation. See p. 94.

sadism. Gaining pleasure, often erotic, by hurting other human beings and animals.

sadomasochism. Sadistic and masochistic tendencies in the same person. It is more common than either sadism or masochism alone.

sapphism. Female homosexuality.

satori. Sudden occurrence of penetrating insights and profound psychological transformation in followers of Zen Buddhism.

satyriasis. Morbidly excessive sexual desire or excitement in the male.

scatophagy. Ingestion of excrement, especially feces.

scattering. Moderately incoherent speech. The term refers to thought that does not follow a logical sequence.

Schilder's disease. A rapidly progressive and widespread loss of myelin in the cerebral hemispheres. The symptoms include mental changes, convulsions, loss of vision, and motor and sensory disorders. The cause is unknown.

schizoadaptation. See p. 94.

schizoaffective reactions. A diagnostic term denoting a schizophrenic illness with predominantly affective symptoms (for example, depression, elation, or excitement); often misdiagnosed as manic-depressive reactions; conversely, some manic-depressive patients, especially when in the manic state, are given this diagnosis.

schizoid. A person with this personality pattern disturbance is characteristically withdrawn, asocial, uncommunicative, and eccentric, without overt evidence of neurosis or psychosis.

schizoid personality. Having the characteristics of a schizoid.

schizophrene. A schizophrenic.

schizophrenese. Any language abnormality used by a schizophrenic.

schizophrenia. One of the major psychoses; a group of psychotic conditions characterized by a pronounced tendency to withdraw from reality, unpredictable disturbances of behavior, various disorders of thought and concept formation, affective incongruities, and various degrees of regression and deterioration. The cause is unknown, but it is thought to contain both biogenetic and environmental determinants. It is classified according to predominant symptomatology into the following types: simple, hebephrenic, catatonic, paranoid, undifferentiated, schizoaffective, childhood, and residual. The term was coined by Eugen Bleuler and is synonymous with dementia praecox.

schizophrenic. A person affected by schizophrenia.

schizophrenic deficit reactions. A poorly understood severe schizophrenic reaction in which thought processes and language are strangely incoherent and usually meaningless; inadequate affective responses, with pronounced overall deterioration.

schizophreniform psychoses. A term used by Langfeldt to denote persons who have an acute onset of basically schizophrenic behavior and symptoms, but who have a good prognosis.

schizophrenogenic mother. A mother who is overprotective, hostile, covertly or overtly rejecting, overanxious, cold, distant, and in many cases, definitely unfit for motherhood. She is unable to give herself to the baby even when she tries. It is a term used by some authors to denote their feeling that the mother is the main dynamic factor in the development of schizophrenia.

schizotype. See p. 94.

school phobia. A state of anxiety in the child brought about by separating him from his parents, caused by his entering school for the first time. It is usually not a true phobia in the sense that the child is not afraid of school; rather it is a form of separation anxiety.

sclerosis, tuberous. An inherited disease of the nervous system, transmitted by a dominant gene, characterized by multiple nodules throughout the brain, spinal cord, and peripheral nerves. It is associated with mental retardation.

scoptophilia. Achieving sexual stimulation and pleasure from looking at primary or secondary sex organs or watching sexual activity in others. It is not considered a perversion or abnormal unless this is the primary means by which the person gains sexual gratification.

scotoma. Blind spot.

scotomization. The tendency to develop a partial unawareness or "blind spot" toward an offending situation.

screen memory. A relatively innocuous memory recalled in place of one more anxiety provoking.

secondary gain. See p. 94.

secondary mental deficiency. Mental deficiency that occurs as a result of cerebral impairment.

seizure. Sudden occurrence of a disease, or signs and symptoms (such as a convulsion) of a disease.

self-aggression. See p. 68.

self-destructive behavior. See p. 68.

self-love. See p. 68.

self-mutilation. Harming oneself. It is seen in widely varying degrees, from neurotic nail-biting to self-castration and self-blinding seen in regressed schizophrenics.

semantic personality disorders. Use of words and language in an apparently normal manner, but without reflecting any of the person's true feeling or meaning.

semeiotic. Relating to symptoms and signs of a disease.

senile psychosis. A severe mental disorder occurring during, brought on by, or aggravated by the senium.

sentence completion test. A projective psychological test technique by which unconscious thought and feeling are revealed in the subject's completion of the incomplete sentences.

separation anxiety. See p. 94.

sexual recrudescence. Increased offensive or aggressive sexual behavior in elderly men. This may be directed against children or may be expressed as voyeurism, exhibitionism, or other sexual deviations.

sham-rage. Outbursts of spontaneous activity that resemble rage in an animal with the cerebral cortex removed.

shell shock. Psychiatric casualties in World War I, partly because many believed they were caused by the trauma of artillery explosions.

sign. An objective manifestation or indication of a disease, not necessarily specific for that particular disease (for example, a rash).

signal anxiety. See p. 94.

situational reaction. An intense psychological response to a real life situation (for example, grief over the loss of a loved one or fear following a serious narrow escape with danger).

skoptsy. Self-castration.

socialized delinquent. A conduct disorder of children that is characterized by such activities as gang activities, keeping bad companions, cooperative and furtive stealing, habitual truancy, and absences from home until late at night.

sociopath. A person with a sociopathic personality disturbance.

sociopathic personality disturbance. An official diagnostic term including those persons who are ill in terms of prevailing social and cultural norms and not only in terms of intrapsychic and interpersonal discomfort. Synonym: psychopathic personality. Included under this category are antisocial, dissocial, sexual deviation, and drug dependency.

sociopathy. Chronic behavior and attitudes that cause conflict with society in a person with no other demonstrable underlying mental illness.

sodomy. Homosexual relations, penis to anus; sometimes, mouth to genitals or sex relations with animals or corpses.

somatization. The process by which fear, anger, tension, or other psychologically determined problems are reflected in disordered physiology (for example, cardiovascular system dysfunction). Another use of the term refers to the somatization of complaints or delusions, in which the patient converts his psychological distress into complaints pertaining to different parts of the body (for example, complaining of palpitation or pain instead of fear).

somnambulism. See p. 69.

speech disturbance. Any speech impediment; interference with normal speech function.

split personality. Multiple personality.

spurious pregnancy. Pseudocyesis.

stereotypy. Repetition of an action. It occurs in an almost endless fashion in some schizophrenics. The motions, though meaningless at first to the observer, generally have some private symbolic meaning to the patient.

stormy personality. See p. 95.

strephosymbolia. Perception of objects or symbols as being reversed, as though seen in a mirror.

stupor. A state of reduced awareness, alertness, and activity. The term is sometimes synonymous with unconsciousness, coma.

stuttering. Spasmodic interruptions in the free flow of speech.

success depression. Onset of depression after achieving success (such as a long-sought goal). It is usually caused by strong unconscious feelings of rage brought about by unconscious attempts to eliminate a rival parent or sibling; or it is a reaction to guilt associated with feeling unworthy of the reward or achievement.

suicide. See p. 111.

survival guilt. Guilt found in someone who has survived an extremely cruel or stressful situation in which others have died; especially seen as part of the concentration camp syndrome.

survivor syndrome. A traumatic neurosis accompanied by strong survival guilt.

symbiotic psychosis. A severe mental disorder found in children unable to emotionally, and sometimes physically, separate from the mother; an inability of the child to differentiate his own ego from his mother's ego.

symbiotic schizophrenia. A form of childhood schizophrenia in which the child is assumed to be potentially normal, but has failed to differentiate his own identity from that of his mother because of failure in maternal handling. Such a child is described as excessively clinging and dependent, and unable to function as an independent unit. It is a form of symbiotic psychosis.

syncretism. Thinking in which the person gives animation to inanimate objects (such as playing with a block of wood and calling it a kitten). This is seen as the first stage of development of thought in the child. It is also seen as a manifestation of regression in schizophrenia.

tachyglossia. Tachylalia.

tachylalia. Rapid speech.

tachyphagia. Rapid ingestion of foodstuff and foreign objects.

tachyphrenia. Accelerated thought processes.

tactile hallucinations. The false perception of touch without an external stimulus. It is sometimes seen in states of delirium.

tangentiality. A defect association in which the stream of conversation wanders from the subject.

tarantism. A dancing mania that appeared in Italy during the thirteenth century and that was attributed to the bite of the tarantula.

taste hallucinations. Gustatory hallucinations.

teleologic regression. See p. 96.

temper tantrums. An explosive outburst of rage in a child or in a psychologically immature adult, characterized by crying, kicking, biting others, head banging, throwing objects, screaming, and cursing. If such behavior persists beyond the age of 2 or 3 years, it is taken to be a sign of psychological distress and illness.

tension. See p. 70.

tension headache. Headache secondary to anxiety and tension; a functional headache.

terror. See p. 70.

terror neurosis. Traumatic neurosis.

test battery. A group of tests used in assessment of

the patient. Such a group may have a standard number of various tests, but these may also be supplemented by additional tests as needed for the individual patient.

Thematic Apperception Test (TAT). A diagnostic psychological test developed by Henry Murray; the patient makes interpretations of scenes depicted on cards, and the content of the interpretations are assumed to reflect his projected conscious and unconscious feelings and thoughts.

theta rhythm. A component of normal EEG tracings; waves of a characteristic frequency of 4 to 7.5 cycles per second.

thoughts-out-loud. A phenonemon in schizophrenia in which the patient experiences his own thoughts as being spoken aloud; auditory hallucinations in which one hears one's own thoughts but may experience them as coming from another person or being.

tic. A muscular twitching, usually involving the facial muscles. The condition may be a result of muscular tension resulting from a psychological problem.

tinnitus. Ringing or any other noise in the ears that is not generated by an external source.

tiredness. See p. 133.

toe-walking. Walking on the tiptoes. It is sometimes seen as a characteristic of some childhood schizophrenics.

tonaphasia. Loss of ability to carry a tune; an aphasia.

topagnosia. Loss of ability to localize tactile sensation. If this occurs when there is no loss of touch sensation on the skin, it is probably caused by a cortical lesion.

topalgia. Pain localized in one area—usually a small area.

torsion spasm. Intermittent, sometimes pronounced, and usually involuntary twitching of the body trunk that is caused by spasmodic muscular contractions. It may be seen as an acute dystonic side effects of treatment with major tranquilizers.

torticollis. Twisting of the neck. It is sometimes pronounced and often involuntary; the cause may be muscular, skeletal, or neurological. It may be seen as part of a dystonic reaction to treatment with major tranquilizers.

toxic delirium. A delirium produced by a toxin.

toxic psychosis. A psychotic state brought about in reaction to a toxin. An example is a severe mental reaction to scopolamine.

trance. A sleeplike state or reduced state of consciousness. It is seen in hypnotized subjects, in certain states of shock, in some epileptic conditions, and in catatonic states.

transvestism. A sexual perversion in which the individual seeks sexual gratification by wearing the clothing of the opposite sex. It is usually seen in males.

transvestite. A person given to transvestism.

trauma. Injury; a hurtful experience.

traumatic. Pertaining to trauma. An early concept of Freud's was that pain or traumatic experiences of the past might produce discomfort or symptoms in later life.

traumatic encephalopathy. Brain damage or disease brought on by trauma to the head.

traumatic neurosis. Abnormal behavior brought about by undergoing severe stress. This stress may involve physical injury, but not necessarily so. It is divided into acute, subacute, and chronic phases, and can easily become crippling to the person if adequate treatment is not obtained quickly. Most investigators feel that traumatic reactions, whether caused by war or an event in civilian life, are essentially the same.

traumatic neurosis, subacute phase. Part of a process of attempting to master an overwhelming traumatic event. In this phase, the person may use a variety of defenses (for example, repression, denial, or projection). There are repetitive attempts to relieve the traumatic event through dreams and vivid flashes.

tremor. Shaking or oscillation of a body part; usually seen in the extremities or head. It is a disorder of muscle tone or control. Such a condition is often caused or aggravated by treatment with neuroleptic drugs.

tribade. A female homosexual who plays the male role in the relationship with another woman. This usually implies that the woman has an unusually large clitoris, which she uses as a penis.

trichophagy. Morbid tendency to eat or chew hair.

trichotillomania. Morbid tendency to pull one's own hair.

tuberous sclerosis. See p. 128.

twilight states. A disturbance of consciousness during which the patient is not prostrate but goes through automatic acts (automatism). It is accompanied by a disturbance of function of the centrencephalic system (Penfield).

tyranny of the shoulds. See p. 97.

ululation. Pronounced sobbing and crying.

unaliveness. See p. 97.

uncinate fits. A seizure caused by a focal discharge in the temporal lobe. The clinical picture usually includes chewing, smacking of the mouth and lips, and hallucinations of taste and smell.

uncleanliness feelings. A part of a symptom complex seen in obsessional persons by which guilt over real and imagined transgressions is symbolically transformed into a feeling of physical uncleanliness.

unclean thoughts. In obsessional and phobic neuroses and depressions, the distasteful or unwanted thoughts that occur despite all efforts to prevent them. Patients suffering from such conditions often identify these thoughts as being unclean.

unconscious conflict. See p. 97.

uneasiness. A kind of tension, the feeling that something is not quite right; a psychological discomfort. It is often seen in mild mental disorders, and it is seen early in severe mental illness.

unio mystica. The feeling that one has achieved a mystic unity with an infinite person. It is seen in severe psychiatric disorders.

unipolar depression. An affective disorder in which the person experiences repeated depressions but no periods of mania or hypomania. Thought to have a strong genetic causative component. (See bipolar depression.)

unreality. The feeling that one's self or one's surroundings are not real. It may be seen in states of depersonalization or dissociation.

unsocialized aggressive syndrome. A type of conduct disorder of childhood diagnosed in children who assault others, are cruel to other children and animals, defy authorities, and are maliciously mischievous. Parents of such children are rejecting and provide limited socializing experience for the child.

unworthiness feelings. A manifestation of self-hate; commonly found in depressive persons.

uprooting neurosis. See p. 97.

uranism. Homosexuality.

urolagnia. Morbid preoccupation with urine; deriving pleasure from urine.

urophilia. Urolagnia.

urorrhea. Enuresis.

urticaria. A pruritic skin condition characterized by red or white wheals that come and go. It is often associated with emotional problems.

vaginismus. Contractions of the pelvic floor muscles, especially during attempts at intercourse. It may be pronounced and prevent intromission of the penis or otherwise cause dyspareunia.

validity. The measure of the ability of the test to measure that which is meant to be measured.

vectorial. An attitude of giving and protecting, especially of parents toward their children.

vectoriasis praecox. Wolman's term for schizophrenia.

vegetative retreat. Meeting dangerous situations by developing an inappropriate visceral response (such as diarrhea rather than coping in an adult manner).

ventriculogram. A diagnostic test in which cerebrospinal fluid is removed and air is injected into the ventricles of the brain and x-ray films are made. The air acts as a contrast medium to better delineate brain structures and any pathological changes.

verbigeration. Senseless repetition of the same words and phrases. It is seen rarely, but mainly it is seen in chronic schizophrenics who may carry this out for days.

verbochromia. Synesthesia. (See p. 70.)

vertigo. The feeling of dizziness. It is usually described as the feeling that one is spinning or that the room is spinning around; it is often associated with nausea, fainting, and falling.

vesania. Obsolete term meaning insanity without fever.

Vigotsky Test. A color-form—sorting test used in detecting brain damage.

virilism. The assumption of male personality characteristics by a female; the development of male secondary sex characteristics in a genetic female, usually caused by a glandular tumor that produces an excess of male hormone.

visual hallucination. The experience of seeing an external object without receiving visual stimulation from an external source.

volubility. Copious speech.

voyeur. One given to voyeurism; a peeping tom.

voyeurism. The achievement of sexual excitation and gratification by watching a nude woman or a nude man and woman having sexual intercourse. It is seen mainly in males.

vulvismus. Vaginismus.

war neurosis. Battle fatigue; shell shock; a form of posttraumatic neurosis.

ward cliques. See p. 98.

waxy flexibility. The tendency of the patient to hold for long periods of time whatever anatomical position in which he is placed. For instance, he may hold his hand over his head for several hours after someone has placed it there. It is most often seen in catatonic schizophrenics. Synonym: cerea flexibilitas.

Wechsler Adult Intelligence Scale. A psychological

test used to measure intellectual ability. It consists of ten subtests; information comprehension, arithmetic, similarities, digit span, vocabulary, digit symbol, picture completion, block designs, picture arrangement, and object assembly. The first six subtests make up the verbal part of the test and are used to derive a verbal I.Q.; the latter four are the performance part and yield a performance I.Q. All test sources together give a total I.Q.

Wechsler Intelligence Scale for Children. A psychological test to measure intelligence in children from ages 5 to 14 years. It is organized and scored in the same manner as the W.A.I.S.

Wechsler Memory Scale. A psychological test used to detect memory and learning impairment, such as might be found in brain-damaged patients.

Wernicke's encephalopathy. A serious nervous system disease caused by deficiency of vitamin B_1 (thiamin), characterized by delirium and dysmnesia with disturbances of consciousness and ophthalmoplegias. It is seen mainly in alcoholics but can occur in any case of prolonged thiamin deficiency.

withdrawal. The act of directing attention and interest away from the social environment; isolation. Also: drug withdrawal; see Abstinence syndrome, p. 16.

Witzelsucht. In patients with damage to the frontal lobes of the brain, a silly euphoria combined with a tendency to play practical jokes with no feelings for others or regard for social taboos.

womb fantasy. Unconscious desire to regress to complete passivity, peace, and security of the womb.

word association test. A seldom used projective psychological test in which the patient gives responses to words called out to him.

word blindness. Inability to perceive words as meaningful symbols; a form of learning defect.

word deafness. Inability to understand spoken words; a sensory aphasia.

word salad. Verbal expressions, including neologisms, that are meaningless to the observer. It may be seen in schizophrenia.

xenoglossy. Speaking in an unknown or foreign language.

xerodermatic mental deficiency. A condition, possibly inherited, in which the skin is extremely dry and thickened; often associated with mental deficiency.

Zeigranik effect. See p. 98.

zooerastia. Sexual intercourse with an animal; bestiality.

zoolagnia. Bestiality.

zoosadism. Deriving pleasure from injuring or hurting animals.

Zwangneurose. Freud's term for obsessive neurosis. Zwang was translated as "obsession" in London and as "compulsion" in New York; subsequent authors used both terms as a compromise; hence, obsessive-compulsive neurosis.

CHAPTER 2

Human behavior terminology

NORMAL MENTAL PROCESSES

Intelligence is the fundamental attribute of the mind from which most of the mental phenomena that might be studied are derived. Likewise, memory is the very cornerstone of intelligence, so that the scope of one largely determines the scope of the other. In most cases, the terms listed as psychopathological are examples of special types of ordinary mental processes. A typical mental process, for instance, is an idea. A typical psychopathological mental process is a delusion. A delusion, on the other hand, is merely one of the many possible kinds of ideas a person might have. In this connection, it is interesting to note that a very rich and sometimes colorful vocabulary of special terms for the abnormal or unusual examples has developed, but only a few specialized terms that specifically designate their normal counterparts. Diagnostically, only one possible category can be used to designate a state of mental health, and that is normal personality, in spite of the fact that there exists a huge number of different types of normal people.

Mental processes can be divided into a few separate classes:

1. Perception: the process by which the mind, through the senses, acquires information about the environment.
2. Thinking: the information processing system of the mind, by which knowledge is converted into solutions for problems.
3. Action: the process by which the brain controls the body to apply skills to the task of implementing decisions.

Although a good case can be made for considering emotions separately, they are so intimately intertwined with the other mental processes that they are also included. Another essential component of the mental processes, or a manifestation of them, is learning. Associated with learning are many other phenomena for which special terminologies have been developed. Issues connected with learning are sometimes referred to as cognitive issues. An old and simplistic view of learning stressed the importance of the stimulus and the response, and researchers in this area use terms such as conditioning or conditioned reflexes. A more contemporary modification of this trend is called behavioral modification.

Motivation is also part of the mental processes in that it is a product of the concepts and ideas each person has to provide him with reasons for doing what he does. Nevertheless, it might also be argued that the original sources of motivation come from extramental sources (such as hunger or sex). Like emotions, however, the actual experience of motive is almost invariably involved with thinking.

The term mental mechanism is used to indicate the means by which a person makes adjustments in his life. Thus repression, according to one set of theories, is a mechanism for coping with painful memories, through a process of burying them in the unconscious, inaccessible to current memory. These mechanisms are methods of adjustment rather than of thinking, although thinking clearly plays a major role in them. Still other theorists refer to these coping mechanisms as defense mechanisms, and different theorists (such as Freud) list a specific number, apparently intended to be an exhaustive list.

PERSONALITY DEVELOPMENT AND ADJUSTMENT

Of central importance in the study and understanding of mental health problems are the role of personality and its growth and development, along with the growth and development of the body itself and the vicissitudes of those experiences associated with adjustment. Furthermore, it is of central importance that the study of personality, growth, and adjustment include normal as well as abnormal human behavioral characteristics.

Personality is the accumulated characteristic behaviors and thoughts unique to each individual. To some extent, personalities can be categorized so that recognizable types can be said to exist. Various theorists have offered their own systems of classification, and the possible types that have been labeled are now so diverse and nonsystematized that no accepted classification system is in common use. Jung, for instance, defined the introvert and the extrovert types. Freud described the anal, the oral, and the genital characters. The American Psychiatric Association diagnostic categories include certain personality types, such as the schizoid personality, that are meant to apply only to certain types of disordered personalities rather than to the general population. Freud and Jung, as well as most other theorists, have stated or implied that their categories referred to normal behavior patterns.

Adjustment is a term that is currently being rather rapidly expanded in its use and application, although it was relatively absent from the writings and discussions of previous generations. It refers to the process and success by which an individual copes with life in the culture. The concept of adjustment is actually derived from Darwin's theories of evolution and refers to a mode of survival in which the individual (animal as well as human being) interacts with the environment. Flexible methods of interaction, based on multiple choices of action from which either successful or unsuccessful choices might be selected, become a function of intelligence. Therefore, the most intelligent species, or the most intelligent individuals within a species, tend to use the most flexible methods, because they have a wider choice of options and the capacity to make better choices. Two sets of factors would, therefore, determine the ultimate effectiveness of an individual's mode of adjustment. In the first place, the environment itself will present its peculiar set of problems to solve and resources—so that problems may be either easy or difficult and resources may be either rich or limited. The other set of determinants is the individual's own set of adjustment skills. The interaction of the two determines the outcome. The term adaptation is frequently used as a synonym for adjustment, although in the earlier evolutionary theories it was more likely to be used to refer to physical rather than behavioral characteristics (for example, external color).

Personality grows and develops along with the growth and development of the child's body, language, education, and so on. The part of growth that is related most directly to personality is the acquisition of experience—the acquisition of knowledge, skills, attitudes, and relationships with others.

Older theories of personality tended to look for important variables within the person himself. Phrenology, the pseudoscience of the nineteenth century, attempted to do this, as did Freud, Jung, Adler, and others. These theories are sometimes called intrapsychic, because all the answers to questions asked were found within the person himself. Later, more contemporary theorists (such as Karen Horney and Harry Stack Sullivan) have become known as culturally oriented instead, because they have studied the issue as one of adjustment with the culture.

THEORETICAL TERMINOLOGY

No field is as rich as the study of human behavior in respect to number or diversity of theories. The theories that have been proposed and that can be found in the literature have come from many divergent sources—religion, philosophy, psychology, folklore, and so on. It is safe to state that any individual or any institution that operates by attempting to influence human beings—whether in trying to sell something, to induce people to obey the law, or to educate them—will inevitably follow policies and procedures based on some theory of human behavior. A given management system in an industry may develop its personnel policy around the basic theory, for instance, that workers are lazy. A police system may operate according to a set of assumptions that all people are corruptible. An educational system may follow a theory of people that assumes that all children hate to learn.

The relevancy of these remarks to the issue of terminology lies in a peculiar characteristic of theorizing: the tradition of dubious merit whereby each new theorist tends to accentuate the novelty of the theory by creating a novel terminology to accompany it. No set of theories in the field has generated as many new terms as has the psychoanalytic theories. It not uncommonly happens that when some time has elapsed after the introduction of a new theory, with its associated, esoteric terminology, the new terms are found to mean the same as an old set of terms. By the same token, then, it also often happens that the new theory itself is merely a restatement of an old one with new terms.

One single characteristic of behavioral theories exists that almost guarantees that they will be incorrect. This is the assumption that there exists some single, universal "law" of "human nature." Instead, it would be correct to state that if there is any law that people follow, there will be other people who will violate it.

A warning is in order for the novice who seeks to learn the terminology of behavioral theories. Do not expect to be able to understand them all, and do not conclude from your failure to do so that you are, therefore, lacking in intelligence. The fact is that many of them simply do not make enough sense to be understand-

able, not to mention the fact that they may also be unbelievable. Also, it is important to be forewarned of a special danger; namely, the hazard of believing a theory because it is understandable. Too often the more understandable, but incorrect, theories are accepted because they seem logical, and not because experience has proved them valid.

In general, theories of human behavior can be classified according to the degree to which they vary from one extreme to another. One of these extremes can be described as mechanistic and the other (for want of a better name) as humanistic. Also, they can be described as being mystical or metaphysical, on the one hand, or scientific or objective, on the other.

At the present time it is quite safe to state that no single theory enjoys any general level of acceptance among professionals. Although there prevails a great variety in the theories endorsed by the various individuals in the professions, there is much less difference in their practices. This is probably because the number of theories available from which to choose is almost endless, but the number of things that may be done in practice is quite limited.

PSYCHOLOGICAL AND OTHER TESTING PROCEDURES

Psychological testing is among the principal diagnostic tools employed by mental health professionals. Psychological tests are usually administered by trained psychologists. Psychometrics refers to procedures used to assess any mental capacity that can be measured quantitatively. Examples of mental functions that might be measured are intelligence, educational achievement, memory, abstract reasoning, and language ability. The term psychodiagnostics refers to those testing procedures that are designed to give useful information for making a psychiatric diagnosis, and includes personality profiles and projective tests.

To be useful, most psychological tests must first be standardized. This is done by measuring the performance on the test of a large number of representative population segments. The level of performance of the individual is then presented as it compares with the average for the group.

To be useful, psychological tests must be both valid and reliable. The validity of a test is the degree of accuracy with which it measures the function in question. It is not always as evident as it might appear that a given testing procedure is a true measure of what is to be measured. For instance, many attempts to measure such things as aptitudes and opinions only reflect how cooperative the subject is or what kind of impression he wants to make. The reliability of a test is the degree of reproducibility of the results. In the case of an intelligence test, for instance, the test would be reliable only if the same person obtained the same or similar results at different times, or if two persons of equal intelligence achieved the same results.

Some tests are administered to one subject at a time by a psychologist. This is especially likely if various parts of the test have to be timed, or if complex instructions have to be given. Other tests can be given to large groups at one time and do not necessarily have to be administered by a trained person. These tests have self-explanatory instructions and are paper-and-pencil tests. Some tests must be individually interpreted and therefore require a great deal of skill and experience to score them. Others can be scored in a fashion so mechanical that it can be done by a machine.

Clinical psychologists are the subspecialists most likely to be trained in administering and interpreting diagnostic and personality tests. Educational psychologists usually confine their testing to intelligence and achievement tests. Industrial psychologists and career counselors usually specialize in aptitude testing. Advertising psychologists may devise or administer opinion tests for market survey organizations.

In addition to the psychological testing procedures employed in mental sciences, there are others used either for research or diagnostic purposes that more closely resemble the kind of tests used in general medicine. For instance, the electroencephalograph is an electronic instrument that records "brain waves," the electrical impulses emitted by neurons within the brain, on a sheet of moving paper. Certain valuable kinds of information about the brain can be found with this method. Also available are a number of biochemical tests which measure such psychological phenomena as the effects of fear on the body. X-ray films are used in a variety of ways to reveal pictographic information about the brain. Radioisotopes are used to make radioactive tracings of the brain's blood supply (brain scan).

REPRESENTATIVE PSYCHOLOGICAL TESTS

A. Aptitude and ability tests (personnel selection)

Academic Promise Tests (scholastic aptitude, grades 6 through 9)
Accounting Orientation Test (high school level)
Bennet Hand-Tool Dexterity Test
Bennet Stenographic Aptitude Test
Crawford Small Parts Dexterity Test
D.A.T. Clerical Speed and Accuracy Test
D.A.T. Language Usage Test
D.A.T. Mechanical Reasoning Test
D.A.T. Space Relations Test
Differential Aptitude Tests (junior and senior high school aptitude)
Engineering and Physical Science Aptitude Test
Farnsworth Dichotomous Test for Color Blindness
General Clerical Test
Graves Design Judgment Test
Medical College Admission Test
Minnesota Clerical Test
Minnesota Engineering Analogies Test
Modern Language Aptitude Test
Revised Minnesota Paper Form Board Test
Seashore-Bennet Stenographic Proficiency Test
Seashore Measure of Musical Talents
Stromberg Dexterity Test
Typing Test for Business

B. Intelligence tests

A-B-C Vision Test
Alpha Examination, Modified Form 9
Barranquilla Rapid Survey Intelligence Test
Bayley Scales of Infant Development (up to 2½ years)
Bender Visual Motor Gestalt Test
Benton Revised Visual Retention Test

Boehm Test of Basic Concepts
Cattell Infant Intelligence Scale (3 to 30 months)
Chicago Non-Verbal Examination
Concept Mastery Test
D.A.T. Verbal Reasoning, Numerical Ability, and Abstract Reasoning Tests
Doppelt Mathematical Reasoning Test
Gesell Developmental Schedules
Goldstein-Sheerer Tests of Abstract and Concrete Thinking
Harris Tests of Lateral Dominance
Kahlmann-Anderson Measure of Academic Potential
Kent Series of Emergency Scales
Miller Analogies Test
Minnesota Test for Differential Diagnosis of Aphasia
Porteus Mazes
Raven Progressive Matrices (nonverbal)
Revised Beta Examination
San Francisco Vocational Competency Scale
Wechsler-Bellevue Intelligence Scale
Wesman Personnel Classification Test
Wide Range Achievement Test

C. Personality inventories

Cornell Index
Edwards Personal Preference Schedule
Minnesota Counseling Inventory
Minnesota Multiphasic Personality Inventory
Omnibus Personality Inventory
Thorndike Dimensions of Temperament

D. Projective tests (diagnostic)

Aphasia Screening Test
Bellak Children's Apperception Test
Bender Visual Motor Gestalt Test
Benton Revised Visual Retention Test
Draw-a-Person Test
Gorham Proverbs Test
Graham-Kendall Memory for Designs
Halstead-Reitan Neuropsychological Test Battery
   Halstead Category Test
   Halstead Finger Oscillation Test
   Halstead-Seashore Rhythm Test
   Halstead Speech Sounds Test
   Halstead Tactual Performance Test
   Halstead-Wepman Aphasia Screening (Reitan Modification)
   Sensory-Perceptual Examination
   Trail Making Test (Forms A & B)

Holtzman Inkblot Technique
Hooper Visual Organization Test
House-Tree-Person Test
Immediate Test
Kent Series of Emergency Scales
Make a Picture Story
Peabody Picture Vocabulary Test
Porteus Mazes
Raven Progressive Matrices (Colored)
Raven Progressive Matrices (Standard)
Rorschach Technique
Rotter Incomplete Sentences Blank
Symonds Picture Story Test
Thematic Apperception Test
Wechsler Adult Intelligence Scale
Wechsler-Bellevue Intelligence Scales-II
Wechsler Memory Scale
Wide Range Achievement Test
Yacorzynski Block Sorting

E. Interest and attitude inventories

Brainard Occupational Preference Inventory
Minnesota Teacher Attitude Inventory
Minnesota Vocational Interest Inventory
Strong Vocational Interest Tests
Thrustone Interest Schedule

F. Achievement tests

Biology B.S.C.S. Comprehensive Final Examination
Davis Reading Test
Gates-MacGinitie Reading Tests
Gray Oral Reading Tests
Processes of Science Test
Test of Science Knowledge
Wide Range Vocabulary Test

G. Paper-and-pencil tests of personality, vocational interest, intelligence and aptitude

Allport-Vernon Study of Values
American Council on Education Psychological Examination
Army General Classification Test
Bennett Mechanical Comprehension Test
California Achievement Tests
   Intermediate and Advanced
      Mathematics
      Reading
      Language
California Psychological Inventory
College Qualification Test
Community Adaptation Schedule

Concept Mastery Test
Cooperative Tests
   English
   Usage, Spelling, Vocabulary
   Reading Comprehension
   Mathematics
   Science
   Social Studies
Culture Fair Intelligence Tests
Differential Aptitude Tests
   Verbal Reasoning
   Numerical Ability
   Abstract Reasoning
   Space Relations
   Mechanical Reasoning
   Clerical Speed and Accuracy
   Spelling
   Language Usage
Edwards Personal Preference Schedule
Forer Structured Sentence Completion Test
Forer Vocational Survey
General Clerical Test
Graves Design Judgment Test
Gray Oral Reading Test
Guilford-Zimmerman Temperament Survey
Interpersonal Checklist
Kessler-PD Scale
Kuder Form DD Occupational Interest Survey
Kuder Vocational Preference
Meier Art Test
Minnesota Clerical Test
Minnesota Importance Questionnaire
Minnesota Multiphasic Personality Inventory
Minnesota Vocational Interest Inventory
Mooney Problem Check List
Motivation Analysis Test
Ohio Literacy Test
Ohio State University Psychological Test
Otis Quick Scoring Mental Ability Test
Otis Tests of Mental Ability
Profile of Mood States
Psychological Screening Inventory
Purdue Pegboard
Revised Beta Examination
Revised Minnesota Paper Form Board
School and College Ability Tests
Sequential Tests of Educational Progress
Shipley Institute of Living Scale
Sixteen Personality Factor Questionnaire
Social Reaction Inventory
Strong Vocational Interests Blank
Survey of Interpersonal Values
Wahler Self-Description Inventory
Work Values Inventory

GLOSSARY

aberration. Abnormal; not typical.

abience. Movement by the organism away from a stimulus; avoidance.

abreaction. A mode through which a patient may openly express, with accompanying emotion, his innermost thoughts or feelings that are either repressed or ordinarily kept concealed. This process is generally considered a desirable part of psychotherapy, but it can also occur outside the therapeutic situation in persons not undergoing therapy; it is a normal phenomenon. The term catharsis is used to refer to the same process, but without reference to the emotional reaction.

abstinence. In classic psychoanalytic theory, the proscription against satisfying neurotic needs during therapy, whether with the therapist or outside the therapeutic scene.

abstract thinking. A high level of intellectual activity in which concepts and generalizations are arrived at, or in which symbols are used as an economic way of organizing thought (as in mathematics). It is often adduced that schizophrenics use little or no abstract thinking. It is often contrasted with concrete thinking.

acclimatization. The process of making an adjustment to a new environment.

acculturation. The mixing or transfer of more than one set of cultural contributions, brought about by a person or ethnic group moving from one culture into another.

acculturation stress. The anxiety experienced by persons moving from one culture into another, as a response to conflicting goals, values, and actions.

achievement motive. D. C. McClellan's term for the concern to improve, to do things better than one has done them before.

acrocinesia. Excessive or exaggerated motion of the extremities.

acting out. Human behavior, particularly when unconventional, that some analytic theorists explain as being an inappropriate carrying out of fantasies or an expression of unconscious feelings and conflicts. It most aptly applies to harmful aggressive or sexual behavior, but also pertains to play and children's play therapy.

acuity. Sharpness, accurateness of perception.

acute. Rapid in onset and brief in duration. Sensitive and discriminating in perception and thinking.

adaptation. In the biodynamic theory of Jules Masserman, adaptation is the conformity of the organism to its environment, determined by its own unique needs, capacities, and experiences as it perceives them.

adjustment. The individual's adaptation to his external and internal environment. It is from an adaptational school of psychologic theory that explains human behavior in terms of adjustment adequacy.

affect. Emotion, feeling: the tone of one's reaction to persons and events. The term is often used in the sense of flat affect, appropriate affect, or inappropriate affect.

affiliation. H. A. Murray's term for the need to be close, form friendships and loyalties, cooperativeness, and give and receive affection from significant others.

affiliative need. Affiliation.

aftercare. Continued treatment of discharged mental hospital patients, which may include foster home placement, vocational rehabilitation, family counseling, and outpatient psychotherapy. Extensive use of these facilities has been found to markedly reduce hospital readmission rates.

aggression. Sometimes used in a broad sense to denote the quality of behavior manifested by a general readiness for and tendency toward forceful action and self-assertion. The term is also used in a narrow sense to refer to hostile actions or statements. Some theorists (neofreudian) have speculated that aggression meant for others can be turned in on oneself to produce a state of depression.

algesia. Sensitivity to pain; usually, hypersensitivity to pain.

alloerotic. Sexual excitement induced by or directed toward others. As opposed to autoerotic.

alloplasty. Adaptation of libido to the environment; libidinal energies directed away from self toward other individuals and objects.

alphagenics. The teaching of a person to control his alpha rhythm, allegedly to gain more control of himself and interpersonal powers. This is probably based on the report that some conditioned control of alpha waves has been reported in scientific literature. It is used with some success in biofeedback procedures in which the subject is trained to increase alpha wave production, hopefully to thereby increase creative thinking and relaxation. (See biofeedback, p. 79.)

altrigenderism. Nonsexual, nonneurotic, nonamorous behavior between members of opposite sex.

ambisexual. Having the personality of one sex and the physical characteristics of another, and sometimes having the physical characteristics of both sexes.

ambivalence. The coexistence of opposite feelings, emotions, and attitudes toward the same subject or person. A typical example is the feeling of dependency accompanied by that of resentment toward another person. Typically one side of the feeling or attitude may be conscious and the other unconscious. This situation is often considered the seat of neurotic conflict fundamental to neurosis. Severe unresolved ambivalence is found in schizophrenia; a classic statement is: "I love my mother; I don't know why I want to kill her."

ambiversion. Introversion and extroversion present equally in a personality.

ambivert. C. G. Jung's term for a person with ambiversion.

amphigenesis. Having normal sexual relations with a member of the opposite sex by one who is primarily homosexual.

amphimixis. Ferenczi's term for the union of anal and genital eroticism.

anaclisis. Emotional dependence on others.

anaclitic. Pertaining to relationships characterized by excessive dependency. Usually used in reference to children who depend too much on one parent. Anaclitic depression is a term used to describe a depressed state in children associated with loss of a parent.

anagogic. C. G. Jung's term for the ideal, spiritual, or moral striving of the unconscious. The spiritual interpretation of words and scriptures pertaining to ideals.

anal birth. Anal, erotic dreams and fantasies expressed in a symbolic wish to be reborn thru the anus.

anal character. See p. 77.

anal eroticism. See p. 77.

anal intercourse. Sexual intercourse using the anal opening of one of the partners.

anal love. See p. 77.

analogue. In Jungian psychology, the equivalent of the archetype (see p. 78) after culture has modified its appearance.

anal phase. See p. 77.

analytic psychology. See p. 100.

anger. The emotion felt toward another person who appears to be opposing or attacking one. Psychologic theories tend to stress the ways in which people handle the emotions of fear and anger, and one or the other of these is often believed to be a basic problem in any psychiatric condition.

anima. See p. 77.

anomie. According to the sociologist Emile Durkheim, a breakdown of social norms, listlessness, and disintegration of society, with increased isolation in many individuals.

antisocial. Human behavior that is destructive to others and that, as such, is frequently illegal. The type of person most likely to engage in antisocial behavior is still occasionally labeled with the old term psychopathic personality. As a diagnostic term, the official nomenclature is sociopathic personality, antisocial type.

anxiety. A diffuse feeling of dread, apprehension; a painful state; a reaction to danger, the source of which is primarily internal and largely unrecognized. The term in its broadest sense is used synonymously with fear, meaning the emotional reaction produced by the recognition of danger. Nearly all the various psychologic theories have attached a specific meaning to the term so that it is used with various connotations. More narrowly, the term is used to refer to something different from fear when the response is directed toward an unreal danger. Freud based a major portion of his theoretical formulation on the various means by which individuals manage anxiety. His defense mechanisms are described as devices that suppress anxiety, and neurosis is seen as a failure to achieve this goal effectively. This and other similar theories generally fail to make an adequate distinction between feelings generated by mental conflict and the fear or anxiety experienced when a danger is either realistically or unrealistically perceived.

apopathetic. Behavior influenced by the presence of, but not directed toward others.

apperception. A term originated by Leibnitz to distinguish conscious perception, awareness of the significance of what is perceived, from perception in general. By the latter he meant the incoming sensory impressions of the environment, whereas apperception referred to that part of the sensory input to which the individual was directing his attention and evaluation. Jung used the term to mean essentially the same thing as understanding. In gestalt psychology, the term gestalt apperceptions signified the totality of meaning attached to fragments of sensations.

appetitive behavior. See p. 78.

approach-approach conflict. A stressful situation in which the person is faced with two equally important goals or choices of action, one nearly identical to the other, and must decide on one or the other.

approach-avoidance conflict. A stressful situation in which the person is faced with two equally attractive goals or choices of action which are the opposite to each other in the action required.

archaic unconscious. See p. 78.

archetype. See p. 78.

arousal. A state of awareness; cortical activity brought about by sensory stimulation. This is thought to be mediated through the reticular activating system. It is the act of arousing.

artificialism. A term used by Jean Piaget to describe a child's feeling that natural occurrences are caused by some human action.

asexual. Without sex. Some schizophrenics have such poor or diffuse identities that they feel sexless.

as if characters. Persons who, having failed to establish a well organized identity, will make strong, but transient identification with one person after another in whom they perceive some desired strength. The attempt that many make to take on the traits they desire represents infantile wish fulfillment.

asocial. Pertaining to behavior characterized by an individual's tendency to remain isolated from social contacts and to be relatively uninfluenced by social pressures. This contrasts with antisocial behavior, which actively engages in contacts with other people, but in a destructive way.

assertion. A deep-seated drive or personality pattern that leads to reacting to stimuli in a definitely forceful way. This term implies the will to overt action but does not necessarily include hostility, as is implied in aggression.

assimilation. The process by which an alien individual absorbs the qualities of a culture into which he has moved. More broadly, it means the acquisition of ideas, traits, and behavior from the environment.

association. The phenomenon whereby one experience or idea reminds one of some other experience or idea. Jung devised a psychological test in which key words were used to elicit associated ideas, thereby revealing material useful in understanding the subject's conflicts. Freud used the term free association as an essential technique of treatment in which the patient was required to express his thoughts as they came into his mind without censoring or organizing them.

associationism. See p. 78.

ataraxy. Peaceful, complacent, calm.

atavism. See p. 78.

attention. The phenomenon of focusing mental process on one particular segment of either incoming sensory impressions or on a particular part of the memory. An essential part of a psychiatric examination consists of the determination of the degree to which the patient pays attention to the interviewer and to the subject under discussion.

attitude. The affective state with which a person habitually confronts his environment. Attitude is determined in early childhood by what Erik Erikson called basic trust. Associated with this is a sense of well-being and optimism and also a clear sense of personal identity. Basic distrust leads to a rigidly hostile, suspicious, and pessimistic attitude toward others.

auditory memory. The ability to recall in response to an auditory stimulus data that have been memorized through hearing it.

auditory span. The amount of information that can be repeated accurately after hearing it one time. It is used as a test for recent memory.

autoerotic. Stimulated to sexual excitement by one's own self. Sometimes used synonymously with masturbation.

autoeroticism. The practice of seeking sexual gratification from oneself and without contact with others; for example, masturbation. According to Freud's theory of sexual development, the child begins life autoerotic and later becomes either homosexual or heterosexual.

autogenic training. A technique advocated by J. H. Schultz to gain control over vegetative functions through elaborate breathing and postural exercises.

autology. See p. 78.

autonomy. Self-determination, independence; without external control.

autoplastic. See p. 78.

avoidance. A mental mechanism whereby the person unconsciously prevents himself from entering into threatening situations or activities.

avoidance-avoidance conflict. A stressful situation in which the person is faced with two equally undesirable goals or choices of action.

barognosis. Ability to detect or recognize weight and differences in weight.

basic personality. Abraham Kardiner's term for the group of personality traits found in all members of a given culture or society secondary to common child-rearing practices.

basic trust. A feeling developed early in life through healthy, loving relationships with parents; based on secure interpersonal ties so that the child can learn that the world is essentially a good place and that people are generally good. It is a necessary basis for a healthy personality.

behavior. The actions carried out by an animal or a human being that can be observed and recorded. It is often used to refer to the patterns of activity that are characteristic of an individual or group.

behavioral science. See p. 101.

bind. A dilemma; a situation in which a difficult decision must be made.

binge. See p. 131.

birth order. The position relationship of one sibling to another within a family.

bisexual. Having the characteristics and qualities of both sexes; hermaphroditic.

bivalence. Ambivalence.

blocking. Sudden, unexplained cessation in a train of thought; may be seen in schizophrenics. Synonym: obstructing.

body build. See p. 79.

body ego. The firmly established conception, memories, ideas, feelings of and toward one's body and self; the ability to perceive one's body as apart from external reality and to appreciate proprioceptive stimuli.

body image. The total array of attitudes, perceptions, and feelings toward the body and its parts. This image is fairly firm and secure in normal people and is altered to various degrees in persons with mental and brain diseases. It is part of the body ego.

body language. A quality of a person's bodily movements; gestures, attitudes, and posture that communicate meaning to others.

body-mind problem. The difficulty encountered in relating mental activity to specific anatomical structures or neurophysiological and neurochemical processes.

bound energy. Libidinal energy under ego control for dealing with reality and not expended on repression or fantasy.

breast-feeding. Feeding of the child from the mother's breast.

broken home. A family situation in which one or both parents is absent. It usually connotes absence by divorce or desertion.

catharsis. Uninhibited verbal expression of ideas and feelings for a remedial effect.

cathartic hypnosis. A therapeutic hypnosis in which the patient is encouraged to divulge repressed and unconscious material that could not be recalled while awake; as opposed to authoritative or directive hypnosis.

cathexis. The attachment of emotion to an object, person, or idea. The emotion may be either positive or negative (love or hate). Freud equated all such emotions with libidinal energies. A cathectic idea is one charged with intense feeling. It is a term from the psychoanalytic school referring to emotion.

censor. See p. 80.

central force. Jung's term for the primal libido; undifferentiated energy or life force.

cerebration. Conscious thinking.

cerebrotonic. See p. 80.

character. Synonymous with personality; a person's typical and habitual manner of dealing with the world. Character has been classified in many different ways, each way being a product of theoretical concepts of human behavior and development. Incorrectly used as meaning something that an individual either has or does not have (for example, strength and honesty).

character analysis. Wilhelm Reich's term for his theory and treatment technique. Character is conceived as an accumulation of defensive armor against a hostile world. Treatment consists of modifying this armor.

character defense. See p. 80.

characterology. The study of personality or personal characteristics. Modern advances in this field owe much to phrenology and other nineteenth century pseudosciences, which really pioneered in emphasizing individual character traits.

chastity clause. A vow undertaken, sometimes unconsciously, by certain usually compulsive or very religious persons to remain chaste. Such a vow may underlie some cases of impotence.

circadian rhythms. Cyclical variations in physiologic and biochemical activity level of function and emotional state of about 24 hours duration. See infradian rhythms and ultradian rhythms.

climacteric. That period of life during which there is a slowing or cessation of sex glandular function. It is synonymous with menopause.

coconscious. The development of a sharing of common experiences, feelings, and thoughts, especially as seen in a group therapy setting. It is a conscious state not in total awareness because the events or thoughts are not in the focus of attention at the moment.

cognition. The act or process of knowing; the ability to know.

cognitive. The quality of mental activity involved in learning and understanding.

coitus. Sexual intercourse between male and female, using the penis and vagina.

coitus interruptus. Withdrawal of the penis from the vagina just prior to ejaculation; usually performed for birth control.

collective unconscious. See p. 80.

communication. The sending of thoughts, feelings, attitudes, and emotions from one person to another.

comparative psychology. See p. 102.

compensation. The mental mechanism or behavior by which the person unconsciously attempts to make up for real or imagined deficiencies.

complementarity. A condition of concord or balance between members of a group in regard to the emotional needs of the group members; especially used in reference to marriage.

complex. A mental state produced by the existence of an unresolved conflict or a group of conflicts; unconscious ideas, drives, and affects that influence conscious behavior, attitudes, and thinking. Various types of complexes have been described, such as castration complex and inferiority complex.

conation. Drives, instincts, needs.

conceptual thinking. A form of mental functioning (for example, the ability to abstract, hypothesize, and synthesize), usually lost following brain damage.

concomitance. See p. 80.

concrete thinking. A primitive type of thinking characteristic of children, retardates, and schizophrenics. The concrete thinker tends to assume a literal, superficial meaning of ideas. The person so affected may not be able to interpret the proverb, "Don't put all your eggs into one basket"; he could conceive it only as something about eggs in a basket. It is opposed to abstract or conceptual thinking.

concretism. Characterized by a tendency to use concrete thinking.

condensation. A mental mechanism whereby the person unconsciously attributes to one thought or idea all the feelings or emotions he holds for several thoughts or ideas (for example, in dreams an object or word may symbolize several persons, objects, or feelings at once).

conditioned reflex. See p. 80.

conditioned reflex psychology. See p. 102.

conditioning. A type of learning in which responses are elicited by stimuli and then are made part of the organism's response repertoire and behavior through either repeated use of the stimulus or use of a reward for these responses. Most conditioning theory is an outgrowth of the work of the Russian physiologist Ivan Pavlov.

conditioning, operant. See operant conditioning.

conflict. See p. 102.

confusion. Broadly, a state of indecision; more narrowly, a state of indecision concerning one's orientation to time, place, or person.

conscience. The capacity to feel guilty: self-censorship; the expectation of disapproval by others.

conscious. The quality of being alert and attentive to reality; therefore, equivalent to the active thinking processes of the mind. Psychoanalytic theory assumes the existence of a separate, additional body of ideation located in the unconscious, where it is readily accessible. The conscious portion is called the ego in this theory.

consciousness. The state of being conscious.

consensual validation. See p. 80.

constancy principle. See p. 80.

constitution. The total physical attributes of each individual. Occasional reference is made to constitutional factors in personality or in psychiatric problems, meaning determinant factors that are not products of experience but that are inherent in the physical attributes of the person.

constitutional. Individual characteristics that are inherited.

constitutional psychology. See p. 103.

constitutional types. See p. 80.

coping. Adjusting or adapting to one's environment.

cosmology. See p. 80.

counconscious. The development of shared unconscious feelings, identifications, and so on, especially as seen in a group therapy setting.

countercathexis. See p. 80.

countertransference. Freud's term to describe the "irrational attitudes of the analyst toward the patient," paralleling the reverse, which he called transference. Usually means the quality of hostility or unprofessional sexual attitudes that the analyst might direct toward the patient.

crisis. A time of acute distress, pain, or suffering.

critical period. A period of time in development during which some deprivation will result in unwanted consequences later in life. This deprivation can be physical, mental, or emotional.

cross-cultural psychiatry. See p. 103.

cruelty. A manifestation of hatred, thought to be a mixture of anger and sexual feelings.

cultural. The qualities of group behavior characteristic of the group.

cultural conflict. A state of disparity between two juxtaposed cultures. An example is the case of the person whose family is of a culture different from the one in which he lives; in his effort to adjust to both, a conflict is produced.

cultural lag. The delay in the rate at which certain social institutions (such as laws) evolve as the culture evolves and changes.

cultural pattern. The complex sets of beliefs and behaviors characteristic of culturally homogenous groups.

cultural school (psychoanalysis). See p. 81.

cultural trait. A single characteristic (such as a particular prohibition) of a cultural group.

culture. The total of persistent patterns of human behavior and its products, which are transmitted to following generations through use of language, art, tools, play, folk tales, and music.

culture stress. The total effect on an individual brought about by an environmental change, such as deprivation, isolation, or rapid changes in cultural setting (for example, moving from a rural to an urban environment).

cunnilingus. A variation of sexual activity (mouth to vulva); considered by some to be an example of sexual perversion.

custom. A cultural group's habitual manner of engaging in a particular kind of behavior, such as the typical marriage ceremony of the group.

dactylology. Sign language using the hands and fingers; used by deaf mutes.

dasein. See p. 81.

daydreams. Fantasy, reverie, wishful thinking. These occur in everyone, normally. In abnormal mental states they may be intensified, prolonged, or uncontrolled, as in schizophrenia or toxic psychoses, or they may be reduced, as in depression or brain injury.

day residue. A latent dream content comprising thoughts and ideas connected with activities and feelings of the dreamer's current waking life.

deanalize. Transfer of instinctual impulses from the anal region to some other mode of expression.

death instinct. See p. 81.

defense mechanisms. See p. 81.

defloration. Loss of virginity in the female; the breaking of the hymenal ring, usually through intercourse.

dejection. A feeling of sadness; usually linked with loss of someone or something, self-esteem, or pride. It is a component of depression.

delinquency, juvenile. Antisocial or abnormal behavior in a young person that may bring him into conflict with society.

denial. A defense mechanism operating from unconscious motivation in which conflict is resolved by consciously rejecting one element of the anxiety-producing conflict. It is said to be manifested by an unconscious disowning of reality. Often there is, in addition, substitution by fantasy. Used more loosely to refer to isolated efforts to deny the existence of a problem by simply ignoring it.

deorality. Transfer of psychic energy from the oral region to some other mode of expression.

dependency. The quality of relying on someone else for decision making, for subsistence, for approval, and so on. This quality is characteristic of developmental immaturity, and is therefore likely to be seen in children, neurotics, and schizophrenics. Also used to mean the reliance on or the acquired need for a drug.

dependency needs. Universally present requirements of (for) love, warmth, affection, reduction of tissue tensions, shelter, parenting; if unmet in the developing individual may contribute to development of psychopathology, marasmus, or death.

depth psychology. See p. 81.

descriptive psychiatry. See p. 104.

desensitization. A process in therapy by which the patient reexamines painful feelings and memories and thereby gradually reduces anxiety through new understanding and formation of new modes of adaptation.

desexualization. Withdrawing sexual energy and attachment from otherwise sexual objects.

desocialization. See p. 104.

destrudo. See p. 104.

determinism. The belief or philosophical stance that nothing occurs from chance alone but rather from specific causes or forces.

developmental psychology. See p. 104.

diffuse. See p. 81.

directive hypnosis. Hypnosis during which the patient is ordered to give up his symptoms or attitudes, as opposed to cathartic hypnosis.

disgust. Unpleasant feeling, one of revulsion; usually associated with unpleasant gastrointestinal sensations.

displacement. See p. 81.

dissocial reaction. A term denoting a person who ignores the social codes and who may come into conflict with the society in which he lives, but does so because he was reared in a group that taught him these different values. An example is a hillbilly engaged in bootlegging, which is acceptable in his community but not in the larger society. The term is included under Personality Pattern Disturbance in the official nomenclature. It is different from the antisocial type of reaction, in which the individual is going against the values and precepts of his social group.

dissociation. A mental mechanism operating outside conscious awareness to bring about separation of a strong emotional charge from an idea, object, or situation. Such an operation splits off a portion of the ego for the purpose of isolating a corresponding portion of a primitive superego, thereby allowing a painless expression of intolerable ideas or behavior. It is used in the official nomenclature to designate more complex psychological phenomena of total or partial personality disorganization that may lead to other specific syndromes, such as double personality, depersonalization, amnesia, somnambulism, and fugue states.

distortion. A mental mechanism by which the meaning of some idea, message, or sensory impression is twisted into a false representation. The psychoanalytic theory assumes that dreams are almost invariably distorted in that they are said to present a false picture through symbolism and condensation.

double-bind. A dilemma forced on a person by presenting him with conflicting messages to which he must respond; a situation in which the person cannot be correct or cannot win, no matter what his response. It is said to be characteristic of interactions within families of schizophrenics and a contributing factor in the genesis of schizophrenia.

drainage hypothesis. See p. 81.

dreams. Fantasies that take place during sleep; a normal phenomenon; nightmare.

dream sleep. Synonymous with rapid-eye-movement sleep.

dream work. See p. 81.

drive. Instinct.

drive behavior. See p. 81.

dyad. A relationship between two persons.

dynamic concept. See p. 82.

dynamics. See p. 82.

dynamisms. See p. 82.

ear pulling. If done habitually, considered equivalent to masturbation (psychoanalysis), a substitute for thumb-sucking (Kanner).

economic concepts. See p. 82.

ecphoria. Reestablishment of a memory trace.

ecstasy. A trancelike state, usually with euphoria, such as would occur during a religious conversion.

ectomorph. See p. 82.

educational psychology. See p. 104.

ego. See p. 82.

ego boundary. The boundary between what is the self and what is not the self, what is psychologically ''me'' and ''not me.''

egocentric. Turned in on oneself, selfish, or self-centered.

egodystonic. See p. 82.

ego ideal. The ideal self; that which one consciously and unconsciously wishes to become; superego.

ego identity. Erik Erikson's term for the internal psychological structure that integrates all past experiences into a coherent whole as part of one's self-concept.

ego psychology. See p. 82.

ego splitting. See p. 82.

ego strenth. The person's tolerance for stress and his ability to function under stress.

egosyntonic. See p. 82.

eidetic image. A sensory impression that is unusually sharp and clear, thought to be more common in children than adults.

Eigenwelt. See p. 82.

elaboration. See p. 82.

elementism. See p. 82.

ellipsis. Omission of an idea, word, thought, or act.

emasculation. Castration; specifically, removal of the testes, but may be used to denote psychological castration as well.

emergency emotions. See p. 82.

emotion. A set of physiological sensations that accompany the individual's current attitude; for example, fear, anger, pleasure, and love.

empathy. The process of objectively observing and understanding another person's difficulties or emotions without experiencing them oneself; in contrast with sympathy, which is a subjective experience in imagination that simulates the other person's feelings.

emperical psychology or philosophy. See p. 83.

enantiopathic. The quality of provoking an opposite feeling.

encounter. In existential psychiatry and philosophy the marked influence in the life of an individual brought about by meeting someone who opens a whole new world of thought, feeling, and perspective to that individual. Such an encounter is seen by the individual as a pivotal point in his life.

endocept. Mental activity intermediary between a level in which there is a prevalence of images and a level characterized by language. Derived from memory traces, images, and motor engrams.

endogamy. Marrying within the clan or tribe.

endomorph. See p. 83.

endopsychic. Occurring within the mind.

end-pleasure. Orgasm.

engram. The underlying chemical and electrophysiological processes in the nervous system that are the correlates of memory. It is a pathway or trace supposedly left in the nervous system by every experience.

entatic. Stimulating; provoking; arousing sexual desire.

enteroception. Proprioception.

environmentalism. See p. 83.

ergasia. See p. 83.

ergasiology. See p. 83.

ergotropy. See p. 83.

eros. See p. 83.

erotic. Productive of sexual excitement.

erotogenic zone. Any part of the body that, when stimulated, gives rise to sexual excitement.

escape from reality. Strong use of fantasy, daydreaming, or denial, or the development of a psychosis; usually a response to painful or stressful situations.

eschatology. Concerned with finality, death, life hereafter.

essence. See p. 83.

esthesotype. MacKay's term for the highest engram; memory traces required for highest mental function.

estrangement. A subjective feeling that one's experiences are occurring as though in someone apart from oneself.

euthymia. Pleasant feeling, well-being.

executive ego function. Management by the ego of the mental mechanisms by which the person's needs are satisfied.

existence. See p. 83.

existential anxiety. See p. 83.

existential guilt. See p. 83.

existentialism. See p. 83.

existential psychology. See p. 83.

exogamy. Marrying outside the clan or tribe.

experimental psychology. See p. 105.

extinction. Loss of the conditioned reflex by eliciting it without reinforcement by the unconditioned reflex and reward.

extrasensory perception. See p. 83.

extrovert. Carl Jung's term for persons who turn their libido outward. The term has come into the popular language to mean the person who is inclined to be active, gregarious, and expressive. It is the opposite of introvert.

factor analysis. See p. 83.

faculty psychology. See p. 83.

familial. Any characteristic or trait that tends to follow family lines.

family stability. The ability of family members to interact in their respective family roles, cope with family conflicts, and restore balance after an emotional upset.

fantasy. Imagination, daydreaming, revery; a type of thinking that is not directly related to current reality and that may not be limited by practical logic. A major step in the development of psychoanalytic theory was Freud's discovery that patients' reports of painful experiences in childhood were products of fantasy, and from that time on Freud was almost solely preoccupied with the study of patients' fantasies.

father substitute. Surrogate; a person other than the legal father with whom one has a conscious or unconscious relationship similar to that with a father.

fear. The emotion experienced when danger is recognized or anticipated. It is felt as a complex of physiological signs that appear to be adrenergic in their mechanism and, that as such, represent a state of readiness for handling danger, thus serving a function in survival.

feelings. Synonymous with emotions and affects.

fetish. An object regarded by an individual or a group to have unusual, magical powers. It is sometimes used loosely to refer to a person's tendency to attach undue importance to an object, an idea, or an activity.

field theory. See p. 83.

first-signal system. See p. 83.

fixation. See p. 84.

folk psychology. See p. 84.

forgetting. The inability to recall certain information. In his treatise on the psychopathology of everyday life, Freud pointed out the unconscious meaning of forgotten names, places, and objects.

free association. See p. 84.

freudian. See p. 84.

fright. Fear that is sudden and startling at onset.

frigidity. The failure to enjoy or reach orgasm in sexual activities, seen especially in women.

frustration. The feeling brought about by the inability to resolve a conflict or to fulfill a need.

frustration tolerance. The ability of an individual to withstand the stress brought on by frustration.

functional. See p. 84.

functional disorder. Abnormality of an organ or organ system that is not caused by physical, chemical, or physiological changes.

functional psychology. See p. 84.

general adaptation syndrome. See p. 84.

generativity. See p. 84.

genital love. See p. 84.

genius. Someone of very superior intellectual and creative abilities, loosely used to denote anyone with very superior skills in a given field. No consensus exists for a definition of the term or criteria for its use.

geographic determinism. See p. 84.

gerontology. See p. 105.

gestalt. A total impression acquired from incomplete fragments.

gestalt psychology. See p. 84.

good me. See p. 84.

group pressure. Influence exerted by the group on the behavior of its members.

guilt. The sensation of remorse and self-blame and the loss of self-esteem because of real or imagined failure or error. Psychoanalytic theory places a great deal of stress on the importance of guilt in the generation of psychiatric problems, and it is alleged that guilt may be either conscious or unconscious. In psychoanalytic terms, guilt may be considered ego fear of the superego.

gustatory. Pertaining to the sense of taste.

habit. Acts or thoughts repeated with sufficient frequency to have become unconscious or unpremeditated.

habitat. The living area or environment of a person or group.

habit-forming. Having the ability to cause dependency.

hatred. The feeling of extreme anger, enmity, and resentment toward another person or object.

Hawthorne effect. See p. 84.

hedonism. A philosophy or way of living that stresses the search for pleasurable experiences.

hedonistic. A way of life dominated by a search for pleasure. The term hedonistic personality is sometimes used to refer to people motivated by such a philosophy, and the term anhedonistic personality is used to describe a type of person who has done very little in his life to bring about a sense of enjoyment. The term is derived from an ancient Greek philosophical school.

heteroclite. A person who does not follow the common rule, as opposed to homoclite.

heteroerotic. Stimulated to sexual excitement by someone of the opposite sex.

heterophemy. Unintentional use of a word when another one is desired, the substitution being unconsciously motivated.

heterosexual. Having the desire for a person of the opposite sex, as opposed to homosexual.

homoclite. A person who follows the common rule; well-adjusted, normal, and healthy; as opposed to heteroclite.

homoerotic. Stimulated to sexual excitement by someone of the same sex.

homogamy. Marriage between close relatives; inbreeding.

hormic psychology. See p. 85.

hostility. The expression of anger. Psychoanalytic theory postulates that hostility can be repressed and manifested in indirect ways. Under any circumstance, hostility is countered by the expectation of retaliation, which is likely to modify behavior.

humanistic psychology. See p. 85.

humor. A technique of normal defense used to convert unacceptable situations into something one can manage psychologically.

hypnagogic. See p. 30.

hypnagogic hallucinations. See p. 30.

hyphedonia. Diminished experience of pleasurable sensation from normally pleasant acts.

hypnopompic. Sleep dispelling.

hypnosis. See p. 85.

hypnosis, authoritative. A type of hypnosis in which the patient is ordered to give up his symptoms, as opposed to cathartic hypnosis.

id. See p. 85.

idealization. A mental mechanism whereby one imagines desirable qualities in another person; qualities that may not actually be present. Freud attached considerable importance to the phenomenon of idealization of the love-object.

idealized self. Horney's term to denote the development of a neurotic life-style wherein a grandiose ideal self-image is invoked as a defense against recognition of the disparity between what the person is and what his neurotic pride tells him he should be.

identical twins. Twins produced from a single ovum and possessing nearly identical characteristics; in contrast to fraternal twins, who resemble each other no more closely than do sibling pairs.

identification. A mental mechanism by which another person is used as a model for one's own behavior. Psychoanalytic theory postulates that unconscious as well as conscious identification can take place. When the process is conscious, one simply imitates and models oneself after an ideal. Unconscious identification is a deeper process of molding oneself to an image of an important person or object. It is most important in early child-

hood when identification is made with the parent or parent figure in formulation and development of the superego.

identification with the aggressor. The unconscious process of imitating a hated or feared person.

identifying link. See p. 85.

identity crisis. See p. 85.

idiogamy. Being potent with only one woman and impotent with others.

idiosyncrasy. Attribute and characteristics unique to the individual.

idiosyncratic credit. The total of positive feelings and reactions of group members toward an individual. They give status and permit deviation from group norms, including assumption of leadership.

illusion. A false perception of an external stimulus (for example, the desert traveler perceiving a heat wave as an oasis).

imago. See p. 85.

impotence. Inability of the male to carry out or enjoy sexual intercourse. It may be partial or complete and is thought to be caused more often by psychological conditions than by physical conditions.

imprinting. A process similar to behavioral patterning or rapid learning occurring at critical points in very early development of the organism.

impulse. A stimulus that provokes thought or action. The term sometimes refers to stimuli presumably originating from instincts.

impulsive behavior. Actions caused by irresistable urges that are usually in conflict with either ethical or social standards. These acts serve no useful purpose for the person and are seen by him as being an abnormal act. Included under this term are kleptomania, pyromania, impulsive gambling, and so on.

incest barrier. A function of the ego, most probably learned, that prevents sexual intercourse between blood relatives. In psychoanalysis, this term has special reference to development of the ego in the child.

incorporation. A mental mechanism whereby a person unconsciously and symbolically takes within himself the attributes of another person; often synonymous with introjection and identification.

indecision. Inability to make a choice. The fear of failure may serve as a major deterrent to being decisive and is frequently seen is psychiatric problems.

individual psychology. See p. 85.

infantilization. Parental behavior that causes or encourages the child to carry out childish behavior beyond the time such behavior normally occurs in children.

infantile sexuality. The existence of sexual drives and feelings during infancy; one of Freud's early discoveries that led to the formulation of his theories of sexuality.

inferiority complex. Alfred Adler's term for feelings that one is less well endowed, less potent, or less intelligent than others. According to Adler's theory of personality development, the child is confronted with the realization of his inferiority, and his personality development becomes strongly determined by his method of trying to overcome it. When the person fails to deal with childhood inferiority adequately, the adult may be left with an inferiority complex.

information theory. A systematic approach to communication using mathematical representation of communication and messages and the systems that carry out these modes.

infradian rhythm. Cyclical variations in physiologic and biochemical activity, level of function, and emotional state longer than one day; may be weeks to months in duration. See circadian rhythms and ultradian rhythms.

inhibition. The process of confining one's thoughts, wishes, or actions to within acceptable limits.

inner directed. See p. 85.

insight. Understanding one's own motives, unconscious, dynamics.

integration. The process of organizing the components of the mind into a workable whole. Disintegration is sometimes said to occur when a patient appears to be failing to behave and think in a systematic way. Reintegration may be used to describe the process of psychotherapy when a new organization is given to a person's thinking.

intellect. Synonymous with mind, wit.

intellectualization. A mental mechanism that is closely related to rationalization. The term means an unconscious overuse of intellectual processes to avoid closeness, feelings, or affective experience and expression.

intrapsychic. Taking place within the mind. Fantasies or neurotic problems generated from within the mind of a person, without direct relationship to reality, may be considered as examples.

introjection. A mental mechanism by which the person unconsciously directs toward himself the feeling for an external object or person. For instance, anger felt toward another person could be turned inward and appear clinically as depression.

introjects. Images, characteristics, and representations of external objects and persons by which the developing child augments the formation of his superego and ego.

introspection. Being preoccupied with one's own inner activity; the action of looking into oneself. It is encouraged in psychoanalytic therapy to develop insight.

introspectionistic psychology. See p. 85.

introvert. Carl Jung's term for one of his two types of personality, the other being extrovert. An introvert is a person whose thoughts and activities are directed toward himself instead of toward others; he is likely to be isolated, introspective, and relatively uncommunicative.

inversion. A mental mechanism by which the person unconsciously changes a feeling for an object or person into the opposite feeling (for example, changing love for someone into hate).

involution. Reduction of and halting of physiological and psychological functions; the opposite of maturation.

irrational. Unreasonable, senseless, insane, illogical.

isolation. A mental mechanism by which the feeling for an object or person is separated from that object or person. In this way, a memory or image can be considered intellectually, because the anxiety-producing emotion associated with that object or person is not felt.

jealousy. The quality of being distrustful, apprehensive, and suspicious of loss, hurt to oneself, rivalry, or unfaithfulness. It probably occurs in everyone and is not considered pathological, especially when provoked.

jocasta complex. See p. 85.

judgment. The quality of one's decision-making processes. The degree of judgment is a function of maturity and the intactness of the cerebral cortex.

juvenile delinquency. Antisocial and deviant behavior in children and adolescents.

kinephantom. The illusion that a moving object has movement other than its real motion.

kinesics. Generally taken to mean the study or use of gestures, posture, affects, and variations in voice in communication.

kinesthesia. The ability to perceive the motion of one's body; synonymous with proprioception.

lambitus. Cunnilingus.

language. A systemized method for transmitting information to others; may include words, gestures, signs, and sounds.

latency period. See p. 85.

latent content. See p. 85.

laterality. The characteristic of using one hand or foot in preference to the other (such as in writing or throwing); handedness.

learning theory. See p. 85.

leptosomal. See p. 86.

leptosome. See p. 86.

lethargy. Lack of energy; a condition of inactivity, drowsiness, and mental dullness.

libido. See p. 86.

life space. See p. 86.

lisping. A speech disorder in which the person cannot articulate a sibilant sound (s, sh, z, ch).

localization theory. See p. 86.

logoklony (logoclony). Stuttering.

logopathy. Any speech defect.

logopedics. The study of speech and speech disorders.

logorrhea. Rapid, voluble speech; extreme form occurs in manic patients.

logospasm. Stuttering; explosive speech.

ludic. Fantastic; false, pretentious.

lust. Strong feelings of sexual desire.

lust dynamism. See p. 86.

maladaptation. Inability of the person to react to his environment in a manner sufficient to assure satisfaction of his needs, reduction of his anxiety, or even continuation of existence.

maladjustment. Maladaptation.

manifest content. See p. 86.

masculinity. Refers to the possession of male secondary sex characteristics (such as, physique, beard, low voice), as well as exhibiting culturally prescribed male behavior.

mass action principle. See p. 86.

masturbation. Self-stimulation of the genitals; usually carried out by hand and accompanied by sexual fantasies. It probably occurs in some form or to some degree in everyone and is not in itself harmful.

material culture. The economic aspects of culture.

maturity. The acquisition of fully adult psychosexual attitudes; usually occurring concomitantly with physical development.

mechanisms. Any of the various types of mental activity that may take place (for example, decision making, opinion formation, memory, fantasy). Interactions among the psychic structures (that is, id, ego, and superego).

memory. The retention of or ability to retain mental images and other information obtained through the senses; in computer terminology, the computer's ability to store information received through an input unit or developed during the processing of data.

menarche. The time of onset of menstruation.

menopause. Cessation of menstrual flow at the change of life; female climacteric.

mental apparatus. See p. 87.

mental chemistry. See p. 87.

mental faculty. Mental skill, ability; a term fundamental to faculty psychology (that is, phrenology), which supposes that each particular type of knowledge or skill is representative of a particular part of the brain's function.

mentalism. See p. 87.

mental mechanism. A psychic operation, most often defensive, occurring without conscious awareness, for the relief of anxiety, reduction of tension, or the resolution of an emotional conflict. The term is synonymous with intrapsychic mechanisms, defense mechanisms, and ego defense mechanisms. The more commonly recognized mental mechanisms are:

compensation	isolation
denial	projection
displacement	rationalization
dissociation	reaction formation
fantasy	regression
idealization	repression
identification	restitution
incorporation	sublimation
internalization	substitution
introjection	symbolization
inversion	undoing

mentation. The process of thinking.

mesmerism. Hypnotism; after Anton Mesmer.

mesomorph. See p. 87.

message. Any symbolic representation carrying information between individuals.

metalanguage. See p. 122.

metaphysical psychology. See p. 87.

metapsychology. See p. 87.

mind. The complex of attributes or abilities enabling one to consider, evaluate, perceive, remember, and decide. Synonyms include psyche, intellect, and wit.

miniature theories. See p. 87.

misanthropy. Dislike of men; commonly taken to mean hatred of mankind.

miscegenation. Marriage between members of different races.

misocainia. Distaste for novelty or change.

misogamy. Aversion to marriage.

misopedia. Hatred of children.

Mitwelt. See p. 87.

mnemic (mnemonic). Pertaining to memory.

mobility (of people). The degree of freedom enjoyed by an individual or class of people to move into different geographic areas or into different socioeconomic levels.

modality. See p. 87.

modus operandi. Manner of performing work.

modus vivendi. Manner of style of living.

mogilalia. Stuttering.

mogiphonia. Difficulty in forming words.

molding. Shaping. (See p. 94.)

monism. See p. 87.

Montessori system. Teaching methods of Maria Montessori (1870-1952), emphasizing individualized attention and attempting to instill knowledge through multiple sensory channels. Her first school to follow the system was established in Rome (1907) for slum children.

mood. An enduring affect or emotional reaction.

mores. Folkways; customs characteristic of a culture.

mortido. See p. 87.

motivation. The conscious and unconscious pressure a person feels to express his desires and wishes.

mourning. The process of grieving for a lost person or object.

narcissism. Self-admiration; self-love. Psychoanalytic theory frequently refers to the pursuit of selfish pleasure and the disregard of others as narcissistic.

need gratification. See p. 88.

negative feelings. Unpleasant emotions, such as fear and hate.

negative therapeutic reaction. See p. 88.

neobehaviorism. See p. 88.

neomnesis. Memory for recent past.

nepenthic. Able to induce peace and forgetfulness.

neurotic traits. A term used extensively in the military service during World War II to indicate the presence of precursors to clinical neurosis (for example, childhood problems of bedwetting, temper tantrums, nail-biting).

neurotigenic. Producing, or able to produce a neurosis.

neutralization. See p. 88.

nexus. Union or linkage of ideas, thoughts, instincts, affects.

nightmare. A discomforting, or terrifying dream.

nirvana principle. See p. 88.

nonreporting. See p. 88.

nonverbal communication. The various means, other than spoken languages, by which a person's meaning is conveyed to others; includes facial expression, tone of voice, gestures, and posture.

noopsyche. See p. 88.

normative. Pertaining to the normal. In psychiatry this is an approach to defining mental illness as a deviation from normal behavior. The major problem with this approach is, of course, the inability to find a universally acceptable definition for what constitutes normal behavior.

objective psychology. See p. 88.

oblativity. Able to relinquish one's mother figure to achieve independence.

obscurantism. The practice of placing obstacles or resistance in the way of change.

obsessive behavior. See p. 88.

olfaction. The sense of or ability to smell.

olfactory agnosia. Inability to recognize odors.

one-trial learning. A form of learning in which the higher mental processes are involved. Much of human learning apparently occurs in this manner.

ontogenesis. The development of the individual.

ontology. See p. 89.

operant behavior. B. F. Skinner's term for his type of stimulus-response studies in animals, in which the response is emitted by the organism rather than elicited by some unknown stimulus.

operant conditioning. A type of therapy founded on the theories of B. F. Skinner in which the desired behavior of the patient is reinforced or rewarded by the therapist after it occurs. The behavior is spontaneous on the part of the patient; undesirable or unwanted behavior is ignored or punished until the person relinquishes that behavior.

operationalism. See p. 89.

oretic. Pertaining to sensations, needs, and drives (for example, hunger, sucking), occurring during infancy and relating to the mouth.

organismic theory. See p. 89.

orgasm. Sexual climax.

orientation. A person's state of knowledge concerning the correctness of time, place, person, and situation.

out-group. A group of persons not currently in social or cultural favor.

overdetermination. A mental mechanism by which more than one need is satisfied by a certain reaction (for example, conversion reaction).

overprotection. See p. 132.

oversensitivity. See p. 132.

pack. Use of hot or cold wrappings in hydrotherapy.

pain threshold. The level of stimulus intensity at which a person can perceive the stimulus as being painful or unpleasant.

panic. Extreme fear; likely to result from the combination of fear and a sense of helplessness.

paradoxical intention. A method used by Victor Frankl in which the person is made to undertake an activity, not with a goal of learning to enjoy that activity, but rather to rid himself of the fear of or desire for it.

passive-aggression. See p. 36.

passive behavior. Psychological inactivity, inertia, laziness, indolence, lack of overresponsiveness, and a yielding to aggression and hostility, or a need for support, guidance, and domination. Passive behavior, which can be pathological and provoke strong aggressive responses from others, should be distinguished from receptivity.

passive-dependent. A way of living characterized by a helpless, clinging attitude.

passivity. This refers to avoidance reactions, but in psychiatry it is used to denote a lack of responsiveness, apathy, and a marked need to be dependent and to receive from others.

pavor diurnus. See p. 37.

pavor nocturnus. See p. 37.

pedigree studies. The examination of family histories in exploring causes or contributions to disease states.

peer group. A group of one's equals.

perception. A recognition of sensory impressions. It is a psychological term meaning more than the mere sensations brought into the brain; it includes the actual recognition and interpretation of those sensations. A major part of experimental psychology has dealt with perception.

personality. An individual's characteristic way of conducting his life. Because of the consistency of individual personalities, various types have been classified by most of the psychologic theories, each in accordance with its theoretical approach to personality development. Personality may be viewed as a pattern of learned adjustment techniques or as a facade that conceals some inner real self.

phantasy. Fantasy.

phenomenalism. See p. 90.

phenomenological psychology. See p. 90.

phenomenology. See p. 90.

phonic recognition. The recognition of sounds, especially spoken words.

pithiatism. Persuasion in treatment of hysterical symptoms.

plateau speech. Flat monotonous speech.

positive feelings. Emotions that have a pleasant connotation, such as love or pleasure.

potency. Ability to obtain and maintain an erection for coitus.

precocious. Early or unusually advanced development; especially used regarding sexual or mental attributes.

pregenital. Phases of psychosexual development in the infant before emergence of genital interests.

preverbal thinking. Thinking that occurs without the use of words; reveries, daydreams. It is thought that most thinking occurs preverbally.

projection. A mental mechanism by which unacceptable thoughts or feelings about oneself are imputed to some other person or object. Through projection, one's own rejected motives, desires, wishes, impulses, and ideas are attributed to others. When overused as a defense mechanism, one shows the clinical picture of a paranoid state.

proprioception. Position sense; awareness of the placing of parts of the body.

protocommunication. Early communication in the infant. For instance, the nipple may be the only meaningful sign to the infant during this phase.

prototaxic mode. H. S. Sullivan's term for the infant's experience of undifferentiated, global, unorganized perception of the world. The first and earliest mode of experience of changing momentary states that are unformulated and incommunicable. See parataxic mode (p. 36) and syntaxic mode (p. 70).

psychalgia. Mental pain.

psyche. The mind; that part of the person that is involved in thinking and feeling.

psychobiology. See p. 109.

psychogenic. Originating from psychological mechanisms, without organic brain pathological condition. For example, psychoneurosis is seen as being psychogenic, whereas senile psychosis is regarded as organic.

psychological stress. Painful demands or struggles that accompany certain life situations.

psychology. See p. 109.

psychophysics. See p. 109.

psychosexual development. Freud's concept of personality development in childhood was the history of the child's struggle with sexuality as he passes through various stages of sexuality: autoerotic, homoerotic, and heteroerotic.

psychotechnology. See p. 110.

pubertas praecox. Early puberty; premature development of adult genitalia and secondary sex characteristics before age 10.

puberty. The age at which the sex glands become functional and the person shows the secondary sex characteristics, such as pubic and axillary hair, beard in the male, and breast enlargement in the female.

pubescent. Coming into the puberty period.

puerperium. The period between childbirth and return of the uterus to normal size; condition of the mother during this time.

pyknic. A physique characterized by short stature, short thick neck, and a stocky round figure; one of four body types characterized by Kretschmer.

quantification. See p. 92.

quantitative personality theory. See p. 92.

quarrel. As used by family therapists, a disagreement over fact; a struggle concerning who has the right to do what to whom.

quid pro quo. Literally, something for something; in marriage theory, a reciprocal relationship.

rage. Extreme anger; may be a result of combined anger and a sense of helplessness and frustration.

rapport. The spontaneous, conscious feeling of harmony; a quality of the state of cooperation between people. Good rapport is a high level of cooperation, and poor rapport is a low level. Good rapport implies that there is understanding and trust between people.

rationalization. A mental mechanism operating outside and beyond conscious awareness by which the ego attempts to make unacceptable impulses, behaviors, feelings, needs, motives into ones that are consciously tolerable and acceptable. By doing so, the ego unconsciously substitutes a false motive for real but unacceptable ones.

reaction formation. A mental mechanism by which the ego unconsciously transforms an unacceptable wish into an overt expression that is opposite to that wish. An example of this is the campaigning against sex and drinking by a person who unconsciously has a strong but repressed wish to participate in or partake of these. It is similar to overcompensation but is broader and more diffuse.

reactive. Caused by or secondary to an event external to the person; opposed to endogenous.

reality. The objective environment; the requirements of society; as opposed to fantasy.

reality-testing. The ability to perceive fact from fantasy; the ability to check one's experiences and reactions. It often requires that one be able to take the role of the other person to understand his feelings, thoughts, and roles. This is severely impaired in psychotics and impaired to various degrees in neurotics and psychoneurotics.

reason. The total ability to use one's intellectual faculties; often used to mean rational or realistic.

reassociation. Renewed or refreshed association occurring in hypnotherapy. Forgotten or repressed memories may thus remain within conscious awareness.

recall. Memory of immediate past. A simple test consists of asking the subject to repeat a series of numbers. The average adult can repeat a list of at least six or seven. Less than this number suggests a defect in memory.

receiving hospital. A hospital or ward designated to admit persons for evaluation and brief therapy of mental disorders. For long-term therapy, the person is usually referred to another resource.

receptivity. Ability to receive impressions and accept instructions; in psychiatry, the willingness to accept friendliness, closeness, information, and so on.

reciprocal role. The ability to place oneself in the role of another in social interaction; usually defective in certain mental diseases, such as paranoid states.

reconditioning. Unlearning old and learning new conditioned reflexes; new learning imposed on old learning.

recovery. Disappearance of all symptoms and signs of a disease.

reduplication. Compensation for a painful loss by insistance that this loss has been replaced (for example, the patient may admit that his right arm is paralyzed but insists that he has another right arm that is not paralyzed). It is seen secondary to brain damage.

reeducation. Treatment or teaching of problem children with focus on behavior and attitudes rather than gaining insight.

reference group. A group that provides the individual with the social or interpersonal standards by which he judges himself.

reflex. An unlearned stimulus response characteristic of a species; a motor reaction involving no thought.

reflexology. See p. 93.

reflex theory. See p. 93.

refractory. Resistant to therapy; stubborn, unwilling.

regression. A mental mechanism by which the ego unconsciously resorts to earlier modes of adaptation (such as thumb-sucking) to relieve anxiety; an attempted retreat from stress toward what is unconsciously regarded as a more dependent and protected position.

rehabilitation. Treatment aimed at restoring the patient to occupational self-sufficiency by giving him the ability to live in a nonpsychiatric or nonmedical setting, at a level of social and occupational competence comparable to that of other adults in the community.

reify. Concretization of abstractions.

reinforcement. Repetition of a stimulus that has previously evoked certain behavior, with the intent of prolonging that behavior.

reintegration. Recombining of a fragmented personality (for example, recovery from a psychosis).

rejection. The act of rebuffing, forsaking, or discarding in some way that demonstrates that one is not interested in or does not desire interaction with another person or thing.

rejuvenation. An attempt to recapture youthfulness or functions one had at an earlier age. It is sometimes seen as a part of abnormal mental states, especially those associated with rapid deterioration of the brain.

relapse. Recurrence of an illness after partial or complete recovery.

reporting brain. See p. 93.

repress. To drive material from the conscious realm to the unconscious; to prevent material that was never in the conscious from coming to the level of awareness.

repression. A mental mechanism by which consciously unacceptable thoughts, feelings, and impulses are relegated to the unconscious. It is the most widely used mental mechanism and is universally employed. What is repressed, however, does not remain dormant or quiescent. Although ordinarily inaccessible to voluntary recall, the repressed material remains active, emotionally charged, and potent. It may contribute to upheaval if (1) new emotional dangers or threats place too great a burden on the repressing process, (2) internal pressures become too great for the continued containment of repressed material, or (3) the repressing ego forces become too weak.

resignation. Submissiveness, acquiescence; Karen Horney's term for the process by which certain persons defend themselves against neurotic trends. In this, the person strives for freedom from conflict and from all emotional feelings by being aloof and detached from others and from material wants. In this way the person attempts to avoid any part of reality that would bring painful inner conflicts into conscious awareness.

resistance. Opposition to change. Many, and perhaps all, psychologic theories emphasize the importance of resistance in patients as an obstacle to treatment, even though each may offer different explanations for this resistance.

responsibility. Trustworthiness and dependability. This is not identical with legal responsibility, which usually signifies punishability.

retention. The mental ability to store data; part of the memory process.

retroactive inhibition. See p. 93.

reveries. Daydreams, wishful thinking, fantasy.

reversal of instinctual wish. A mental mechanism by which the instinctual wish is manifested by an opposite action, thought, or feeling (for example, hating a love-object). It is essentially the same as inversion.

reward and punishment. As part of instrumental learning and conditioning therapy, the reward of desired behavior, thinking, and feeling and the punishment of undesirable responses. Theoretically, the organism is rid of troublesome behavior, thought, or feeling, and its learning processes are facilitated.

riddance principle. See p. 94.

rigidity. The quality of resistance to change; often applied to patient's ideas (obstinacy) or to behavior (compulsions).

ritual. A ceremoniallike activity having a special meaning to a person; often used as an unconscious defense against unpleasant feelings, such as a ritual of handwashing to rid oneself of guilt that has been symbolically transformed to a feeling of being dirty.

role. Patterns of expected behavior of the individual within a group.

role assignment. The tendency of a person, such as a patient, to expect another person, such as a therapist, to carry out certain anticipated patterns of behavior; also, the pattern of behavior required of an individual by a group.

role diffusion. Rapidly changing assumptions of values, behavior, allegiances; characteristic of adolescents.

role expectancy. Patterns of behavior and attitudes anticipated by the group for an individual.

role fulfillment. The individual's meeting of requirements placed on him by the group in regard to behavior expected of him by the group.

rootedness. The firm feeling of belonging to and being accepted by a place, a group, or a community.

rote learning. Learning by repetition. This implies that there is little understanding of what is being learned, that it is done in a mechanical fashion. It is used in retraining brain-damaged persons.

rudimentation. See p. 94.

rumination. To mull over, think deeply, ponder, meditate. It also means to regurgitate, rechew, and reswallow stomach contents.

secondary process thinking. The reality-oriented, mature, rational thinking of normal adults.

secondary sensation. Synesthesia.

second-signal system. See p. 94.

security. The securing and assurance of material and bodily needs. Psychodynamic security means, according to Fairbairn, security of the personality as such, and is attained only by adequate ego growth.

self-abuse. Masturbation.

self-aggression. Aggression against the self as manifested in suicide or other self-destructive behavior.

self-blame. Accusations, recriminations against the self; usually seen as a part of guilt feelings.

self-concept. The total psychological picture one holds of oneself; an image or representation of all the attributes and qualities a person believes himself to have.

self-destructive behavior. Any act that causes damage or pain to oneself. It may mean psychological and social pain and damage as well as physical harm.

self-effacement. The act of or tendency toward keeping oneself in the background; to shy away from recognition. Horney's term for a solution to neurotic conflict in which the person is compelled to be loving and lovable, self-sacrificing, compliant, and dependent, to be approved of, and to give in. In this, the person identifies with his despised self and sees others as being more intelligent, superior, and competent than he. He unconsciously invites mistreatment almost as a way of life.

self-esteem. The totality of one's evaluation of oneself.

self-hate. The act or quality of holding oneself in contempt, of identifying with the bad part of introjected objects. It may be seen as a predisposing personality trait in depression, in which anger and rage are directed toward the self.

self-image. The totality of qualities and traits a person holds in a mental picture of himself.

self-love. A narcissistic attachment to oneself. When overdeveloped, it represents part of the poorly developed personality and hampers the person's ability to appreciate others and to treat them as objects of love.

self-segregation. Restriction of behavior or mobility, or isolation of an individual or a group by the individual or the group.

self-systems. The experiences that a person has of being a distinct unit apart from his surroundings; the feeling that he exists in the world as a meaningful whole, able to act and be acted upon. Such a feeling is likely to be absent in psychotics and weakened in other, less severe, mental states.

semantic confusion. A ploy sometimes used in arguments by normal persons and often seen in schizophrenics; the alteration or repeated alteration of the meaning of words one is using.

senescence. The quality or state of growing old.

senility. Usually touched physically or mentally by the aging processes. This period is now variously placed as beginning at 65 to 70 years of age.

senium. Old age; usually defined as starting at age 65 to 70 years.

sensationism. See p. 94.

sensitivity training (group). A recent movement more or less under the auspices of the National Training Laboratories of the National Education Association. It consists of a type of group therapy, but it is not necessarily for people having specific psychological problems. Its proponents claim that the experience facilitates communication among people.

sensorium. A person's total sensory capacity. A patient is said to have an intact sensorium when he is oriented correctly for time, place, and person. A delirious patient may show a defective sensorium.

sensory deprivation. A reduction in the quantity of sensory stimulation, with or without a change in the pattern of stimulus.

sensory filtering. Inhibition or selective admission of sensory input into the organism; for example, a cell of the retina of the eye when stimulated by light may inhibit the firing of a neighboring retinal cell, thereby altering the total visual input to the brain.

separation individuation. A period of psychological maturation in which the developing child begins to see himself as an individual apart from his parents and begins to accept separation from his parents.

sexual intercourse. Physical contact between persons involving the genitals of at least one of those persons; but usually physical contact of the genitalia of the two persons.

shame. An emotion closely related to dejection, fear, inferiority. It is usually evoked by being caught in forbidden or unacceptable activities or wishes.

shaping. See p. 94.

sib. Short form of sibling.

sibling. Brothers and sisters; children having the same parents.

sibling reaction. The behavior of a child in reaction to the arrival of a new baby in the home. Such a reaction may be positive or negative, even to the point of severe disturbance.

sibling rivalry. Competition between brothers and sisters for parental affection, ministrations; the wish to be the favored child. This may intensify to a desire on the part of one child to dominate or eliminate the other siblings. Incomplete resolution of such intense wishes may lead to maladjustment in later life.

sick role. The limitations and alterations of an individual's behavior within the group caused by an illness or an injury.

sleep. A neurophysiological state, easily reversible, in which there is cessation of sensorimotor interaction with the environment. There appears to be two kinds of sleep: rapid-eye-movement sleep (REM sleep) and non-rapid eye-movement sleep (NREM sleep).

sleep paralysis. An inability to move or cry out occurring in the transition period between sleep and arousal; seen in normal people and also associated with narcolepsy.

social class. A large segment of a population with certain common socioeconomic characteristics (such as, education, occupation, area of residence).

social groups. A collection of persons who interact and whose behavior is partly determined by these interactions. A football team and a school class are examples of a group.

social integration. The degree to which the individual is united or bound to the group.

socialization. A complex process by which the individual acquires the skills to adapt to demands and restrictions of society or of the group.

social regulation. Ways by which the group keeps the individual within the limits set by the group norms.

somnambulism. Sleepwalking; the act of walking about and even carrying out interpersonal relations while in a sleep-wake state. The person appears to be awake, but has amnesia for the time he spends in this state.

somnolence. Drowsiness, sleepiness.

soteria. An object or possession that gives the person a feeling of security. Such an object could be an amulet or a religious medal.

subconscious. Usually synonymous with unconscious.

sublimate. To use sublimation.

sublimation. A mental mechanism by which painful or unacceptable drives, feelings, or wishes are unconsciously diverted into a socially acceptable expression, usually through pleasurable or creative activities.

subliminal. Below the threshold of perception.

substitution. A mental mechanism whereby an unacceptable object, feeling, thought, or goal is unconsciously replaced by a more acceptable one. It may include material from the unconscious deflected from its original source to some other target. In this point of view, many neurotic symptoms are seen as substitutes for an unconscious problem.

suggestibility. The quality of being easily influenced. Therapeutic techniques that use hypnosis often suggest new ideas or activities to replace unwanted ones. People who respond to this technique are said to be suggestible.

suggestion. In hypnosis the subject is instructed to feel, behave, or talk in various ways. These instructions are generally called suggestions. In psychotherapy the therapist uses suggestion to subtly imbue the patient with an idea or belief that his symptoms are being relieved. This is generally used on less disturbed individuals with mild symptoms and not on psychotic persons.

symbol. An object, word, sound, line, or body movement that is used, taken, or shaped to mean something other than itself.

symbol formation. The process by which properties of a particular object or word are taken, used, or shaped to represent something other than themselves.

symbolic activities. Behavior, motion, postures, speech, and tones of voice carried out to convey messages or to classify other forms of communication.

symbolic distortion. Misuse or misinterpretation of symbols. At the syntactic level, symbols are not used according to ordinary rules; semantic level distortion occurs when a symbol does not convey the facts it is supposed to represent; at a pragmatic level, the sender and receiver attach different meanings to a symbol.

symbolization. The capacity to represent; the ability to take items of experience or to intend materials of the environment to mean or exemplify something other than themselves. It is a mental mechanism by which unacceptable wishes, thoughts, feelings, or urges are unconsciously converted into an idea or object having a similar but disguised meaning. Dreams, particularly, were claimed by Freud to be filled with symbols. In psychoanalysis some theorists claim that certain objects invariably symbolize specific sexual problems in all people, while others claim that the meaning of symbols is more individualized.

sympathy. Having emotional feelings similar to those present in another person as a result of imagining oneself in the other person's place.

synesthesia. A feeling of more than one sensation at the same time; a visual sensation. For example, the color blue may be accompanied by the sensation of cold, the color red by the sensation of heat. It is also called secondary sensations.

syntaxic mode. H. S. Sullivan's term for consensually validated experiences, observations, and judgments and an interpersonal system of communication. See parataxic mode (p. 36) and prototaxic mode (p. 65).

systematic desensitization. J. Wolpe's term for the behavior therapy technique of deep muscle relaxation to reduce the effects of gradually increased anxiety-producing stimuli.

tactile. Pertaining to the sense of touch.

teasing. See p. 132.

temperament. See p. 133.

tenderness. Gentleness, warmth, loving, responsiveness. In the theories of Harry Stack Sullivan, this is a felt state produced in the mother by infants signaling a need for tension reduction. In the infant, the entire collection of tensions that require intervention of mothering are called the need for tenderness.

tension. A state of local or general muscular tightness when the body is in a state of readiness for action. People who are either fearful or angry for long periods of time may be constantly tense and are, therefore, likely to develop symptoms resulting from muscular fatigue. A very large share of the complaints that psychiatric patients present to the physician concern the uncomfortable consequences of tension.

terror. Intense fear.

T-group. Group therapy in which all participants are encouraged to intensively feel, verbalize, and, within limits, display their feelings, thoughts, and emotions to the group. It is also called sensitivity training group and basic encounter group.

thermagnosia. Inability to perceive heat and cold.

thermesthesia. Ability to detect heat and cold.

thinking. The process of reasoning or problem solving in which memory, judgment, and current perceptions are sorted and weighed in the search for explanations or choices of action.

threats. A real or imagined danger to the individual; a real or imagined source of severe discomfort.

thumb-sucking. The habit seen in some children and occasionally in adults of sucking one's thumb; a response to anxiety. It is usually taken to be, especially in older children, a sign of some unresolved mental conflict.

tiredness. See p. 133.

togetherness. The state of not only being within a group, but feeling a part of the group as well. Ackerman uses this term to denote the earliest stage of personality development in which the child is psychologically in union with the mother.

toilet training. The process by which the mothering one teaches or encourages the child control of anal and urethral sphincters. Freud and some of his followers thought that a too severe or demanding mother led to the development of the anal personality because of unresolved conflict during this developmental period.

tomboy. A young girl who exhibits boyish mannerisms, enjoys participating in boyish games, and wears boys' clothing. This is common and not usually significant in young preadolescent girls, but it may be an indication of identity problems if it persists into late teens.

tool reaction. See p. 96.

topesthesia. The ability to localize a tactile sensation.

torpillage. Use of pain in treatment.

transactional psychology. See p. 97.

transference. The irrational attitude of the patient toward the therapist. Seeing the therapist as a father is the typical example. Freud stated that the essence of psychoanalysis was the "analysis of transference."

transitional object. An object carried with a child as he moves away from a secure base. Such an object may be a toy with which he can identify a feeling of security. It is similar to a fetish or a soteria.

transposition. A mental mechanism whereby unacceptable ideas, feelings, and urges for external objects are interchanged (for example, a father jealous of his son and incestuously attracted to his daughter would be overindulgent of the son and punitively strict with the daughter). Compare with displacement, inversion, and reaction formation.

triad. A relationship between three people.

trophotropic. See p. 97.

trust. Confidence in or reliance on some quality or attribute of another person or on the truth of a statement. This is a necessary component of any viable relationship, especially a marriage.

typological psychology. See p. 97.

typology. See p. 97.

ultradian rhythms. Cyclical variations in physiological and biochemical activity, level of function, and emotional state shorter than one day. See circadian rhythms and infradian rhythms.

unconscious family. A term used by family therapists to denote the unconscious change of roles within a family; for example a father may be playing the wife and mother role; the son, the father role, and so on.

underachievement. Poor academic or other performance not explained by lack of intellectual ability, physical handicap, or organic reading difficulties. It can be caused by emotional and environmental problems in the home, the school, or at work.

undifferentiated ego mass. In family therapy, the prohibition within a family against any of its members becoming or forming a completely separate ego structure apart from that family; a deindividualization of the family with weakening of all members' discrete ego boundaries.

undoing. A mental mechanism by which the individual unconsciously attempts to undo some harm by doing the opposite of what his unconscious wishes demand (for example, offering kindness toward someone whose destruction is unconsciously wished).

unstriped muscle response. See p. 97.

uxorious. Wifely.

vaginal orgasm. Sexual climax during intercourse without stimulation of clitoris.

value conflicts. The incongruity of the original and the new cultures; a cause of stress in families moving into a foreign culture.

value systems. Beliefs and practices organized into a system; organized rules of conduct for members of the society.

value testing. Acquired discriminative functioning by which the individual judges relationships between himself and the external world and objects in the external world with each other.

verbalization. To use words; the patient's talking out of problems, ideas, and conflicts in therapy.

virgin. See p. 133.

viscerotonic. See p. 98.

visual-motor organization. The ability to take objects of unassorted colors and forms and sort them by matching certain traits, such as color or shape, and carrying out the actual sorting of these objects.

volition. The ability to control or will; the conscious control of drive behavior.

ward cliques. See p. 98.

Weltschmerz. Sadness, pessimism, a feeling of woe.

wet dream. See p. 133.

wish. A desire or craving.

wit. The ability to reason, judge, conceptualize; mental alertness, quickness, and humor.

working through. Arriving at a solution of a problem in therapy through exploration of the problem and tracing it to unconscious sources.

CHAPTER 3

Treatment terminology

TREATMENT

In general medicine, the concept of treatment tends to be kept within rather narrow limits and generally refers to measures taken by the physician to bring about some desired improvement in the patient. Treatment and cure are not the same, however, for many forms of treatment are not designed to bring about a cure, but are meant simply to help make the patient more comfortable. Thus, two general types of treatment may be classified: (1) specific treatment, a measure designed to counteract the process of a disease and effect a cure, and (2) symptomatic treatment, measures designed to relieve a patient's discomfort. Physicians may also perform many other patient-related functions that are not in themselves considered treatment. The practice of preventive or prophylactic medicine (for example, immunizations and routine testing) is designed to prevent illness. The admission of a patient to a hospital may be for the purpose of placing him in an environment suitable for undergoing treatment, and it may in itself constitute treatment by removing him from a pathology-creating environment and giving him an opportunity to regain emotional equilibrium. While patients are in a hospital, other measures may be offered that are designed to relieve monotony, reduce weight, and so on, and thus may be referred to as adjuvant treatment. Therapy is a synonym for treatment.

In the mental health field, the term treatment has not been used as narrowly as it has been in general medicine. Perhaps often in a misleading way, many procedures that are performed on or for the patient are called treatment when there appears to be very little justification for so doing. The tendency to overuse the term harkens back to the days when the field of mental health had very little to offer patients that was helpful to them, so a tendency was established to call virtually any procedure involving the disturbed patient "treatment," and thereby create the illusion of progress in the absence of progress. Furthermore, it has become common to employ the classifications of therapeutic (good treatment), nontherapeutic (not treatment), and countertherapeutic (bad treatment) to refer to many measures according to whether they are beneficial, useless, or harmful to the patient. In many ways, the use of the term treatment, or therapy, in mental health professions comes closer to the layperson's use of the term than it does in other branches of medicine. The layperson refers to the ways in which, for instance, the mother treats her child or the way the supervisor treats his workers; these uses of the term have no relationship to disease or cure. Similarly, in mental health the mere process of a professional's interacting compassionately with a patient might be called a treatment measure and often yields positive results.

In recent years there has been an attempt to broaden the concept of treatment in mental health. Many different kinds of professional and nonprofessional people have entered the field, in addition to the traditional physician and nurse. Thus, occupational therapy, recreational therapy, music therapy, and drama therapy have been added not only to the repertoire of (usually hospitalized) patients' activities, but they have also been added to the list of procedures called treatment.

Since the use of the term has steadily expanded in scope, it has become necessary to establish categories that indicate different kinds of treatment for mental disorders. These include:

Psychotherapy: any kind of treatment taking place between a therapist and a patient in which only psychological methods are used.

Organic therapy: the kind of treatment measures common to general medicine, such as medication and surgical operations, but used for psychiatric problems.

Group therapy: a type of psychotherapy in which a therapist or several therapists treat a group of patients together, encouraging discussion among the patients of emotional and psychological issues.

Adjuvant therapy: any kind or set of procedures used to supplement a patient's activity program (usually in a hospital) such as arts and crafts activities.

Custodial treatment: hospital care of a severely mentally ill patient centered on feeding, housing, and protecting the patient from the difficulties of life in an open environment.

Supportive therapy: treatment with limited goals, having in mind a general encouragement or morale-boosting program.

Symptomatic treatment: a treatment approach that focuses on specific symptoms in an attempt to alleviate them without attacking the cause.

Analytic or analytically oriented treatment: psychotherapy in which the techniques or theories followed conform more or less to a psychoanalytic school of thought.

Ambulatory treatment: treatment of patients outside the hospital in a private office or clinic.

Institutional treatment: treatment in a hospital.

Milieu therapy: the process of employing the entire setting of a hospital and the entire day of the patient's time in a total treatment program.

The therapist has the primary responsibility for managing a patient's treatment program. More narrowly, the therapist is one of the two people in the psychotherapeutic relationship, the other person being the patient. A patient is sometimes said to be in treatment or in therapy during a certain period of time in which he attends psychotherapeutic sessions on a more or less regular basis, usually while otherwise conducting the normal affairs of life.

In summary, in the mental health field a very wide variety of procedures are referred to as treatment. Thus, the term is used to mean something that would more properly be called management.

PSYCHOPHARMACOLOGY

Psychopharmacology is the study of that class of drugs that affect the central nervous system and that show therapeutic benefit in management of mental disorders.

Drugs used in psychiatry can be divided into three categories on the basis of their clinical effects. These categories, while not pharmacologically or biochemically exact, are nevertheless useful to the clinician in trying to organize his thinking about this ever proliferating group of drugs. The list of drugs in each category is, of course, incomplete and is given as a ready reference guide rather than as a comprehensive compendium of available agents.

Antipsychotic agents

Antipsychotic drugs, or neuroleptics, will reduce or abolish the "core" symptoms of the psychotic process (delusional thinking, hallucinations, agitation, or withdrawal). These manifestations are common denominators of nearly every psychosis. The antipsychotic compounds are mild sedatives and tend to inhibit motor activity. These drugs are nonaddictive, but, because of the nature of psychosis, are often administered to patients for protracted periods of time.

The phenothiazines are the most widely used of this assemblage and chlorpromazine

ANTIPSYCHOTIC AGENTS

Generic name	Brand name	Outpatient dose mg/day	Inpatient dose mg/day
Phenothiazines			
Aliphatic derivatives			
Chlorpromazine	Thorazine	75-200	200-1600
Promazine	Sparine	75-200	200-1000
Piperazine derivatives			
Perphenazine	Trilafon	8-24	12-72
Trifluoperazine	Stelazine	4-10	6-30
Prochlorperazine	Compazine	15-60	30-150
Acetophenazine	Tindal	40-80	60-160
Piperadine derivatives			
Thioridazine	Mellaril	75-200	200-800
Mesoridazine	Serentil	25-200	75-400
Dibenzoxazepine			
Loxapine	Loxitane	20-50	60-250
Butyrophenone			
Haloperidol	Haldol	2-8	4-16
Dihydroindolone			
Molindone	Moban	15-60	75-225
Thioxanthenes			
Thiothixene	Navane	6-15	20-60
Chlorprothixene	Taractan	30-60	75-600
Rauwolfia alkaloid			
Reserpine	Many brands	0.5-2.0	0.75-12

(Thorazine), the prototype of this group, is probably the most often prescribed of these. The widespread success of chlorpromazine has stimulated efforts to improve the therapeutic efficacy of the neuroleptics, but to date, no other compound has been definitely shown to possess any distinct advantages over it. All the phenothiazines possess qualitatively not only the same clinical effects but also the same side effects. However, there are quantitative differences in such variables as rapidity of onset of action, milligram dosage, motor control, etc., and side effects such as neurotoxicity, sedation, hypotension, etc.

Although these drugs are prescribed mainly for treatment of psychosis, in some nonpsychotic patients lower dosages of the drugs work well as antianxiety agents. They have an added advantage over the antianxiety compounds in that none of the drugs listed in the antipsychotic group are known to produce dependency. The most pronounced beneficial effect is in the schizophrenic reactions, with improvement following an almost exponential curve. There is rapid change in the first few weeks, a gradual leveling off in the sixth to twelfth week, and little change after that. Hyperactivity and withdrawal disappear first, usually after a few doses, while delusions and hallucinations may persist, with less intensity, for several weeks.

The physiological site of action of these compounds is not definitely known. Chlorpromazine stimulates the amygdaloid nucleus and a portion of the limbic system and depresses the hypothalamus. Additionally, it has some depressing effect on the reticular activating system and on anticholinergic, adrenolytic, and antidopaminergic actions. The antidopaminergic action in central nervous system, specifically in the mesolimbic area, is thought to be the most relevant to its antipsychotic effect.

The rauwolfia derivatives are now little used

ANTIANXIETY AGENTS

Generic name	Brand name	Average dose mg/day
Barbiturates		
Phenobarbital		60-500
Dibenzazepines		
Chlordiazepoxide	Librium	16-100
Diazepam	Valium	5-40
Oxazepam	Serax	30-120
Others		
Hydroxyzine	Atarax, Vistaril	75-400
		75-400
Meprobamate	Equanil, Miltown	1200-2400
		1200-2400

in psychiatry, primarily because of the side effects of hypotension and neurotoxicity, especially extrapyramidal symptoms.

The butyrophenones and thioxanthene derivatives to date have demonstrated no real advantage over the phenothiazines except in cases when the patient may have shown a previous hypersensitivity to a phenothiazine. The same can be said for the more recently developed dibenzoxepine and dihydroindolone antipsychotics.

The side effects of these drugs are numerous and sometimes serious. The prescribing physician should be acquainted with these. The *Physicians' Desk Reference* is a ready source of such information and may be consulted for this purpose.

Antianxiety agents

Antianxiety drugs all have muscle relaxant, anticonvulsant, and sedative properties. Each of these qualities, of course, contributes to the compound's ability to reduce anxiety, but heavy sedation is not usually desirable in treatment of anxiety. For this reason, the barbiturates, paraldehyde, and chloral hydrate are seldom used for this purpose, though phenobarbital is often used because of its relatively low cost. However effective these agents are in reducing anxiety they have almost no effect in modifying psychotic symptoms.

The major indication for prescription of these compounds is anxiety. Additionally, they are of real usefulness in controlling the symptoms of postalcoholic states, and postpartum and postoperative agitation not involving psychosis. They are especially useful in postalcoholic states (where phenothiazines may lower convulsive threshold) and in postpartum and postoperative states where they are less likely to cause autonomic side effects (hypotension, etc.) than are the phenothiazines.

These drugs may be habituating, and withdrawal symptoms will occur after prolonged usage. Because they possess euphoriant properties they are frequently abused, and should, therefore, be prescribed on a limited basis.

Antidepressant agents

Antidepressant agents are of several pharmacological categories, the most prominent of which is the tricyclic antidepressant group. They work especially well in the retarded and "hypoactive" depressions. All allegedly exert their effect by increasing central sympathetic activity.

The stimulant drugs are not widely prescribed as antidepressants because of the possibility of addiction and the rapid build-up of tolerance to their euphoriant effects. They are frequently abused, and are capable of profoundly affecting perception and behavior. The MAO inhibitors are also losing popularity in psychiatry, not only because of their side ef-

ANTIDEPRESSANT AGENTS

Generic name	Brand name	Outpatient dose mg/day	Inpatient dose mg/day
Stimulants			
Dextroamphetamine	Dexedrine	15-30	30-60
Methylphenidate	Ritalin	10-30	30-60
MAO inhibitors			
Phenelzine	Nardil	15-30	15-75
Tranylcypromine	Parnate	20-30	20-30
Tricyclic derivatives			
Amitriptyline	Elavil	50-150	75-225
Desipramine	Pertofrane	75-150	75-200
Doxepin	Sinequan, Adapin	75-300	75-300
Imipramine	Tofranil	50-150	75-225
Nortriptyline	Aventyl	50-150	50-200
Protriptyline	Vivactil	15-40	15-60

fects but also because of the advent of the tricyclic derivatives, which are safer and generally more effective.

The demethylated tricylic derivatives are gaining popularity because their onset of action seems to be faster (most show some lifting of mood in 6 to 10 days as compared to 12 to 30 days for the parent compounds and the MAO inhibitors), and possess no side effects not seen with their tertiary amine parent compounds. They are indicated mainly in depression and especially in those depressions showing psychomotor retardation. They do tend to aggravate some of the schizophrenic symptoms and sometimes make even nonpsychotic persons more agitated, restless, and uncomfortable. Physiological side effects are generally the same as those of the phenothiazines and are sometimes serious. Again, the *Physicians' Desk Reference* is a ready source of such information.

An extensive vocabulary (for example, psychedelic) has grown up in connection with drug abuse problems, and much of it has come from very unscientific sources. As a result, the common use of many of these terms often has very misleading implications. For instance, the very concept of addiction, although still commonly accepted by the public, is now being challenged; and, in recognition of this, the terms drug abuse and drug dependency are more in professional favor.

GLOSSARY

abortifacient. A medical term for any drug or chemical that can or is meant to produce an abortion.

abreaction. See p. 52.

abstinence. See p. 52.

abstinence syndrome. See p. 16.

aftercare. See p. 53.

after-shock. Secondary hypoglycemia as a complication of insulin coma treatment.

agrypnotic. A stimulant; a drug that counteracts lethargy.

akathisia. See p. 17.

Alanon. Relatives of alcoholics; organized philosophically and structurally similar to Alcoholics Anonymous; anonymous to encourage discussion and resolution of problems common to them all.

Alcoholics Anonymous. See p. 100.

alienation from self. An important concept in the theories of psychopathology formulated by Karen Horney. It is a process by which an individual moves from his genuine self to create a pseudoidentity. The person may be unaware of bodily sensations and may have an emotion without being aware of its nature and meaning.

alimentary orgasm. A term used by Sandor Rado connoting satisfaction of oral needs, especially by depressed persons.

alloplastic. A term used in adaptational theories to denote that the organism tries to alter the environment to fit its needs. In psychoanalytic theory it denotes aberrant social conduct.

alphagenics. See p. 53.

Ala-teen. Teen-aged children of alcoholic parents; organized philosophically and structurally similar to Alcoholics Anonymous to provide group support toward developing a better understanding of their parents' problems and better methods for coping with them.

amelioration. See p. 100.

amobarbital. A medication prescribed for sleep at bedtime, for sedation, and as an antianxiety agent. When used chronically, it can lead to drug dependency.

amphetamines. A group of drugs that are central nervous system stimulants, producing euphoria, appetite suppression, and postponement of fatigue. They are widely abused by a growing number of persons. Chronic heavy use can lead to hallucinations, psychosis, and dependency.

anaclitic. See p. 53.

anaclitic therapy. Treatment that revolves around the patient's anaclitic or dependency needs. In a structured manner, the patient is given emotional support, protection, and warmth. It has been used successfully in such psychosomatic conditions as ulcerative colitis, but its use has been limited.

anal character. A term used by Freud in an attempt to define a constellation of traits found in obsessive characters that he felt resulted from conflict during the period of bowel training. It is usually synonymous with obsessive character.

analeptic. A medication that acts to stimulate the central nervous system. Caffeine and amphetamine are examples.

anal eroticism. Gaining sexual arousal or gratification from activities, such as bowel movements, associated with the anal area; may be manifested by traits ranging from preoccupation with defecation to a need for anal intercourse as one's primary mode of sexual gratification. Psychoanalysts attach great significance to events occurring during the bowel training period, especially learning to experience pleasure from defecation, anal cleansing, and so on.

anal love. In psychoanalytic theory, implies ambivalent or sadistic feelings growing out of the anal phase of personality development.

analogue. A term used by Carl Jung to denote an archetype that has been modified by culture.

anal phase. In psychoanalytic theory, a phase of psychosexual development usually begins in the infant at termination of the nursing phase, with attention and interest being given to the pleasurable sensations of retaining and passing feces and with parental attempts to teach control of these functions.

analysand. One who is undergoing psychoanalysis, particularly when he is a student in training rather than someone with serious psychiatric difficulties.

analysis. A type of psychotherapy developed by Freud and followed with varying degrees of similarity by others with different theories. In time, the term has come to refer to a school of thought in addition to a treatment technique. The followers of the freudian school confine the term to mean that type of psychotherapy that employs free association, in which analysis of the transference is fundamental, and in which the objective is to make the unconscious conscious. Nonfollowers of Freud may use the term to apply to psychotherapy, regardless of their philosophical commitment.

analytic group therapy. Psychotherapy carried on, in, and by a group using the principles of psychoanalysis, with insights for the individual being stressed and minimal participation by the therapist (as opposed to directive group therapy, in which the therapist is more active).

analytic psychology. See p. 100.

anamnesis. See p. 100.

anima. Carl Jung's term for the soul, or the individual's inner self; in contrast to the persona, the external facade the individual presents to the world.

animal magnetism. The term used by Anton Mesmer in his eighteenth century teachings of mesmerism to mean hypnotism. The magnetism was some force or power that passed from the therapist to the subject during hypnosis. Largely because of Mesmer, hypnosis became the basis for a largely fraudulent, though sometimes effective, means of influencing hysterical patients with imaginary ailments.

Antabuse. Trade name of disulfiram; a drug used as a deterrent and in aversive therapy for alcoholism. Drinking alcohol during treatment with this drug can cause severe, sometimes dangerous, toxic reactions, including flushing, sweating, headache, respiratory distress, nausea, vomiting, tachycardia, shock, coma, and death.

antianxiety drugs. Medications that lessen anxiety. The group includes a pharmacologically and chemically heterogeneous group, all of which are sedatives, muscle relaxants, and anticonvulsants. They are classified apart from those drugs in the antipsychotic drug groups, because they do little to meliorate a psychosis. They are also called minor tranquilizers.

antidepressants. A group of drugs that alleviate depression; mood elevators. Generally, they are divided into three groups; stimulants, monamine oxidase inhibitors, and tricyclic types.

antipsychotic drugs. Drugs that reduce psychotic symptoms (such as delusions, hallucinations, withdrawal, and hyperactivity). They do not cure a psychosis but allow some control over the major symptoms, thereby permitting the patient to function more normally both in and out of the hospital. They are also called major tranquilizers and neuroleptics.

aphrodisiac. Any substance that arouses sexual desire; usually understood to mean a drug, although the ability of drugs to do this is probably more folklore than fact.

apomorphine. A drug obtained by treating the morphine molecule with strong mineral acids; used mainly as an emetic.

appetitive behavior. The initial portion of a sequence of actions that are believed to be instinctive and are presumed to occur through development of internal tensions. After the initial exploratory or appetitive actions (such as seeking food, water, or sexual partner), in which the animal appears restless and agitated, consummatory behavior follows.

archaic unconscious. A psychoanalytic term to describe those experiences in infancy and early childhood that never reach the level of clear consciousness. They are distinguished from other experiences and wishes that were once explicitly conscious but were for various reasons diminished by repression.

archetype. In Carl Jung's theory of personality, certain images and ideas of man, such as the bad father or devil and the good and omnipotent father or God, which he postulates are holdovers from the past experiences of mankind.

assertive training. Overcoming habitually inhibited behavior through encouraging expression of spontaneously felt emotions in actual situations; a behavioral therapy technique.

associationism. An early school of thought in psychology. Its chief tenet was a theory explaining

memory on the grounds that what is remembered is that which is associated with pleasant or unpleasant experiences.

asylum. See p. 101.

atabrine. A drug used in the treatment of malaria; important in psychiatry because of the drug-induced psychosis it can produce in susceptible persons.

ataractic. Tranquilizer.

atavism. Manifestation in an individual of an ancestral form of behavior.

atomistic school. A term indicating a focus on physiological or sensory studies of isolated bits of behavior and a failure to study more complex and realistic forms of behavior; used by opponents of the early laboratory psychologists as a derogatory term.

atropine. An anticholinergic belladonna alkaloid used as a prescription medicine to reduce intestinal spasms and in potent sedatives to produce sleep.

attitude therapy. Mental hospital milieu therapy program to help ensure a consistent approach by the entire staff to the patient. After evaluation and diagnosis of the patient, the treatment team assigns an attitude or treatment approach (for example, firmness, no demand, active friendliness, passive friendliness, matter-of-factness) for the patient that is carried out consistently by the entire hospital staff.

authoritative hypnosis. A type of therapeutic hypnosis in which the patient is ordered to give up a symptom or an attitude; opposite of cathartic hypnosis.

autology. Study of onself.

autoplastic. A term used in adaptational theories to denote that the organism attempts to fit its needs to the environment.

aversive therapy. A form of conditioning in which performance of undesired behavior is followed by an unpleasant or painful stimulus, such as Antabuse therapy of alcoholism. A person who drinks alcohol while taking antabuse becomes violently ill; in this way drinking comes to be associated with unpleasantness and may thus be easier to give up.

averted schizophrenia. A term used by Arieti to denote that in certain individuals schizophrenia does not occur despite all apparent factors militating in favor of its development.

bad me. Harry Stack Sullivan's term for that portion of the personality that is organized around early experiences of anxiety and tension secondary to disapproval by the mothering person.

balneotherapy. Treatment through use of various types of baths; not widely used in psychiatry now.

barbiturates. A group of drugs that act as depressants of central nervous system activity. Some are prescribed as sedatives and some as anticonvulsants. Prolonged and heavy use can lead to dependency.

basic anxiety. Horney's description of a profound insecurity and apprehensiveness in children of overprotective, dominating, irritable, and erratic parents.

behaviorism. A school of thought in psychology that was named by J. B. Watson in 1913 and that was derived from the conditioned-reflex studies of Pavlov. The behavioral school is concerned with studies of the activities of individuals (usually animals) and tends to ignore the study of the thinking process on the grounds that it is not amenable to objective investigation.

behavior therapy. Methods of altering those portions of the patient's activities that are deemed unacceptable; based on the theory that psychopathology is a result of learned inappropriate behaviors that are reinforced or shaped by external forces.

benzedrine. Amphetamine.

bibliotherapy. The use of reading material selected and recommended by the psychotherapist for the patient as an adjunct to therapy.

biodynamics. The theoretical system of Jules H. Masserman in which he has attempted to integrate psychoanalytic, behavioral, and neurophysiological information obtained from research and clinical experience in both man and animals.

biofeedback. Providing information to a patient from one or more of his physiologic processes (for example, blood pressure, pulse rate, brain waves, muscle activity) in learning control of these processes. Useful in therapy of certain mental conditions especially those in which tension, hypertension, headaches, and other visceral conditions are problematic.

biological psychiatry. Psychiatric theory that includes emphasis on physical, neurological, chemical, genetic as well as psychodynamic, social, and other contributions to the understanding and treatment of the patient.

birth trauma. An essential component of Otto Rank's theoretical formulations. He sought for the prototype anxiety—that is, the first fearful experience in a child's life—and concluded that it was invariably the process of birth itself, and that this was invariably a painful experience that is unconsciously retained throughout life.

bisexual theory. The belief that sexual desires for both sexes exist in everyone.

body build. Ernest Kretschmer described four body types, the athletic, the leptosomatic, the pyknic, and the dysplastic, which he related to certain normal and abnormal personalities having predispositions to mental illness.

body language. Messages conveyed by body motion, postures, facial expression; learned communication modes that can serve instead of or in addition to the spoken mode. Can be used to emphasize or negate messages transmitted by other modes.

breast envy. Melanie Klein's term for the occurrence in a child of a primitive type of envy toward the good breast, which he felt to contain every desired quality that the baby feels he lacks. Klein felt this was the source of strong envy seen in certain persons later in life.

bromide. A sedative medication containing a salt of bromine. These are contained in many patent medicines and, as such, are often a source of overdosage and poisoning (bromidism).

bulbocapnine. A drug that will produce catatonic-like symptoms in animals.

caffeine. A stimulant used medicinally; found in coffee, tea, and in some soft drinks.

camisole. A canvas jacket used to restrain patients.

camphor convulsive therapy. A treatment introduced in the early 1930's using injected camphor to produce convulsions. It was replaced by electrically induced convulsions (electroconvulsive therapy, ECT) and is now seldom, if ever, used therapeutically.

carbon dioxide therapy. CO_2 therapy.

case history. See p. 101.

case method. See p. 101.

case work. See p. 101.

castration complex. Freud's oedipal theory maintains that the child's fear of punishment for wanting the opposite parent is conceived by the child to be the danger of castration. Ineffective struggle with this problem is said to lead to a castration complex. Synonym: castration anxiety.

catamnesis. See p. 101.

categorical demand. A psychoanalytic concept of a severe, uncompromising superego seen in rigid, inflexible personalities.

catharsis. See p. 55.

cathartic hypnosis. See p. 55.

censor. A hypothetical mechanism in freudian theory that monitors the drives and instincts striving to leave the unconscious to have access to conscious awareness.

cerebrotonic. William H. Sheldon's term for psychological traits of the ectomorph, who is described as being inhibited, very sensitive, and given to thinking and speculations; as opposed to viscerotonic.

character analysis. See p. 56.

character defense. Defense mechanisms built by neurotics and designed to keep anxiety under control. These mechanisms become expressions of the individual's way of facing life; hence, part of his character. The term was originated by Freud but was greatly elaborated by his daughter, Anna Freud.

chemopallidectomy. Destruction of part of the basal ganglia by injecting a chemical, usually pure alcohol, into it as treatment of certain diseases (such as parkinsonism and hemiballismus).

chemotherapy. The use of medicines in treatment.

child guidance movement. See p. 101.

child psychiatry. See p. 101.

child psychology. See p. 101.

client-oriented therapy. A therapeutic process wherein the therapist consistently reflects the patient's feelings to him but does not suggest, direct, prescribe, or interpret. It is a highly permissive mode of treatment and does not work with severely ill psychotics and inured sociopaths.

clinic. See p. 102.

clinical psychology. See p. 102.

CO₂ therapy. Inhalation of CO_2 to the point of unconsciousness; a type of treatment for psychosis that was originated by Meduna and is still used to a limited extent. The therapeutic indications for this are similar to those for convulsive and insulin therapy.

coconscious. See p. 56.

codeine. A narcotic drug derived from the juice of the opium poppy. Papaver somniferum. Prolonged use can lead to dependency.

cold pack. A device used to calm excited and agitated patients. The patient is placed in a tub and surrounded by cold blankets or wraps. It is not widely used now.

collaborative therapy. Stereoscopic therapy.

collective unconscious. Carl Jung's term for a reservoir of unconscious psychic phenomena common to all people and inherited by each generation from their ancestors.

concomitance. Hughlings Jackson's doctrine that for every mental state there is a correlative physical state within the nervous system.

conditioned reflex. The Russian physiologist Ivan Pavlov's findings that a dog could be trained to salivate at the sound of a bell if the bell had been previously associated repeatedly with the presentation of food. Salivation to food is called an unconditioned reflex. Salivation to the sound of the bell is the conditioned reflex.

conjoint therapy. A form of group psychotherapy in which one or more therapists (usually no more than two) treat several patients at once. This is used to treat some or all members of a family together.

consensual validation. General agreement; Sullivan's term for the validation one receives through use of the syntactic mode of communication, as opposed to a lack of validation when one uses the paratactic mode.

constancy principle. In psychoanalytic theory, the assumption that psychic energy is constant and that a person strives to keep excitation at a low level.

constitutional types. Kretschmer's classification of people according to their physical habitus (for example, the pyknic type—the broad, thick, stocky habitus; the asthenic—the tall, thin, narrow habitus; the athletic—one of optimal proportions; the dysplastic—a miscellaneous group). Each type was ascribed certain personality characteristics (for example, cyclothymic personality associated with the pyknic build, and the schizoid personality found in the asthenic type). These correlations have not been substantiated, and little attention is paid to the concept today.

consultation. See p. 103.

convalescent home. See p. 103.

cortisone. A hormone produced in the body by the adrenal cortex.

cosmology. The theme of ancient Greek philosophy during the fifth to eighth centuries B.C. The visible, material world was considered the proper subject for investigation.

counconscious. See p. 57.

counseling. See p. 103.

countercathexis. In freudian theory, the psychic energy that has been reallocated to maintain the neurotic symptoms.

countertransference. See p. 57.

crisis clinic. See p. 103.

crisis intervention. Psychiatric treatment giving immediate attention to persons undergoing acute psychological distress may include short-term follow-up care and referral to appropriate other agencies or therapists for continuing care.

cultural school (psychoanalysis). Contemporary schools of thought in psychoanalysis that have departed from the freudian emphasis on instinct and have attached more importance to the role of the culture in which the person lives. Harry Stack Sullivan and Karen Horney have been leaders in this new departure.

custodial care. See p. 103.

dasein. A term used in existential psychiatry that refers to the way of existing of an individual human being.

daseinanalysis. A type of psychotherapeutic treatment derived from existential psychology, in turn derived from existential philosophy in recent years. Ludwig Binswanger, a Swiss psychiatrist, has promoted the method, in which emphasis is placed on interpersonal relationships with the goal of finding a direction suited to the patient's attempts at self-realization.

day care. See p. 103.

day hospital. See p. 103.

death instinct. In his post-World War I theoretical speculations Freud adopted the concept of the death instinct to replace the earlier concept of the pleasure principle as the foundation of human behavior. According to this concept, man is seen as primarily self-destructive, and his principal motivation is to return to a state of minimal tension (death).

defense mechanisms. Freud's term for the techniques a person might employ to ward off anxiety. Anna Freud specified the following defense mechanisms: regression, repression, reaction formation, isolation, undoing, projection, introjection, sublimation, displacement, and turning against oneself. It is essentially the same as character defense. It includes unconscious, automatic, and defensive psychologic processes by which emotional conflicts are alleviated or resolved in order to bring relief from intense anxiety and tension. These processes act in the service of the ego to resolve conflict arising from opposing drives or from conflict between the id and the superego (internal or intrapsychic danger). These are present in everyone and are regarded as normal or pathologic according to their efficacy, the way in which they are employed, and whether their use makes constructive or destructive contributions to the individual's psychologic economy. Synonym: mental mechanism.

degeneration hypothesis. Benedict Morel's (1809-1873) teaching that the mentally ill were degenerative deviations from normal types and that these traits were hereditary.

depth psychology. Freud's term for psychoanalysis, which emphasizes the study of unconscious processes, in contrast to other systems that deal with superficial behavior; a concept derived from psychoanalysis, referring to the deep probing of the unconscious in place of preoccupation with reality.

destrudo. The energy of the aggressive instinct; as opposed to libido or the sexual energy.

detoxification. Restoration of physiological function after it has been seriously disturbed by overuse of opiates, alcohol, barbiturates, and other dependency-producing drugs.

diffuse. In psychoanalytic theory, the separation of the basic drives or instincts to where they act independently.

directive group therapy. Treatment of a group of patients, mainly using lectures and group discussion, with active participation by the therapist.

displacement. A defense mechanism in which the emotion meant for one person or idea is unconsciously directed toward another (for example, the hostility felt toward a parent is expressed, instead, toward people in authority).

dissociation. See p. 58.

distortion. See p. 58.

dopamine. A chemical identified in brain tissue and thought to be one of the substances that transmits impulses from one nerve to another across the synapse. It has been found to be deficient in such states as Parkinson's disease.

double-blind. See p. 119.

drainage hypothesis. McDougall's concept to explain psychological phenomena. A substance, neurine, was said to exist in various quantities in the brain and to flow hydrostatically from areas of high pressure to areas of low pressure.

dreams. See p. 58.

dream sleep. See p. 58.

dream work. The processes by which the latent dream content is transformed into manifest content (for example, by condensation, displacement, and symbolization) in analytic therapy.

drive behavior. In psychoanalytic theory, behavior that is caused by the instincts or psychobiological drives. For instance, aggressive behavior could be a manifestation of destrudo.

drug holiday. Omitting administration of medication

for short periods (usually 1 to 2 days) each week. Most psychiatric medications are long-acting so that such omissions do not lower the amount of the drug in the body to levels too low for therapeutic effect; reduces total weekly dose of drug without reducing therapeutic effect.

drug interaction. Alteration of the effect of one drug by another taken simultaneously. May be additive or potentiating, may reverse the therapeutic effect, and may result in serious side effects.

DSM-II. Second edition of the American Psychiatric Association's Diagnostic and Statistical Manual of Mental Disorders (1968).

dynamic concept. The assumption that the true meaning and motivation behind human behavior, particularly the psychoses, is unconscious and therefore hidden not only from the observer but from the person himself.

dynamic psychiatry. See p. 104.

dynamic psychology. See p. 104.

dynamics. In psychoanalytic theory, the hidden or unconscious meanings of or motives for feelings and behavior.

dynamic therapy. Psychoanalysis.

dynamisms. Harry Stack Sullivan's term for the relatively enduring patterns of coping with life situations and interpersonal relations: also refers to the psychic forces behind an action.

dysplastic. A physique characterized by abnormalities, especially caused by endocrine dysfunction; a body type described by Kretschmer.

dystonia. See p. 26.

economic concepts. A division in psychoanalytic theory that deals with the manner and degree in which psychic energies are discharged.

ectomorph. William H. Sheldon's term for the thin, angular, and asthenic body type. This person is said to have a cerebrotonic personality orientation.

educational psychology. See p. 104.

ego. The self or the conscious portion of thinking processes; that portion of the personality or mind in contact with the environment. It functions as an executive apparatus, modifying and compromising between the blind biological drives (id) and the learned prohibitions and the superego.

ego analysis. Intensive psychoanalysis of methods employed by the ego to attempt resolution of intropsychic conflict especially in developing and using mental mechanisms.

egodystonic. Sandor Rado's term for ideas that are unacceptable to the individual; also called ego-alien.

ego psychology. Freud's term for the study of the conscious self. He referred to his own work as having been preoccupied with the study of the unconscious and left to others the task of pushing the field further into the study of the ego. His daughter Anna attempted to do this, along with others, such as Erik Erikson, David Rapaport, Ernst Kris, and Heinz Hartmann, who refer to their studies as ego psychology.

ego splitting. Psychoanalytic term describing the segregating of undesirable characteristics from the personality; also called dissociation. It is seen in the split or multiple personality (such as that in the *Three Faces of Eve,* Jekyll-Hyde).

egosyntonic. Sandor Rado's term for ideas that are acceptable to the individual.

Eigenwelt. In existential psychiatry and philosophy this denotes the person's own world; the world of a man to himself.

elaboration. The process of expanding on a subject. Psychoanalytic theory refers to the secondary elaboration of a dream, meaning the extension of the original content into the actual story as remembered by the dreamer.

electra complex. Freud's term for the female equivalent of the oedipus complex. It is postulated that in the female there are unconscious wishes for sexual union with the father that are coupled with the unconscious wishes to destroy the mother. It is further postulated that the coexistence of these unconscious fantasies creates a basic conflict that, when not adequately resolved, becomes a basis for neurosis. (See oedipal complex.)

electroconvulsive therapy. Electroshock therapy.

electroencephalogram. See p. 26.

electronarcosis. Electrosleep.

electroshock therapy. A treatment technique that consists of applying electrodes to the patient's scalp and passing an electric current through the brain that is sufficient to cause a convulsion. It is used in treating depression.

electrosleep. Therapy in which barely perceptible pulses of electric current are passed through the patient's brain, inducing relaxation and sleep, but not convulsions; reported to be efficacious in treating various mental disorders.

elementism. The study of discrete and small units of psychological events at the expense of studying complex behavior; atomistic.

elopement. A patient's unauthorized departure from a hospital or other residential treatment facility.

emergency emotions. Sandor Rado's term for denoting such feelings as fear, rage, guilty fear, and guilty rage; as opposed to welfare emotions.

empirical psychology or philosophy. The kind of philosophy or psychology, similar to Locke's, that places the entire emphasis of the study of human behavior on the individual's experience.

encounter group. Group therapy emphasizing emotional awareness, rather than intellectual insights; stresses development of coping behavior in the here and now.

endomorph. William H. Sheldon's term for the body type that has a large body cavity, a round face, fragile extremities, weak muscles, and an inclination to obesity.

environmentalism. Psychological theory that places more importance on the role of the environment in shaping the individual than do other types.

epinephrine. A biogenic amine believed to be a transmitter for substances at the synapse of certain types of nerves; especially the sympathetic nervous system.

ergasia. Adolph Meyer's term for an organism's total behavioral functioning.

ergasiology. Adolph Meyer's general theoretical approach to psychiatry. He emphasized the importance of studying the whole person. The new terminology he designed never came into general use.

ergotropy. Hess' term denoting those activities that enable the organism to display an externally directed behavior; activities of a proposed diencephalic and subcortical system that bring sympathetic and somatic motor activities to focus on preparing for positive action. (See trophotropic.)

eros. In psychoanalytic theory, the combined instincts of love and life as postulated by Freud; counterposed to eros is thanatos.

essence. In existential philosophy, the possibilities of existence open to an individual. Not actualizing one's essence is a source of existential anxiety and existential guilt.

existence. In existential philosophy, the actualization of the essence.

existential anxiety. Anxiety that is neither realistic nor neurotic but an element in the normal human existence; anxiety generated mainly by man's knowledge that he, a being, can also become a nonbeing; that is, can cease to exist.

existential guilt. Guilt that is neither realistic nor neurotic but that is a part of the structure of human existence and that is attributed to failure in realizing one's essence or potential.

existentialism. A philosophical school that originated 100 years ago with the Danish philosopher Kierkegaard and was revived in France by Sartre, Jaspers, and Heidegger. The philosophy challenges older concepts of the relationship between thought and existence. Recent exponents of the philosophy adopt a pessimistic, disillusioned view of man's worth as an individual and claim that man only struggles but never achieves a sense of unity and belonging that he seeks. In the United States a school of psychiatry has developed that takes its impetus from existensialism. According to this school, schizophrenia is seen as the example par excellence of what Sartre claims to be the true description of all people: an isolated, worthless mass of protoplasm struggling fruitlessly for impossible goals.

existential psychology. Daseinanalysis.

extrapyramidal effects of drugs. Increased muscle tone, tremor, and choreo-athetoid movements; some of the more common side effects of treatment with major tranquilizers. They are thought to be caused by the drug's action on the extrapyramidal portions of the central nervous system.

extrasensory perception. Ability to sense the thoughts in someone else's mind. A psychological study by Rhine at Duke University claims that proof of such phenomena has been demonstrated. These claims are currently the subject of considerable controversy.

factor analysis. Charles Spearman's theory of intelligence based on two factors—one being intelligence itself and the other being a set of special abilities.

faculty psychology. The concept that intelligence is made up of several independently operating parts of the brain, each one a faculty. The pseudoscience of phrenology was founded on this doctrine.

family care. See p. 105.

family history. See p. 105.

family therapy. A type of group psychotherapy in which all members of an immediate family are involved at once. Usually this is done on an outpatient basis, but it has been tried where all are admitted (at the same time) into a hospital for treatment.

field theory. Gestalt psychologists' term for the dynamic interaction of different areas of intelligence, each one affecting the other.

first-signal system. In pavlovian theory, the total of all internal and external stimuli to which the or-

ganism responds with conditioned and unconditioned reflexes.

fixation. Freud's term for a person's overemphasis or
dependence upon some childish tendency. When a
person characteristically employs such childish
ways of doing things, he may be referred to as
having an infantile fixation or an overemphasis on
oral means of expression, which is described as an
oral fixation.

folk psychology. Wundt's term for cultural psychology. He saw the study of culture, however, as
genetic rather than social.

foster family. See p. 105.

free association. A psychotherapeutic technique
used in psychoanalysis in which the analysand is
encouraged to verbalize whatever thoughts, feelings, and associations of these that come to mind
during the therapy period.

freudian. Pertaining to the writings, theories, techniques, and followers of Sigmund Freud. As the
psychoanalytic movement became splintered into
several diverse groups following somewhat different theories or treatment approaches, those who
remained faithful to the original concepts were referred to as either freudian or orthodox.

functional. A term in common use that refers to a
medical (or pseudomedical) condition that is not
based on organic pathology. In psychiatry,
psychotic states may be divided into functional and
organic types. Schizophrenia is an example of a
functional psychosis, and a drug intoxication state
is an example of organic psychosis.

functional psychology. Psychological theory of the
view that human behavior is, above all, adaptational and that it either succeeds or fails as it contributes to social adaptation.

fusion. Psychoanalytic term for union of the instincts.

general adaptation syndrome. A a term used by
Hans Selye to denote the total of nonspecific endocrine and hormonal reactions to stress.

generativity. Erik Erikson's term for the concern of
persons with having children, in guiding social organizations, and in other fields of endeavor concerned with shepherding the growth of ensuing
generations.

genital love. In psychoanalytic theory, synonymous
with mature, adult love.

geographic determinism. The point of view or
theory that cultural traits are influenced by geography.

geriatric psychiatry. See p. 105.

gestalt psychology. Study directed chiefly toward
sensory processes and the mechanisms by which
images and concepts are developed from blends of
sensory cues; a school of thought in psychology
chiefly identified with the names of Wertheimer,
Kohler, and Koffka. The school of psychology
was developed originally by Wertheimer, Koffka,
and Kohler in Berlin and was then brought to this
country where Kurt Lewin joined the ranks. It
views psychological phenomena holistically rather
than fragmentally. Perception, for instance, is typically a gestalt process in which the individual tries
to fit sense signals into a whole image.

good me. Harry Stack Sullivan's term for that part of
the personality that is organized around the
pleasurable and rewarding experiences of early
life. It is the portion of himself that one discusses
when he uses the term "I."

graphology. The practice of studying handwriting in order to ascertain personality traits of the
writer.

group therapy. Psychotherapy in which the therapist
engages with groups of patients in the therapeutic
process. Use is made of the various members of
the group in helping each individual understand his
problem. It is not necessarily identified with any
particular school of thought.

halfway house. See p. 105.

hallucinogen. Hallucinogenic drug; a chemical substance that can produce delirium in human beings.
Many toxic chemicals can do this, but the term is
usually restricted to a certain group of drugs used
experimentally, such as LSD. The mechanism of
action is probably through a poisoning or stimulation of sensory pathways, which results in false
sensory stimuli reaching the brain. Some researchers have erroneously equated the state produced by hallucinogenic drugs with schizophrenia.
The latter, however, is a defect in conceptualization, while the experimental states are defects in
perception.

hashish. Marijuana.

Hawthorne effect. From industrial psychology
studies of the Hawthorne plant in the 1920s by
Elton Mayo, it was found that workers tended to
respond with increased production to any kind of
environmental change, even when the change was
to some original state.

hemispherectomy. Removal of one of the cerebral
hemispheres.

heroin. A semisynthetic derivative of opium;
diacetylmorphine. It has no medical uses, but is
well known as a drug of abuse. It is highly addic-
tive and is known to cause one of the most intract-

able habits or addictions. It is also known as horse, H, the big H, junk, and smack.

hormic psychology. Purposive psychology; McDougall's term for drive. He said that there are a discrete number of different drives that motivate human beings.

hotline. Telephone assistance used in crisis intervention; usually a center that is staffed 24 hours daily with trained lay persons and that uses professionals in advisory capacity.

humanistic psychology. John Cohen's term used to stress the importance of seeing psychology as the study of the whole man, not merely of his physiology.

hydrotherapy. The use of long tub soaks to calm the anxious, agitated patients; also, the drinking of mineral waters.

hypnosis. A state of semiconsciousness in which the individual is responsive to only a limited type of stimuli (such as commands from the hypnotist) and that is, necessarily, brought about by the influence of one person or another. The technique has had frequent upsurges in popularity, beginning with Anton Mesmer in the late eighteenth century.

hypnosis, authoritative. See p. 61.

hypnotics. Medications that produce sleep, sedation, and tranquilization. Some have anticonvulsant properties (for example, barbiturates and meprobamate).

iatrogenic. Caused by treatment; toxicity and other medical problems arising from the treatment measure used on a patient. Neurotic states are frequently referred to as iatrogenic when they appear to result from medical treatment.

id. Freud's term for the instinctual components of a person's psyche; refers to a major part of the unconscious (the remainder being the superego).

identifying link. Arieti's term denoting a predicate used by a psychotic person to link several otherwise unrelated subjects, especially when using paleologic thinking.

identity crisis. Erik Erikson's term describing the behavioral manifestations of an adolescent who is trying to determine his sense of who he is and what he is to become; especially when in doing this he comes into conflict with family or society.

imago. Carl Jung's term for the image one person forms of another.

implosion. Behavior therapy using vivid accounts of dire consequences resulting from the feared object; such presentations are repeated until the object does not evoke fear or anxiety in the patient. Used in therapy of phobias.

individual psychology. Alfred Adler's type of psychoanalysis, which developed after he broke away from Freud. His theory stresses the importance of people's seeking power as a compensation for childhood inferiority complexes. Adler paved the way for development of the cultural school of analysis under Sullivan and Horney.

Indoklon. An ether gas that produces convulsions and that is sometimes used where electroconvulsive therapy is indicated. Generic name: flurothyl.

indole compounds. A group of compounds that include the biogenic amine serotonin and psychotomimetics (such as LSD and bufotenin).

inner directed. David Riesman's term for persons who have a capacity for self-assertion, both against tradition and against their fellows in competition.

inpatient, outpatient. See p. 106.

institution. See p. 106.

instrumental conditioning. Operant conditioning. (See p. 64.)

insulin coma therapy (ICT). Insulin treatment.

insulin treatment. Periodic injections of insulin to produce coma; a treatment method introduced in the 1930s by Manfred Sakel. It was usually used in schizophrenia. The treatment is rarely used today.

introspectionistic psychology. An informal school of psychological thought that relied upon internal, logical analysis of thinking rather than on studies of objective behavior, in order to obtain knowledge of psychology.

jocasta complex. In psychoanalytic theory, the mother's incestuous attachment to her son.

kinesics. The study of the meaning of body movement, posture, facial expression.

kinestherapy. Use of mechanical devices, exercise, massage, and manipulation in treatment.

lapsus. A slip or mistake (for example, a slip of the tongue [lapsus linguae] or of the pen [lapsus calami]). Psychoanalytic theory holds that such occurrences are evidence of unconscious conflict.

latency period. The period of a child's life, between the ages of 6 and 12, when little or no psychosexual development is apparent. Freud used this term to denote that the drives were by no means inactive during this period, even though they were not apparent.

latent content. Freud's term for the deep, hidden, unconscious meaning of any dream or fantasy.

lay therapist. See p. 106.

learning theory. A body of theory using the view that behavior, feelings, and thought patterns are acquired through experience and, as such, can be studied and modified. The conditioning therapies are an outgrowth of this general body of theory.

leptosomal. Ectomorphic.

leptosome. Kretschmer's term for a physique characterized by a spare, angular, and narrow build with a thin chest.

leucotomy. Lobotomy.

liaison. See p. 106.

libido. Freud's term for the putative energy that provides the drive for the sexual instincts. Other terms having essentially the same meaning are sexual hunger, psychic energy, and élan vital. The concept that sexuality is endowed with energy is fundamental to freudian theory, since it is used to explain the process of repression as a struggle and the state of the unconscious as a dynamic rather than a static phenomenon. The concept assumes that the energy is constantly being generated in the individual and must, therefore, be released in some fashion. The ways in which this release takes place become then the determinants of behavior.

life chart. See p. 106.

life space. A term used by Kurt Lewin for the space or sphere of influence of an individual in which that person lives and moves.

lithium. A metal used in psychiatry in its carbonate salt form to treat cyclic affective disorders (for example, mania, hypomania, and depression).

lobotomy. Severing some of the connections between the frontal lobes of the brain and the thalamus; claimed to be effective in making schizophrenic patients more tractable. It is also called prefrontal lobotomy, leucotomy, and transorbital lobotomy. The effect of the operation on patients was usually that of increased indolence, lack of initiative, and loss of memory. It is rarely used now. This operative procedure was devised by the Portuguese neurosurgeon Egas Moniz in the 1930s.

localization theory. Psychophysiology based on the discovery that specific areas of the brain govern complex behavior activity.

logotherapy. A modification of the existential psychology approach to psychiatric therapy, with an aim of therapy being to help the patient find his own individual reason for existence. Viktor Frankl of Vienna has been the promoter, and he refers to his approach as the ''Third Viennese School,'' following those of Freud and Adler.

lust dynamism. Harry Stack Sullivan's term for the patterns of interactions motivated by and revolving about sexual feelings and interests.

lysergic acid diethylamide (LSD). A psychomimetic; may produce a psychoticlike state when taken. No generally accepted therapeutic use has been shown for it.

lytic cocktail. A mixture of tranquilizers given in the treatment of alcohol and sedative drug withdrawal states (delirium).

maintenance drug therapy. Continuation of medication to prevent relapse or exacerbation.

major tranquilizers. Antipsychotic drugs.

malevolent transformation. Harry Stack Sullivan's term for a learned response of the person whose need for tenderness is frustrated. He responds with undesirable behavior whenever he feels the need for tenderness and affection.

malignant identity diffusion. Erik Erikson's term for events in the development of some young persons who later become criminals or are otherwise deviant. Since these young persons lack proper models with which to identify, they must therefore identify with unacceptable models.

Malleus Maleficarum. *The Witches' Hammer;* an infamous book written in the Middle Ages by two monks, Sprenger and Kramer, that had strong influence in causing the mistreatment of people thought to be witches, sorcerers, and heretics. This work had a deleterious effect on the treatment of the mentally ill.

manifest content. Psychoanalytic theory postulates that a dream or a fantasy may have two different components; the apparent one being termed the manifest content, or that which is actually reported, and the other being the latent content, or the hidden meaning.

marathon group. Group therapy meeting carried on for very extended (8 to 72 hours) periods of time; fosters closer interaction, candor, and openness that is helpful especially when this is developed in conjunction with regular group psychotherapy.

marijuana. A euphoria-producing drug derived from the flower of the hemp plant *Cannabis indica;* may be dependency producing and may produce a psychoticlike state. The active component is thought to be a cannabinol.

marriage counseling. A form of therapy usually carried out by ministers, but also done by psychiatrists, psychologists, and social workers. It can be premarital, to help prevent problems before marriage; or marital, to married couples seeking help for troubled relationships.

mass action principle. A principle proposed by Karl Lashley's theory relating loss of brain tissue to changes in behavior: that the loss of function of the brain depends more on how much tissue is lost rather than on what specific areas are lost.

megavitamin therapy. Administration of large doses of vitamins (originally B$_3$ but later extended in some clinics to all vitamins) in the treatment of schizophrenia; an unproven therapy. Also called orthomolecular therapy.

mental apparatus. Id, ego, and superego.

mental chemistry. John Stuart Mill's term used to draw an analogy to chemistry to explain the phenomenon of association.

mental hospital. See p. 107.

mental hygiene. See p. 107.

mental incompetence. See p. 107.

mentalism. Psychological theory or school of thought that stresses the thinking processes rather than external physical phenomena.

mental status. See p. 107.

mescaline. The most active of hallucinogenic chemical agents, found in the buttons of the mescal cactus, *Lophophora williamsii.*

mesmerism. See p. 63.

mesomorph. William H. Sheldon's term for the person who has large bones, is muscular, and is athletic. He described the mesomorph as being somatotonic.

metaphysical psychology. Psychological theory that places emphasis on the soul and religion.

metapsychology. Freud's term for his later (1920s) theories that went beyond psychology; for example, the topographic concepts (id, ego, superego, geography of the psyche).

methadone. A synthetic narcotic-analgesic; used psychiatrically in the substitute-therapy of heroin addiction. It also produces dependency, but apparently not to the degree that morphine, heroin, and other narcotics do.

methionine. An amino acid that, when given in combination with a monomine oxidase inhibitor, may produce or exacerbate schizophreniclike symptoms.

metrazol therapy. Convulsive therapy; not now used.

milieu therapy. A therapeutic approach to hospital psychiatry in which the entire hospital environment is designed to facilitate rehabilitation. This includes occupational therapy, recreational therapy, team approach, work assignments, and education of all who work in the hospital to participate in the care of patients.

miniature theories. The tendency to narrow studies and speculations into small components of the psychological whole; occurred during the bitter theoretical controversies in psychology between 1900 and 1940.

Mitwelt. The co-world of an individual; his social world in which he participates with other individuals. (See Umwelt.)

modality. The manner or mode of treatment; classes of sensory activity, such as seeing and hearing.

monism. Attempts to unify body and soul into one concept. In the ancient controversy over the mind-body problem, the opposing schools became divided along lines known as dualism and monism. The dualistic approach (for example, that of Descartes) sees the human being as made up of two independent and irreducible components— body and soul.

moral treatment. Humane treatment. A philosophy and technique of caring for the mentally ill that came to the fore in the nineteenth century. Emphasis is given to humane and kindly treatment, removal of restraints, work, religion, socialization.

morphine. A narcotic-analgesic medication derived from the juice of the opium poppy. It is known to produce strong dependency and to be widely abused. It is used in medical practice to alleviate severe pain (such as postoperative pain).

mortido. Wish for death; opposed to libido.

nalorphine. A drug that acts as an antagonist to morphine. Because of this property it is used to treat morphine poisoning and is sometimes given to addicts who supposedly have been off morphine. Withdrawal signs seen after nalorphine is given are considered presumptive evidence that the supposedly withdrawal addict has started taking narcotics again.

Nancy school. A group of followers who worked with Hippolyte Bernheim at the University of Nancy, France, in the 1880s. Work was done on the experimental use of hypnosis in treating hysterics. In contrast to an opposing school under Charcot, the Nancy school saw hysteria and hypnosis as solely psychological phenomena.

narcoanalysis. A technique used extensively during World War II for patients with combat fatigue. Subnarcotic injections of barbiturates were administered and the patient was encouraged to express painful fantasies or memories.

narcoplexis. A deep, lengthy drug narcosis therapy, with the patient given active psychotherapeutic interpretations using material during narcoanalysis from the patient's past. It is rarely used.

narcosynthesis. Narcoanalysis.

narcotic. Pertaining to or able to produce sleep; a

group of drugs having powerful analgesic and sedative effects and able to produce pronounced dependency.

need gratification. In psychoanalytic theories, the one basic tendency of the organism; that is, to reduce tension brought about by a need (such as the need for food, sex, or water).

negative therapeutic reaction. Freud's term for the phenomenon of a person who gains insights through psychotherapy, but who is unable to make use of them.

neobehaviorism. The later developments of behavioral psychology into learning theory and reinforcement (such as those of Thorndike and Clark Hull).

neofreudianism. The later developments of psychoanalytic theory and practice that did not depart from but modified Freud's concepts (for example, those of Franz Alexander).

nonfreudians. Karen Horney, Erich Fromm, and Harry Stack Sullivan, among others, who built upon and extended the theories of Freud. They recognized the importance of environment on psychological development and incorporated social and environmental concepts into psychoanalytical theory.

neuroleptic. A major tranquilizer or antipsychotic agent.

neurology. See p. 107.

neuropsychiatry. See p. 107.

neuropsychology. See p. 107.

neutralization. The concept of Heinz Hartmann that instinctual drives, especially aggression, can be deenergized, with this energy being made available to the ego for other functions, (such as coping and defending against anxiety).

neutralizer. In group therapy, a member who controls aggressiveness, impulsiveness, and destructiveness and other members.

night hospital. See p. 107.

nightmare. See p. 64.

nihilism. A philosophical term referring to the attitude that nothing is worthwhile. In depressed patients, a nihilistic attitude is one in which life is viewed as useless and nothing seems worth any effort.

nirvana principle. A tendency, postulated by Freud, of an organism to discharge internal tension and to seek a state of rest.

nitrous oxide. An anesthetic gas; commonly called laughing gas.

nodal behavior. In child group therapy, the peak of disruptive behavior (such as levity and aggressive-

ness) followed by a quiet period (anti-nodal behavior). These periods of behavior become shorter as therapy progresses.

nomothetic psychology. Types of psychological inquiry that seek lawfulness, orderliness, or rationality in psychological and behavioral processes.

nonreporting. Sandor Rado's term for unconscious; chosen because of the ambiguity of the term unconscious as used in classical theories of psychodynamics.

noogenic neurosis. A concept used mainly in existential psychiatry to refer to a life without meaning.

noopsyche. Stransky's term for the intellectual or cognitive portion of mental processes.

noradrenaline. Norepinephrine.

norepinephrine. A catecholamine thought to play an important role in the brain as a neurotransmitter; an adrenergic pressor drug.

not me. Harry Stack Sullivan's term for that portion of the personality that is dissociated out of conscious awareness, because that portion is associated with early experiences that fill one with dread, horror, awe, or loathing. These feelings can come into consciousness as dreams or nightmares or into pathological states, such as schizophrenia. These experiences are nearly always experienced as being unreal and, therefore, "not me."

noumenon. Kant's term to indicate the real state of an event or object. In contrast, the mind never knows quite what reality is, but only its approximation (that is, the phenomenon).

object choice. External recipient of libido.

object love. In freudian theory, the libidinal energy that has attached itself to a thing or person outside of the self.

objective anxiety. Freud's term for fear.

objective psychology. A grand view of psychological methods, referring to those that tend to study external manifestations of behavior. Subjective psychology includes then the introspectionists.

obsessive behavior. Sandor Rado's term for obsessive-compulsive neurosis. This is usually divided into obsessive symptoms (such as acts, feelings, and thoughts) and obsessive character traits. These are usually egoalien (that is, the patient considers them to be strange and disturbing and incompatible with himself).

occupational psychiatry. See p. 107.

occupational therapy. See p. 108.

oedipal complex. The central core of Freud's theory of neurosis. He described the child as going through a stage of life in which incestuous wishes toward the parent of the opposite sex and destructive fantasies about the other parent create a conflict in the child's relationships. When this conflict is inadequately resolved, there remains an oedipal complex, producing psychological difficulties later. (See electra complex.)

oedipal theory. A midpoint in Freud's evolution of psychoanalytic theory. According to this view, the child passes through an oedipal period, during which he has conflicting and ambivalent attitudes toward his parents (for example, he desires the opposite parent and wishes to destroy the parent of the same sex). Failure to resolve the conflict satisfactorily becomes the foundation of neurosis.

oneirology. Study of dreams.

one-way mirror. See p. 108.

ontoanalysis. See p. 108.

ontology. Study of the nature of being.

open-door. See p. 108.

open group. A therapy group to which new members can be added; as opposed to closed group.

open hospital. See p. 108.

operant conditioning. See p. 64.

operationalism. The view that terminology should be derived from behavioral or experimental models in which all theory can be defined in terms of repeatable and identifiable operations.

opiates. Narcotic drugs derived from the opium poppy *(Papaver somniferum);* broadly, any narcotic.

opium. A mixture of narcotic analgesics obtained from the juice of the opium poppy. *Papaver somniferum.* It contains morphine, codeine, and dilaudid, among other compounds. Its use produces dependency when abused.

orality. A personality state; an outgrowth of a period of psychosexual development that Freud termed the oral phase. Supposedly, personality traits such as smoking, chewing gum, some homosexual practices, and obesity secondary to psychogenic overeating are evidence of such oral drives or needs.

oral phase. According to Freud's theory of personality development, the earliest stage in the infant's life. At this time, the infant explores the world, primarily with his mouth, and gains his principal satisfaction orally. Freud equated these actions to early sexual satisfaction. Frustration at this level of development could result in overemphasis of oral activities later on.

oral sadism. Sexual pleasure or aggression expressed through biting or eating.

organ eroticism. Undue erotic attachment to one's own body parts because of libidinal investment in that body part.

organic therapies. Various chemical, hormonal, and physical treatments (for example, electroshock therapy) that affect the brain and its activity.

organismic theory. A gestalt approach to the study of behavior; a psychological theory of K. Goldstein.

organ language. The symbolic meaning of psychophysiological disorders.

orgone. Wilhelm Reich's term for a life-force that he hypothesized and around which he devised a therapeutic approach that he called orgone therapy.

orthopsychiatry. See p. 108.

other directed. David Riesman's term for persons who developed an attitude of dependence on one another within relatively homogeneous cultural settings.

outpatient. See p. 108.

overcompensation. Alfred Adler's term for excessive attempts to overcome inferiority feelings (for example, a very small person being overly aggressive).

pain barrier. A mental mechanism postulated by Sandor Rado that works to prevent recall of memories and feelings that are painful.

pain dependence. A term used by Sandor Rado to describe a chronic disturbance in which the person, as a result of his own rage being turned against himself, feels constantly in the need of punishment. Consequently, he finds ways to inflict moral, mental, and even physical pain on himself in order to satisfy this need.

palliative. In medical treatment, a procedure that offers comfort or relief, but not a cure.

pananxiety. See p. 35.

panneurosis. A term used by Hoch and Pollatin in their description of psuedoneurotic schizophrenia to mean that the patient has an all-pervading anxiety structure; not just one or two neurotic symptoms but all symptoms known in neurotic illness are present at the same time.

pansexualism. Freud conceived of the child as passing through various stages of sexual maturation, including autoerotic, homoerotic, and heteroerotic. This range has been called pansexualism.

paranoid pseudocommunity. A concept of Norman Cameron that defines the belief of the paranoid person that there exists a group or community of real or imaginary persons who plot against him.

parapraxia. A "slipup" or minor accident that was

thought by Freud to be motivated by unconscious feelings or drives. Because these slips reveal feelings and urges about which the patient is usually unaware, they are useful in psychotherapy.

parapsychology. Studies of extrasensory perception.

parataxic distortion. False ideas concerning another person, based on unrelated past experiences, such as blaming someone in the past for harm done by someone else in the past.

parataxic messages. Harry Stack Sullivan's term for uncommunicative, misleading, and unintelligible messages.

partial hospitalization. See p. 108.

participant-observer. Harry Stack Sullivan's term denoting that the psychotherapist is not detached from the therapeutic situation, but rather is involved in it, using himself, his feelings, and his reactions as diagnostic and therapeutic tools.

part instincts. A term used by Freud to describe erotic impulses that arise from pregenital zones. Kissing and stimulation of the anal area are examples of activities associated with the part instincts.

patient government. See p. 108.

pavor diurnus. See p. 37.

pavor nocturnus. See p. 37.

penicillin. An antibiotic medication used to treat a variety of bacterial infections. Psychiatric complications (such as deliria, confusion, and depression) secondary to its use are uncommon but can occur.

penis envy. A girl's desire to own a penis. Freud speculated that a major psychological threat to a boy was castration fear, and an equivalent feeling in girls was the resentment experienced from the knowledge that they had no penis. Psychoanalysts describe masculinelike women as being motivated by penis envy.

pentothal interview. Narcoanalysis.

persona. Carl Jung's term for a person's external appearance and behavior (personality); in contrast to anima.

person language. One division, used by J. H. Woodger, of scientific language that relates information about people.

personology (need press theory). H. A. Murray's theory of personality, which is heavily influenced by psychoanalysis and which attempts to blend the physiological and psychological into a holistic concept.

persuasion. Directive psychotherapy, most often associated with Paul Dubois of Berne, based on principles of intellectual, explanatory, and moralizing discussions.

peyote. The dried buttons of the mescal cactus, *Lophophora williamsii,* which will produce hallucinations when smoked. Mescaline, a hallucinogen, is the active agent in peyote, but it contains at least 15 less active chemicals.

peyotl. A name sometimes given to the mescal cactus, *Lophophora williamsii.*

phallic phase. Freud's third stage of personality development (the first and second being the oral phase and the anal phase), which is associated with the child's discovery of his own sexual characteristics.

phallic woman. A woman who is active in trying to play the man's sexual role, especially during heterosexual intercourse; too coarse, masculine, manipulative, or lacking in feminine qualities.

pharmacotherapy. Treatment with medicines.

phenomenalism. Phenomenology.

phenomenological psychology. The study that examines the minute phenomena of behavior, such as individual sensations. The term has been applied to the type of psychology promoted by the early experimental psychologists.

phenomenology. Existential psychotherapy in which the patient is studied as he exists at that present moment, with little emphasis on the patient's past or his unconscious motives. An attempt is made to eliminate the therapist's preconceived theory and presuppositions. It developed from the philosophy of Edmund Husserl.

phenothiazines. A group of drugs, some members of which are useful in psychiatry as major tranquilizers or antipsychotic agents. Their efficacy as an antipsychotic agent apparently depends on there being 3 carbon atoms between the ring nitrogen atom and a side-chain nitrogen atom.

phrenology. A pseudoscience developed during the early nineteenth century as a result of Franz Gall's theory that individual differences in people are reflected in the pattern of protuberances of the skull. The movement enjoyed widespread popularity in its time, and, although having no scientific basis, it did have the effect of stressing the importance of individual differences.

physiotherapy. The use of physical methods and mechanical devices in treating psychiatric patients. These include massage, passive and active exercise, and light, heat, and cold applications.

physique types. Correlation of such constitutional factors as body build with personality type, temperament, and mental disorders. Such concepts are usually associated with Sheldon and Kretschmer.

pithiatism. See p. 65.

placebo. An inert medicine given for its psychological effect.

placement. See p. 108.

play therapy. Therapy carried out in a playroom well stocked with toys that the child, through play, uses to express conflicts and feelings that he is unable to communicate to the therapist in a verbal or any other more direct manner.

pleasure principle. Freud's postulate that human beings are motivated to seek pleasure and to avoid pain; contrasted with the reality principle.

pneumatology. An obsolete term for psychology, referring to the pneuma, or spirit, which resided in the body.

polymorphous perversion. Use of all forms of sexual expression. Freud felt that the infant and young child normally showed polymorphous perversion and matured into heterosexual orientation and practices later.

posthypnotic suggestion. Commands given during a hypnotic state that are carried out by the subject after the hypnotic trance is terminated.

power instinct. Alfred Adler's theory postulating that the driving motivation in human behavior is attempts to acquire power over others as a compensation for inferiority feelings.

prealcoholic symptomatic phase. In E. M. Jellinek's schema of alcoholism, a time during which the person drinks socially but soon begins to drink daily and excessively.

preconscious. A part of the mind, midway between the conscious and the unconscious, that has some of the properties of each. The preconscious may contain, for instance, material that is ordinarily dormant but that can be recalled under certain circumstances. The concept was an invention of Freud's to explain phenomena that could not be accounted for otherwise.

pressor agent. A drug or compound that causes an increase in blood pressure.

preventive psychiatry. See p. 108.

pride system. Karen Horney's concept of the dilemma of the neurotic personality. The person's expectations of himself, his idealized image, become so invested with pride that he is unable to relinquish or modify this image. In addition, he feels contempt for what he is, and this pride and self-hatred—two sides of the same coin—form the pride system.

primal repression. In freudian theory, a postulated mechanism by which primitive urges, which have never reached the level of consciousness (such as possible archaic cannibalistic urges) are kept out of conscious awareness. This contrasts to the repressed unconscious.

primal scene. Sexual intercourse of the parents as viewed by the child. Psychoanalytic theory attaches great importance to the young child's witnessing or hearing sexual activities of his parents and alleges this to be significant in the development of the oedipal complex.

primary gain. Warding off of anxiety (from unconscious sources). Psychoanalytic theory postulates that the neurotic state serves this principle purpose, and this is the primary gain. Other benefits that might accrue from the neurosis are called secondary gains.

privileged communication. See p. 109.

proception. Buchler's term for the self.

prognosis. See p. 109.

progress notes. See p. 109.

prosthesis. See p. 109.

protodiakriasis. Monakow's term for the loss of the ability to discriminate between living and lifeless matter; a condition that is often seen in infantile autism.

protophrenia. Bourne's term for severe mental, physical, and emotional deterioration caused by affect deprivation in children.

prototaxic communication. In the theories of Harry Stack Sullivan, this is the earliest mode of communication of the infant.

pseudoinsight. Manufacture of insightful statements to please the therapist, with no real feeling or understanding to support such statements.

psilocybin. A psychotomimetic or hallucinogenic drug.

psychedelic drugs. Literally, drugs that affect the mind; usually refers to those drugs that cause hallucinations and other psychoticlike mental abnormalities. Examples are LSD, psilocybin, and mescaline.

psychiatric aide. See p. 109.

psychiatric hospitals. See p. 109.

psychiatric interview. See p. 109.

psychiatric nurse. See p. 109.

psychiatric patient. See p. 109.

psychiatric social worker. See p. 109.

psychiatric team. See p. 109.

psychiatrist. See p. 109.

psychiatry. See p. 109.

psychic apparatus. Id, ego, and superego.

psychic determinism. The concept that behavior is caused by psychological processes. Opponents to Freud's theories, especially of the philosophical type, used this as a way of characterizing Freud and condemning his theories.

psychic driving. D. Ewen Cameron's treatment method exposing the patient to repeated positive or negative statements through recordings of his own voice, where possible, morning and night, over a period of many weeks and months; not in wide use.

psychoanalysis. Sigmund Freud's treatment technique and psychological theories. The technique requires that the patient lie on a couch and by free association relate his thoughts to the analyst, who is usually nondirective and passive. The theory is based on an acceptance of major unconscious factors in human motivation and behavior with conflict between opposing psychological forces.

psychoanalyst. See p. 109.

psychodrama. See p. 109.

psychodynamics. Dynamics.

psychologism. Husserl's term for the false notion that subjects such as mathematics and logic are dependent on psychological laws. He states that, instead, they are universal an independent.

psychophysical parallelism. Operation of the mind and the body parallel each other; they are closely correlated with each other, but are otherwise independent.

psychosocial assessment. Utilization of information about the patient's environment, work, family, and so on in making an evaluation of his psychiatric status. It is used in addition to the therapist's examination of the patient in making the evaluation and in planning or initiating treatment.

psychosocial moratorium. Erik H. Erikson's term for the fact that the adolescent will often ask implicitly to be allowed to postpone a decision as to what adult sexual role he will assume.

psychosocial therapies. Milieu therapy, especially hospitals and the community, group, and family.

psychosurgery. Brain surgery performed for treatment of psychiatric conditions.

psychosynthesis. Recombining the components of the mind into a whole; usually the last phase of psychoanalysis, in which the components are at first taken apart and examined.

psychotherapy. Generally all psychological treatment techniques—including psychoanalysis; often specifically used to denote a one-to-one interview method between physician and patient.

psychotic insight. Silvano Arieti's term denoting a sudden acquisition in a schizophrenic of understanding of what is behind the strange things that happen to him. Arieti feels this development gives a poor prognosis for the recovery from the psychotic state.

psychotomimetic drugs. Drugs that produce an abnormal mental state that mimics a psychosis (for example, LSD and amphetamines). Synonym: hallucinogens.

psychotoxic. Having or able to have an adverse effect on the mind; able to cause disturbance of mental function.

psychotoxicology. Industrial and occupational psychiatry based on the finding that the earliest sign of intoxication by certain industrial compounds is a change in cognitive functioning.

psychotropic compounds. Any drug that has an effect on the mind; usually those drugs used in the treatment of mental illness.

punishment dreams. Freud's postulate that the ego anticipates condemnation by the superego and attempts satisfaction of the demands of the superego by giving expression to punishment fantasies via dreaming.

purposivism. Psychological theory that stresses the importances of motivation.

quantification. Experimentation and measurement in psychology. Midnineteenth century scientists tended to criticize psychology as being unscientific because it was not qualifiable. In response to this, experimental psychology became directed toward physiological studies, particularly of the senses, because here quantification seemed feasible. By so doing, however, the study of the thinking processes was neglected. When psychometrics was introduced (by Binet and others) after 1900, quantification of more psychological types of studies became fashionable. Even today, however, there tends to be more reverence for what is measurable than for what is important.

quantitative personality theory. Personality theory derived from experimentation and measurement.

quarrel. See p. 66.

quinacrine. An antimalarial drug that may induce a psychoticlike state.

rationalism. Psychology that used introspection as the source of knowledge.

rauwolfia alkaloids. Medicinal compounds derived

from the root of the plant *Rauwolfia serpentina*. One derivative, reserpine, has been used in psychiatry as a major tranquilizer, but is not now widely prescribed.

reactology. Psychological study that attempts to translate Marxist ideology into social phenomena; followed in Russia. Kornilov described seven types of human reactions: natural, muscular, sensory, discriminatory, selective, and reactions of recognition and of logical order.

reality principle. Freud's term for the practical demands of society, which represent the reality principle and which are often in conflict with the individual's own wishes.

real self. Horney's term for a central inner force or principle that is common to all, yet unique in each individual, and is a source of personality growth, energy, interest, effort, depth of feeling, and resourcefulness. An optimal environment would favor health development of one's real self. Unfavorable environmental circumstances lead to development of an idealized self.

recapitulation theory. In his development, the individual passes through the stages of evolution experienced by the species. "Ontogeny recapitulates phylogeny."

receptor. Sullivan's term for that part of a zone of interaction that receives sensory stimuli.

reciprocal inhibition psychotherapy. Weakening the bonds between neurotic symptoms and the anxiety-provoking stimuli by teaching or conditioning responses that are antagonistic to anxiety in response to those stimuli; a form of behavior therapy.

reconstructive therapy. A psychoanalytic procedure based on adaptational psychodynamics that is used to treat patients who are functioning at a level of infantile dependency.

recreational therapy. Play and sports activity carried out in a meaningful way to enhance the patients' creative skills, resocialization, and recovery.

redintegration. Hollingworth's term for the provocation by part of a complex stimulus of the entire response previously elicited by the complex stimulus (for example, reawakening memories, attitudes, and affects in response to an odor associated with the entire original event). It is sometimes synonymous with reintegration.

reductionism. Psychological theory that reduces the scope of interest to atomistic phenomena; opposite of a holistic approach.

reflexology. The study of autonomic nervous system physiology and of the effects of drugs and environmental factors on this system.

reflex theory. A system of thought that assumes that the primary element of behavior is response to external stimuli.

registered nurse. See p. 110.

reinforcement. See p. 67.

reintegration. See p. 67.

relapse. See p. 67.

relaxation therapy. Teaching and helping the patient to reduce bodily tensions and gain some control over his thought content in order to reduce his anxiety level; advocated by Edmund Jacobson.

release effect. Sudden manifestation of repressed feelings and affects (such as joy, tears, excitement, hostility, fear); a phenomenon in narcoanalysis.

remission. Reduction or disappearance of symptoms and signs of a disease.

remotivation. Reawakening, enhancing communication skills, interest in the environment, vocational skills in chronic, withdrawn hospitalized patients through group therapy carried out by hospital personnel, especially nursing staff.

repetition compulsion. Ernest Jones' term for a tendency in neurotic patients to repeat similar mistakes in their lives (such as bad marriages ending in divorces). Jones implied that this tendency was in response to a self-destructive impulse.

reporting brain. Sandor Rado's term for those portions of the brain concerned with conscious awareness.

repressed unconscious. In freudian theory, a postulated body of remembered experiences and wishes that at one time were explicitly conscious, but that were then, for various reasons, eliminated from consciousness by repression.

residential treatment. See p. 110.

resistance. Conscious or unconscious defense by the patient against allowing repressed or unconscious thoughts into conscious awareness; an impediment to psychotherapy.

rest-cure. Weir Mitchell's advocation of rest, massage, fattening diet, and mild exercise; not widely used.

restraints. See p. 110.

retroactive inhibition. Inhibition of an old response by the learning of a new response (for example, learning a new language will reduce ability to recall words and symbols of the old language).

retroflexion. Turning backward; Rado's term for inversion.

reverse vulnerability. Lederer and Jackson's term for a method of defense against becoming involved with another. In marriage, for instance, this could be the excessive withholding of responses that are expected and often needed by the other spouse. The person is afraid that unless he withholds something from the other, that the other will expect too much from him all the time.

revolving door. See p. 132.

reward and punishment. See p. 67.

riddance mechanisms. Sandor Rado's term for repression. (See p. 67).

riddance principle. Rado's term for automatic activity (such as vomiting, coughing, scratching) that rids the body of irritants.

rudimentation. Lorenz's term for the fragmentation and deautomatization of the consummatory act in human beings. In animals, mounting, intromission, and ejaculation are all reflexive by nature. In human beings, only the final pelvic thrusts and ejaculation are automatic.

rut formation. Wendell Muncie's term for tics occurring as a motor neurosis; the movement loses its original meaning as a reaction to psychological discomfort and becomes a habit.

schizoadaptation. Silvano Arieti's term for a compensatory style of life in persons with predisposition to schizophrenia. This adaptation, while somewhat removed from a normal one, may act to prevent a further deterioration into a schizophrenic psychosis.

schizotype. Silvano Arieti's term denoting a person with impairment of pleasure appreciation and a defect in proprioceptive awareness; deficits that are probably genetically determined and that contribute to the clinical syndrome of schizophrenia.

school psychiatry. See p. 110.

scopolamine. A rapid-acting anticholinergic and central nervous system depressant used in combination with narcotics as preoperative and pre-ECT medication. Overdose can produce hallucinations; single doses have been reported to cause psychotic-like states in susceptible individuals.

Scottish school. Thomas Reid, in the eighteenth century, advanced the concepts of Locke and founded a center in Scotland that later included Duglad Stewart and Thomas Brown. Until William Ames, psychology in the United States tended to follow the Scottish tradition.

secondary gain. Any benefit other than reduction of anxiety that might accrue from being neurotic (for example, attention or sympathy, financial rewards, and avoidance of responsibility). Synonym: epinosic gain. (See p. 26.)

second-signal system. A pavlovian term denoting development of responses to signs and symbols that stand for stimuli in the first-signal system.

sedation threshold. The amount of a hypnotic agent, such as amobarbital, required to induce slurred speech and EEG changes in the direction of drowsiness.

sedation without drowsiness. A major and very important difference in the clinical effects of the antipsychotic agents, such as the phenothiazines and butyrophenones, as compared with the hypnotics, such as the barbiturates. This fact gives the antipsychotics an advantage over the hypnotic agents in treating psychoses.

sensationism. Empirical psychology that states that sensory experience represents the foundation of all learning.

sensitivity training (group). See p. 68.

sentence frames. An incomplete sentence; one in which various classes of words may be substituted to complete the sentence and give association to various member words of the class. It is a term used in communications theory.

separation anxiety. 1. In children, a reaction to temporary loss of the parent, especially when this loss occurs under stressful circumstances such as hospitalization. 2. Otto Rank's concept of a fundamental fear in people associated with forced or necessary separation from the mother, the origin of which begins with the birth trauma.

sequelae. Medical term for complications following an illness, injury, or treatment measure (for example, weakness following a stroke).

serotonin. A biogenic indole alkylmonoamine found in brain tissue and thought to be a neurohumor.

shaping. B. F. Skinner's term denoting the induction of changes in the behavior pattern of an organism by immediately rewarding the behavioral responses desired by the therapist.

shock treatment. A general class of treatment used in psychiatry, including insulin shock, electroshock, and metrazol. Devices in the past century that induced pain and surprise are sometimes regarded as early examples.

side effects. Unwanted and sometimes unexpected effects of a therapeutic mode. Examples are hypotension and dizziness caused by tranquilizers.

signal anxiety. Freud's term for the anxiety that is evoked by perception of potential inner or outer danger and that calls out psychological defense measures (such as repression) to prevent painful memories from reentering conscious awareness.

social breakdown syndrome. Patient's symptoms that are caused by conditions within the treatment milieu and facility and are not part of the illness. Contributing factors include teaching the chronic sick role, labeling the patient, reducing social and work abilities. Rehabilitation is aimed toward revising this.

socializing activity. Any action or activity that results in the interaction of an individual with other members of the group; a goal for the individual in group therapy.

social psychiatry. See p. 110.

social psychology. See p. 110.

sociotherapy. Treatment emphasizing environmental, social, interpersonal factors (for example, therapeutic community, milieu therapy, attitude therapy) rather than intrapsychic factors.

sodium amytal. One of the barbiturate compounds; a sedative used in narcoanalysis.

sodium pentothal. One of the barbiturates; a sedative medication used in narcoanalysis.

sodium permanganate. An oxidizing medication used in gastric lavage as treatment for drug overdose.

sodium phenobarbital. A barbiturate; a strong sedative and anticonvulsant used in the treatment of epilepsy, hypertension, and anxiety.

somatic therapies. Various chemical, hormonal, and physical treatments for mental illness; also called organic therapies.

somatotonic. The mesomorph; an individual with vigor, resistance to fatigue, and powerful drive.

somatotypes. Body types allegedly associated with specific character traits, as in the theories of Kretschmer and Sheldon.

somnifacient. Able to induce sleep.

soporific. Having the quality of inducing sleep; sometimes, a tranquilizer.

space medicine. See p. 111.

space psychiatry. See p. 111.

stereoscopic therapy. A term used by Martin and Bird to denote their method of family therapy conducted by two therapists, each of whom sees one spouse. By conferring at intervals, each therapist has a double view (therefore stereoscopic) of his patient. It is also called collaborative therapy.

stimulant. A drug that increases alertness, awareness, and mental and motor activity (for example, caffeine, amphetamine).

storefront clinic. A community mental health clinic in a building as near as possible to the population it

serves. Typically held in an empty store in ghetto or rural areas staffed by lay indigenous workers under the supervision of professionals from the main clinic.

stormy personality. Silvano Arieti's term for a type of preschizophrenic personality; one who shows sudden, violent, and drastic personality changes, as compared with the stability of the schizoid.

streptomycin. An antibiotic produced by the fungus, *Streptomyces griseus.*

structural concepts. The id, ego, and superego as elaborated by Freud in his theories. These concepts largely replaced the topographic concepts in freudian theory.

structuralism. Psychological theory placing emphasis on physical structure of the nervous system and body rather than on the thinking processes.

style of life. Alfred Adler's term designating the individualized way each person asserts himself and guides his actions.

subcoma insulin treatment. Hypoglycemia induced by small intramuscular doses of insulin; manifested by weakness, profuse sweating, and drowsiness, but not coma. It is given for various psychiatric states.

succinimides. A type of drug used in the treatment of epilepsy.

succinylcholine. A drug that blocks transmission of the impulse from the nerve to the muscle; a neuromuscular blocking agent. In psychiatry, it is given immediately prior to electroconvulsive therapy to reduce the magnitude of the convulsions, spasms, and increased muscle tone caused by the electric shock.

suggestibility. See p. 69.

suggestion. See p. 69.

suicide. See p. 111.

suicide risk. See p. 111.

superego. Freud's term for that part of the unconscious that has an inhibiting influence on the ego to prevent expression of instinctual drives. It is sometimes equated with conscience. It includes the ego-ideal, which is that complex of characteristics of important real and fictional persons that has been obtained through identification and incorporation and that contributes to the foundation of character.

supportive psychotherapy. Treatment reinforcing the patient's psychological defenses; the patient is reassured, counseled, inspired, persuaded, reeducated without exploring the conflicts in depth.

suppression. A deliberate attempt to forget or hide an unacceptable wish, thought, or feeling. In psychoanalytic theory, this differs from repression in that it is a conscious process, while repression is assumed to be an unconscious process of forgetting or concealing.

sympathin. Epinephrine.

sympathomimetic. A drug that stimulates activity of the sympathetic nervous system.

symptomatic relief. Abolishing symptoms of a disease or condition by therapy that does not necessarily affect the underlying disease process. An example is relieving the itch of measles rash.

Synanon. See p. 111.

systemic desensitization. Treatment using muscle relaxation training, identifying anxiety-producing stimuli specific for the patient, deliberately provoking anxiety using these stimuli, and counteracting the anxiety via relaxation techniques. A behavioral therapy.

talon principle. The biblical principle of "an eye for an eye, a tooth for a tooth." In psychoanalytic theory, the term refers to the expectation of retribution in kind for destructive thoughts or wishes.

teleologic regression. Arieti's term for a return to a lower, more primitive or earlier level of function for the purpose, in schizophrenia, of removing excessive anxiety and reestablishing some kind of psychic equilibrium.

teleology. A property of any theory of nature that sees a man-centered purpose or direction toward some goal.

telepathy. Transference of thoughts by mystical means from one person to others. Although a small group of psychologists have produced what they claim to be proof of the existence of telepathy, this is not widely accepted.

temporalize. To be concerned with time; to use time as the reference; to situate in time. Binswanger uses the term to denote the individual's relation to time.

tension reduction. In psychoanalytic theory, the one basic tendency of all organisms; synonymous with need gratification.

teonauacatl mushroom. Mushroom (*Stropharia cubensis*) found in Mexico that produces hallucinations and disorders of visual perception when eaten.

thanatos. Freud's term for one of his later (post-World War I) theoretical developments that refers to the death instinct. Whereas prior to this time, he saw the pleasure principle as the major motivation in human behavior, he later described the death instinct as the opposing factor. Self-destructive activities could not be explained by the early pleasure principle, but the adoption of the death instinct concept offered an explanation. The repetition compulsion of Ernest Jones would be considered, in this framework, to be a manifestation.

therapeutic attitudes. The therapist's behavior toward and his approaches to the patient; a nonjudgmental, nonpunitive approach; a fundamental respect for the patient as a human being, with the flexible combination of permissiveness and limit-setting carried out in the course of a therapeutic relationship.

therapeutic community. Maxwell Jones' term for attempts to make the whole of time spent in a mental hospital to be a treatment time. Every effort is made to integrate various details of mental hospital life into a continuous program of treatment. Such an approach requires cooperation and teamwork from all mental hospital personnel: professional, paramedical, maintenance, food service, and so on.

therapeutic occupation. Usually taken to mean an extension of occupational therapy; a full-time and often permanent placement of a patient in a work position that is found to be suitable for him physically, mentally, and emotionally. Such arrangements are usually coordinated through vocational rehabilitation services.

therapist. A person, usually trained professionally, who administers treatment to the patient.

therapy. The process of treatment of the patient.

thiamin. Vitamin B_1; a necessary dietary ingredient. Deficiency of this vitamin is thought to contribute to brain diseases associated with chronic alcoholism.

thymoleptics. Synonym for antidepressants or mood elevator drugs.

thymopsyche. Stransky's term for the affective mental processes.

token economy. An incentive therapy program using applied principles of operant conditioning through work-payment techniques within wards, classrooms, halfway houses, and other institutional settings. Patients engaging in desired behavior are given tokens (conditions reinforcement) that can be exchanged for items, privileges, or other specified rewards (positive reinforcement).

tolerance. The need for increased doses of a certain drug in order to achieve the same effect originally brought about by smaller doses of the drug.

tool reaction. Lorenz's term for the fact that certain locomotor and manipulation patterns can be used to serve more than one instinctual drive. In human beings, almost all techniques, such as begging, biting, and sucking, are tool reactions, whereas in animals they usually appear in the service of a single drive.

topectomy. Excision of portions of the cerebral cortex in treatment of severe and intractable mental illness; now rarely used.

topographic concepts. Freud's theories of the unconscious, preconscious, and conscious layers of the mind.

torpillage. See p. 70.

total push. A treatment approach, usually in hospital psychiatry, in which every possible resource is employed to help in patients' rehabilitation. This includes occupational and recreational therapy, nursing care, and work with families.

toxic. Having the quality of a poison; able to produce sickness or death.

toxin. A noxious or poisonous agent, usually in the form of a chemical or drug: can originate from within, such as from cell breakdown, or from outside the body, such as from nerve gas.

tradition directed. David Riesman's term for persons who maintain a matter-of-fact attitude toward tradition.

tranquilizers. A class of psychotropic drugs that may be divided into major tranquilizers (antipsychotic drugs) and minor tranquilizers (antianxiety agents).

tranquilizing drug. A central nervous system depressant alleged to be useful in lessening anxiety or tension.

transactional analysis. Psychotherapy aimed at understanding interplay between patient and therapist (ultimately between the patient and his world of reality) using role therapy. See transactional psychology.

transactional psychology. A theoretical approach that sees events involving the individual as occurring within a total system of interdependent subsystems that are intimately and complexly interrelated. It is a recent trend in psychiatric theory and practice and was particularly represented by Eric Berne. The transaction, the central core of the patient's character, is the nature of his relations with others.

transference. See p. 70.

transference neurosis. Freud's term for the type of neurosis that is psychologically determined.

traumatic constitution. Adolph Meyer's term for posttraumatic personality disorder.

triage. See p. 111.

trimethadione. An anticonvulsant medication used in the treatment of epilepsy.

trophotropic. Hess's term for parasympathetic activity; anabolism, excretory functions, reproductive functions, and conservation of energy. (See ergotropy, p. 83.)

twilight sleep. Therapy in which the patient is maintained on a sedative drug, usually one of the barbiturates, in sufficient dosage to keep him in a light sleep state for several days and nights. It is used for more severe mental states, but is not widely accepted in this country at present.

typological psychology. Constitutional psychology based on the theory that personality is related to the type of body fluid.

typology. A study of types; especially associated in psychiatry with Kretschmer.

tyramine. A naturally occurring amine; a sympathomimetic drug. It is an indirectly acting pressor agent.

tyranny of the shoulds. Karen Horney's term for the need of the neurotic person to actualize his idealized image and mold himself into his image of perfection by a system of shoulds, oughts, musts, and must nots.

Umwelt. In existential psychiatry, the surrounding world of an individual; the environment. See Mitwelt.

unaliveness. Fromm's term for a psychological condition in which the person seems not fully alive, as if his total personality is not functioning. The person is not fully aware and not fully responsive.

unconscious. Memories and impulses that were repressed because they were unacceptable to the ego. The repressed wishes are charged with energy that seeks release and may make themselves known in disguised forms. It is a state of total unawareness of sensory stimuli.

unconscious conflict. Confusion, feelings and ambivalence, and inability to resolve a problem, without being consciously aware of these processes. Such processes underlie many emotional problems, and a great deal of effort in therapy is spent helping the patient discover these and resolve them.

undifferentiated ego mass. See p. 71.

unstriped muscle response. In conditioning theories, responses of smooth muscle to stimuli.

uprooting neurosis. Hans Strauss' term for the reaction to a sudden change of residence to a strange land with strange language and socioculture differences, or even a change into a hospital setting. In older persons, especially, this can be cause of mental problems.

urethral eroticism. The urethra is regarded as an erogenous zone by psychoanalysts, who define such activity as undue enjoyment of urination as urethral eroticism; such childhood behavior as letting one's own urine squirt into one's mouth is taken to be evidence of secondary autoeroticism or urethral eroticism.

urethral zone. In psychoanalytic theory, an erogenous zone centering around the urethra is seen as a main determinant of personality. Accordingly, unusually pleasant or unpleasant experiences involving this zone lead to a psychological fixation of this area, or zone, that in turn shapes character formation. As an example, some psychoanalysts claim that an intense burning ambition of those who formerly suffered from enuresis is caused by the influence of such a urethral fixation.

ur phenomenon. A German term used in existential psychiatry and philosophy to denote that the experience of the dasein is original and not derived, having its source on the level of experience, which is prior to the dichotomy of subject and object.

vanillylmandelic acid. A methylated, deaminated metabolic product of norepinephrine.

ventilation. A form of psychotherapy in which the patient tells his thoughts and feelings; sometimes termed ''getting a load off my chest''; catharsis.

verbalization. See p. 71.

viscerotonic. W. H. Sheldon's term for the personality type associated with the endomorph; a relatively uninhibited, emotionally expressive, pleasure-loving personality. See cerebrotonic.

visiting nurse. See p. 111.

vitamin B$_{12}$. A dietary factor necessary for blood production. Impairment of absorption from the gastrointestinal tract leads to a deficiency of this vitamin, with consequent macrocytic anemia and other symptoms, including mental changes (such as confusion, paranoid states, and depression).

vocational rehabilitation. See p. 111.

walk-in clinic. See p. 111.

ward cliques. The grouping of patients on a ward through mutual attractions or interests, or because of organization by a leader. These are sometimes detrimental to overall patient care and are, therefore, discouraged; but they can be used by an alert staff as a therapeutic mode.

ward rounds. See p. 112.

welfare emotions. Sandor Rado's term for such feelings as pleasurable desire, joy, affection, love, and pride; as opposed to emergency emotions.

wetpack. An encasing of wet sheets and blankets that covers the patient from head to foot; used to calm excited and agitated patients. It is not widely used now.

wish fulfillment. The satisfaction of desires that are unacceptable to the superego and that have been repressed into the unconscious. In freudian theory, dreams and fears are examples of fulfillment or attempts at fulfillment of such wishes.

wish, unconscious. Wishes and desires once conscious but now held by repression within the unconscious mind. According to psychoanalytic theory, such wishes become evident through slips of the tongue and dreams.

working through. See p. 71.

xanthines. A group of chemical compounds, some derivatives of which include caffeine (a stimulant drug found in coffee and tea) and theophylline (used as a medication).

xerostomia. Excessive dryness of the mouth; most often seen as a side effect of treatment with major tranquilizers, but also occurs as a neurotic symptom and as a normal fear reaction.

yohimbine. A derivative from the bark of the yohimbe tree; a chemical of interest mainly because of a common but unproved belief that it is an aphrodisiac.

Zeigarnik effect. Memory for interrupted tasks, as described by the Russian psychologist Bluma Zeigarnik.

Zen Buddhism. An oriental religion stressing self-actualization. This system has had much influence on the thinking of psychoanalysts such as Karen Horney and Erich Fromm.

CHAPTER 4

Administrative and legal terminology

ADMINISTRATIVE AND INSTITUTIONAL TERMINOLOGY

Although most administrative and institutional terms associated with matters of mental health are equivalent to those terms as they are used in a general medical context, some terminology related to hospital procedures, record keeping, and similar activities are more specifically associated with the structures within which attention is directed to people who suffer emotional and thought disturbance.

The relationship of general medical practice to law has become prominent only recently. Legal issues have been associated with the care of mentally ill patients for many years. The process of confining a mentally disturbed individual against his will and requiring him to accept treatment for his condition is called commitment. There is no equivalent impingement on individual rights and due process in the practice of general medicine, with the rare exception of mandated quarantine for carriers of some potentially epidemic diseases. Commitment of an individual to a psychiatric facility is based on the judgment of physicians and the court that the individual is dangerous to either himself or others as a result of his mental disorder. The procedures and requirements for committing a patient vary from state to state, and in some instances the judgment of a psychiatrist is not required.

LEGAL TERMINOLOGY

Many strictly legal terms are in wide use in the field of mental health because so many of the clients served by mental health professionals experience legal difficulties as a consequence of their adjustment problems. This is not to imply, however, that they are necessarily criminals; most of the cases of a legal nature are those concerned with marriage and divorce, adoption procedures, negligence, litigation, and disability qualifications. Mental health professionals, especially psychiatrists, are also frequently called on to testify in court as experts on issues such as: (1) a defendant's competence to stand trial or his mental competence at the time of commission of a crime, (2) custody suits in which there is a dispute over the defendant's fitness to be a parent, (3) disability claims or negligence claims, and (4) a person's mental competence to sign a will. Furthermore, representatives of mental health clinics or other mental health services are often asked by courts to provide either some kind of evaluation of or guidance for offenders who are placed on probation. Forensic, or legal, psychiatry is a recognized subspecialty of the psychiatric discipline.

A knowledge of the technical meaning of the legal terms that arise in the course of correspondence concerning clients, either in reports concerning their mental health status or the literature concerning many kinds of mental health problems, becomes necessary for a full understanding of the implications. For those mental health professionals who become deeply involved in community work, a sophisticated understanding of the general issue of constitutional civil rights is also important. A not uncommon problem presented by many mental health clinic clients, for instance, is either an excessive demand for nonexistent civil rights or failure to find access to those rights that do exist.

Any kind of patient record maintained in a hospital, clinic, or physician's office can be subsequently subpoenaed for use in a court proceeding. The possibility of this happening requires the utmost care in maintaining adequate records that can be supported by the physician in a court of law. Thus, for example, standardized, coded diagnostic terms are used even when everyday professional discussion of cases might use different kinds of terminology. Discussions in case conferences might become highly speculative and theoretical, and remarks made in this context might be difficult to defend in an intensive cross-examination. For legal as well as medical reasons, therefore, record keeping should be complete, accurate, and reflective of the clinician's most careful judgment.

GLOSSARY

abandoned child. Legal term for a child whose parents or guardians have been charged with desertion.

abatement. Legal term for abolishment; for example, abatement of a nuisance.

abjuration. Legal term for an oath taken in renunciation of a previously avowed affiliation. Such is the case of the alien who disclaims loyalty to his mother country.

abnormal psychology. The study of deviant thinking and behavior such as might be found in psychiatric patients, criminals, and the mentally retarded.

abrogate. Legal term meaning to repeal or annul.

abscond. Legal term for hiding or secreting oneself from a given location.

accessory. Legal term for a person who assists another in the commission of an offense. If the action is completed after the fact, it is done with the intent of defeating justice; if before, it is done without the accused's presence at the time of the offense.

action. Legal term for a law suit.

adoption (legal). Legal term for the act of accepting a child as a member of the family and assuming the responsibilities of a parent.

affinal. Having identical origin; related by marriage.

age of consent. The age at which one is considered by the law to be able to give consent to marriage or sexual intercourse.

Alcoholics Anonymous. A self-help group of abstinent alcoholics that provides emergency and continuing care to alcoholics. It is a strong and widespread organization in the United States.

alias. Legal term for an assumed name.

alienation (law). Legal term for transfer of confidence or affection from one person to another, such as from a spouse to an extramarital partner.

alienist. An obsolete term for a psychiatrist who testified in court on questions of mental competence.

alimony. Legal term for the monetary allowance required by the court for one party in a divorced marriage to pay regularly to the other.

allegation. Legal term for a declaration or assertion that something is true.

ambisexual. See p. 53.

amelioration. The process of bringing about an improvement by means of relief measures.

American Law Institute Formulation. A.L.I.'s Model Penal Code (section 4.01): "a person is not responsible for criminal conduct if at the time of such conduct as a result of mental disease or defect he lacks substantial capacity either to appreciate the wrongfulness of his conduct or to conform his conduct to the requirements of law."

amicus curiae. Legal term for "friend of the court." A witness might testify as an expert at the behest of the judge, for instance, instead of for the defense or prosecution.

anal intercourse. See p. 53.

analytic psychology. Carl Jung's theoretical approach, using mystical and religious elements in addition to the freudian instinct psychology, to the study of psychiatric problems. He extended Freud's concept of the unconscious to include the racial unconscious—a body of inherited but unconscious problems—and gave a broader definition to libido as being inclusive of all life instincts, rather than just sexuality. His theorizing had a religious and mystical quality. His school of thought has not been represented to any great extent in American psychiatry but has influenced certain popular writers.

anamnesis. The patient's account of his life history.

answerable. Legal term meaning the obligation to make a payment, such as for damages.

appellant. Legal term for one who makes an appeal from a judicial decision.

appurtenance. Legal term for improvements or equipment that belong to a building.

arraignment. Legal term referring to the event in court when the defendant pleads guilty or otherwise to the charge.

assault. Legal term referring to conduct that carries with it the threat of injury to another person.

assign. Legal term for transfer of ownership to a person.

assumption of risk. Legal term referring to the dangers voluntarily accepted when about to undertake a task. Workmen may be assumed, for instance, to accept certain risks of employment.

asylum. Obsolete term for a hospital, usually as an abbreviation for insane asylum or mental hospital.

attachment. Legal term for the court action that takes over possession of a person's property.

attainder. Legal term for the loss of civil rights following imposition of punishment for serious crimes.

bail bond. Legal term for the bond given the court by an accused to guarantee his appearance for trial.

bailiff. A sheriff's assistant and official in a court.

barratry. Legal term for the excessive practice of bringing litigation against others.

battery. Legal term for the unlawful touching of another person, such as when there is an intent to do harm.

bawd. A person who operates a house of prostitution.

bedlam. Bethlehem Hospital; the oldest hospital in England (London, 1377). It became infamous because of the miserable conditions in which the patients were kept. It is now used as a descriptive term for severe hospital or environmental conditions. By association, it has become a noun referring to disorderly or chaotic behavior.

behavioral science. A broad group of sciences that includes psychology, sociology, anthropology, and psychiatry.

bench. Legal term for the judge when he is presiding in court.

beneficiary. Legal term for one who is the recipient of a gift, a legacy, or insurance.

bestiality. See p. 21.

Bicetre Asylum. A mental hospital in Paris, France that was made famous by Phillipe Pinel (1745-1826), who first instituted there humane treatment for the insane in Europe.

bind over. Legal term for requiring a person to appear for trial, usually referring to the action of the grand jury.

bridewell. An obsolete term for a house of correction.

Briggs Law. A Massachusetts law requiring psychiatric examination for lawbreakers who repeatedly commit major crimes.

business agent (union). A union representative who negotiates grievances or contracts with employers.

capias. Legal term for an order to arrest someone.

capital crime (or offense). Legal term for a crime that carries the death penalty.

care and protection proceedings. Legal intervention through court proceedings on behalf of the welfare, health, and education of a minor child when the parents or caretakers cannot or will not provide for these.

carnal abuse. Legal term for illegal sexual offenses toward a minor.

case history. The record of contacts between agency and client in medical or social work.

case method. Teaching in medicine or social work by use of actual case histories.

case work. The clinical work of the psychiatric social worker; includes group therapy, counseling of families of patients, rehabilitation, and job placement.

catamnesis. Medical history of a patient during and following an illness.

caveat emptor. "Let the buyer beware," meaning that the buyer assumes the risk of ownership after he purchases the merchandise.

central index. Social service exchange; a community-wide repository of information on all clients serviced by local agencies.

certifiable. Legal term for the status of a person who is ruled eligible for commitment to an institution.

chancery court. A court that has jurisdiction over equity cases.

chattels. Legal term for personal property other than real estate.

check-off. The procedure by which the employer collects union dues from those employees who are union members.

child guidance movement. A movement, begun by William Healy, that led to care of the child as a patient.

child psychiatry. A branch of psychiatry dealing with care and treatment of mentally ill children and adolescents.

child psychology. Pediatric psychology; the study of childhood development and behavior.

chiromancy. Foretelling one's fortune through signs alledgedly read in the palm of the hand; palmistry.

chiropodist. A person who offers minor services in the care of the feet.

chiropractic. A type of pseudomedical practice in

which the practitioner typically makes spinal adjustments; considered to be a cult.

citation. A legal term ordering a person to appear on a certain day for some purpose or to show cause why he should not.

civil malpractice. Legal term for the type of malpractice observed when no criminal negligence is involved.

civil rights. Those rights guaranteed the individual by the constitution or by the government.

clinic. A medical service agency where various specialists offer diagnostic and treatment services. It is often erroneously referred to as a place where free medical care is given.

clinical nurse specialist in psychiatric nursing. A registered nurse with advanced preparation, at the masters or postmasters level in psychotherapeutic nursing care; assigned to the nursing unit in a nonadministrative capacity to provide and promote better nursing care; gives direct care to patients and provides consultative service to the nursing staff regarding nursing care. Would serve as a member of the Interdisciplinary team, conduct in in-service education, as a role model dealing with difficult patients, as a coordinator of student activities, and to initiate and participate in research; works in such facilities as inpatient prehospital and posthospital, nursing home care, and hospital-based home-care programs.

clinical psychology. A branch of professional psychology that is involved in the treatment of patients with psychiatric problems. It developed as part of a psychiatric team including a psychiatrist, a social worker, and a psychologist. The function of the first was to treat the patient, of the second to deal with the family and community, and of the third to do psychological testing. Since then, the clinical psychologist has become more autonomous and functions alone as a therapist. It is the application of psychology to clinical psychiatry. The clinical psychologist originally confined his role to psychological testing, but now participates in some clinics in actual treatment of psychiatric problems.

codicil. Legal term for an amendment to a will.

cognizance. Legal term for the recognition of some fact.

cohabitation. Living together, usually without being married.

collective bargaining. A technique of negotiating union contracts with employers, in which the bargaining takes place industry-wide or at least with a number of related companies.

commitment. The legal processes involved in bringing about a nonvoluntary admission to a mental hospital. In law, the same term also applies to the process of incarceration in prison. Since the process is a legal procedure, it is invariably associated with certain legal safeguards. It is sometimes erroneously assumed that physicians make commitments, when, in fact, only courts can legally do this. It is a legal term for deprivation of liberty, such as to a prison or mental hospital. Constitutionally, this can only be done through due process of law.

common-law marriage. Legal term for a relationship between a man and a woman not formally married, but that is of sufficient duration to constitute a de facto marriage.

community property. Legal term for the statutory provision that husband and wife share equal ownership in property acquired during the marriage. California, for instance, has such a law.

commutation of sentence. Legal term for the lessening of a court-awarded sentence, usually by the state's governor, such as the lessening of the death penalty to life imprisonment.

comparative psychology. The study of thinking or behavior or both of different species of animals.

compensation neurosis. See p. 23.

competence. A legal term measuring the capacity to use reasonable judgment in the conduct of one's affairs.

competency to stand trial. Determination of a defendant's state of mind at the time of trial. Competency is assumed if the accused understands the nature of the charges against him, the consequences should he be convicted, and is able to assist his attorney in his defense.

complaint. Legal term for the statement of the complainant's or plaintiff's case.

conditioned reflex psychology. Psychology derived from the physiological experiments of Pavlov. The stimulus-response psychologists are a group who practice according to this psychology.

confiscation. Legal term for the court seizure of property without compensation, as might be done in the case of stolen goods.

conflict. The coexistence of opposing ideas or feelings on the same subject. Such a state may lead to indecision, anxiety, or aberrant behavior.

consanguinity. Relationships between people having common ancestry. Most states specify the degree of consanguinity within which marriage can take place (for example, siblings, first cousins, and so on).

conscientious objector. A person who objects to service in the armed forces on grounds of conscience. Exemption from military service is usually made with the understanding that the person will give some kind of equivalent service.

constitutional psychology. A movement started by Ernst Kretschmer's attempt to link constitutional body types (configuration of the body) with personality types.

consultation. Seeking of advice by the therapist or the patient from someone else, usually from an expert or a specialist.

content psychology. Franz Brentano's emphasis on the difference between an act (or hearing, for example) and the content (of what is heard).

contract. Legal term for an agreement between two parties, whereby one does something in exchange for compensation from the other.

contributory negligence. Legal term referring to the degree to which a claimant in a negligence suit might himself have contributed to the cause of the accident.

convalescent home. A nursing home or institution where people who do not require the highly specialized and expensive facilities of a hospital may recover from illness and injury.

conviction. Legal term for finding the defendant guilty.

correspondent. Legal term for a person who is required to respond with another person to an action. Usually this means the third party in a divorce suit.

coroner's jury. Legal term for a jury selected to establish the cause of death when this is in doubt. It does not include the prosecution of an accused for murder or negligence, however.

corporal punishment. Punishment administered in the form of physical application of force, such as whipping or execution.

correctional institution. Any of the various types of prisons, including so-called training schools, reform schools, workhouses, and so on.

counseling. A use of guidance and supportive techniques; used by psychologists, social workers, pastors, and others mainly in aiding persons not severely psychologically disturbed.

counterclaim. Legal term for the claim made by party A against party B, after B has already made a claim against A.

court calendar. The schedule of cases appearing before a court.

credit union. A cooperative society, usually of workers, set up to lend money to its members.

crime. An act of commission or omission that is against the law; a legal definition meaning breaking of the law.

criminal. Something relating to the nature of crime; one who has been identified as having committed a crime.

criminal malpractice. Legal term for the type of malpractice in which damage results from action that is itself illegal (for example, illegal abortion).

criminal responsibility. The term derived from the legal concept that all persons who commit crimes are not equally responsible (for example, children, who are not regarded by the law as subject to the same conditions as adults in the commission of crime; mentally retarded, who are treated as children in Anglo-Saxon law; and, more recently, some psychotic persons). Such persons are considered not responsible for crimes committed. The various state criminal codes provide for legal tests of the degree of responsibility. Generally, the term applies to a defendant's state of mind at the time of the alleged crime. The defendant cannot be convicted if it is proved that he lacked ability to formulate criminal interest at the time of the crime.

crisis clinic. A type of psychiatric treatment clinic where persons undergoing acute psychological distress can receive immediate attention and short-term follow-up care; as opposed to the conventional psychiatric clinic, where the patient is placed on a waiting list and seen for treatment after several days or weeks.

cross-cultural psychiatry. The studies of differences and similarities in epidemiological patterns of mental illness in various cultures.

cross-examination. Legal term for the questioning of a witness by the attorney on the other side of the adversary proceeding. If the witness represents the defense, then cross-examination is by the prosecution.

cruelty. See p. 57.

custodial care. The provision of food, housing, and other physical care, without psychiatric or medical treatment, for a person in an institution.

day care. The provision for supervised care during the day, such as care for small children of working mothers.

day hospital. An alternative to full-time hospital care that requires less dislocation of the patient's life. Typically, the patient appears during certain hours of the day at a treatment center but sleeps at home.

decedent. Legal term for a dead person.

decree. Legal term for a decision from court in cases of equity, such as a divorce decree.

de facto. Legal term for something that actually exists or is being practiced, even though not legally acknowledged.

default. Legal term for failure to appear in court or to answer a court order.

defendant. A legal term for the person accused of a crime.

de jure. Legal term for a situation that is practiced or is in existence as a result of the passing of a law.

descriptive psychiatry. A type of psychiatric study or practice that merely describes what is observed without attempting to theorize about cause.

desertion. Legal term for the act of absenting onself from a responsibility.

desocialization. Diminished social contact, depreciation of social values, meanings, and values; often seen in persons with an intellectual deficit.

detention home (center). A temporary shelter for people, usually children, awaiting court action.

developmental psychology. The psychological study of the maturation process in children. Stanley Hall referred to his type of psychology as genetic psychology, and portrayed the development of a child in evolutionary terms.

deviant sexual behavior. See p. 25.

differential psychology. The emphasis on individual differences in psychology. Francis Galton's concepts of hereditary genius were of this type.

direct examination. Legal term for the initial questioning of a witness in court for the purpose of uncovering facts.

disorderly conduct. Legal term for a charge against a person alleged to have disturbed the peace or engaged in improper conduct.

disposing mind. Legal term for the state of mind of a person drawing up a will, indicating that he is doing it with the intent of disposing of his property (not under duress, for example).

dispossess. Legal term for the lawful deprivation of a person's right to reside in a given place.

documentary evidence. Facts supported by written documents.

domestic relations court. A special court or a special court term devoted to hearing cases pertaining to family conflicts.

double jeopardy. Legal term for the charging of a person with the same crime more than once. This is prohibited by the Constitution.

due process of law. Legal term for the formal and regular exercise of legal authority. The Constitu-

tion prohibits the deprivation of civil rights unless done through due process.

Durham Rule. A criminal law based on the court decision that if the unlawful act is the result of mental illness, the accused will not be held criminally responsible for the act. In the District of Columbia, it has been replaced by the American Law Institute Formulation.

dying declaration. Legal term for verbal dispositions of property when the subject is knowingly on the verge of death. The assumption is made that under circumstances of this sort there would be no motive to defraud or lie.

dynamic psychiatry. Therapy using or subscribing to psychoanalytic techniques and theories.

dynamic psychology. Those qualities of human thinking and behavior that demonstrate the unconscious motivations and mechanisms described by psychoanalytic theory. It is not to be confused with the term dynamics as used in psychoanalysis. Robert Woodworth called his type of psychology by this term. He meant, simply, that psychology is properly the study of causes and effects of thought and action.

easement. Legal term for the granting of rights to use a right of way, for instance, through another person's property.

educational psychology. The application of psychological studies of learning in children and training of teachers.

emancipated minor. A minor considered to have the rights of an adult when demonstrated that the minor is in fact exercising general control over his or her life.

embezzle. Legal term for the fraudulent use of funds or property entrusted to one for safekeeping.

engineering psychology. Human engineering, human factors, or other similar terms referring to the application of psychological study methods to industrial and design problems.

epinosic gain. See p. 26.

escrow. Legal term for the entrusting of funds to a third party, pending completion of a contract by the two principals.

euthanasia. The practice of mercy killing; in the case of a person with some hopeless medical state, assisting or passively permitting that person to die. Movements occasionally appear to legalize the practice.

exhibitionism. See p. 26.

ex parte. Legal term for a procedure conducted in the absence of one of the parties.

expatriation. A court order or act by the immigration department to return an alien to his parent country.

experience psychology. Empirical psychology (See p. 83.)

experimental psychology. The laboratory study of psychological phenomena, usually physiological studies of animals, though human psychological investigations are also carried out under the controlled conditions of the laboratory.

false confession. See p. 27.

family care. Placement of discharged mental patients with a suitable family; a type of after-care.

family history. The record taken of the relevant information concerning members of a client's or patient's family in case work or medical practice.

felony. Legal term for a serious crime; misdemeanor is the term for a minor crime.

forensic psychiatry. The legal aspects of psychiatry. This usually takes the form of making determinations of mental competence for legal purposes (such as competence to make a will and criminal responsibility).

fornication. Sexual intercourse between a man and woman not married to each other.

foster family. A family selected to give care to a discharged mental patient. The family is usually not closely related and is often paid or supervised regularly to assure reasonable standards of care for the patient.

foster parents. Substitutes for natural parents.

fraternal twins. Twins born from the same pregnancy but of separate ovum-sperm union; not identical and may be of opposite sexes.

fraud. Legal term for deliberate misrepresentation that does damage to another.

Ganser's syndrome. See p. 28.

garnishment. Legal term for a court judgment prescribing that an employer will deduct certain amounts from a worker's pay to discharge a debt.

gault decision. A landmark court decision stating that juvenile court proceedings must follow due process and fair treatment guaranteed under the fourteenth amendment. The juvenile must be given proper notice of the charges, must be represented by counsel, protected against self-incrimination, and allowed to confront and cross-examine witnesses.

geriatric psychiatry. A branch of psychiatry that deals with the special mental and emotional problems of the aged.

gerontology. The study of old age.

grant-in-aid. Funds given by federal or state governments to lower jurisdictions to help finance local services.

graveyard shift. The nighttime (after midnight) work shift.

group perversion. See p. 28.

guardian. Legal term for a person legally appointed to act in the interests of another person not deemed capable of taking the responsibility. Such might be the case of a child or a mentally incompetent person.

habeas corpus, writ of. Legal term for a court order to free a person from confinement on the grounds that commitment was made for insufficient reasons or was accomplished without due process of law.

habitual offender. A person who frequently comes to the attention of a court for misconduct.

halfway house. An institution that functions as an open hospital and as a day center within the community to which patients from traditional psychiatric hospitals are sent. The patients are encouraged to work, become involved in community activities, and continue in some form of psychotherapy, thereby gradually becoming readjusted to being out of the hospital.

Harrison Drug Act (1914). Federal legislation aimed at control of narcotics through policing and taxing rather than through education and treatment. It requires licensure of physicians and anyone else involved in the dispensing of narcotic drugs.

hearsay evidence. Legal term for evidence a witness reports as having come from another person.

highway hypnosis. See p. 131.

homosexual. See p. 29.

hypothetical question. Legal term for a technique often used in eliciting testimony from an expert witness who has no personal knowledge of the crime or alleged negligence. The attorney presents the facts "as if" they represented an actual case and asks the expert to state his opinion.

impeach. Legal term for the process of charging an official with neglect of duty.

incest. See p. 30.

incommunicado. Legal term for the condition of isolating a person from any communication with his associates, attorney, and others.

incompetence. A legal term meaning the lack of capacity to use reasonable judgment in the conduct of the affairs of life. Forensic psychiatry is largely concerned with questions of mental competence.

incompetent. Legal term for the condition found in a person that declares him unable to act in his own interests by reason of mental defect or psychosis.

indemnify. Legal term for the process of compensating for loss.

indenture. Legal term for a contract binding two persons.

indictment. Legal term for the written statement that is prepared by the prosecution, that is approved by a grand jury, and that charges a defendant with a crime.

industrial psychology. Psychology, especially experimentation applied to industrial work. This includes the study of worker's behavior, motivation, performance, and work environment.

inebriate. See p. 131.

injunction. Legal term for a court order prohibiting some action, such as a strike.

inpatient, outpatient. Persons obtaining hospital treatment are distinguished according to whether they stay longer than 24 hours. If longer, they are inpatients; if shorter, they are outpatients; although the latter might return for repeated visits.

inquirendo de lunatico. Legal term for a formal court hearing to determine a person's sanity.

insanity defense. A ploy most often used in crimes that carry the death penalty, in which the defendant is held unaccountable for his actions because of his mental condition. The premise is that when an alleged criminal has not shown intent to do harm by reason of insanity there is lack of criminal responsibility and thus he cannot be convicted.

institution. Any organized place or service in which clients are likely to be housed for substantial periods of time, such as a hospital, prison, school, nursing home for the aged, or orphanage.

instrument. Legal term for any legal document; psychological term for any test or measuring device.

invalidism. See p. 37.

involuntary servitude. The condition of forced labor.

irresistible impulse. An inner psychic disturbance that drives the person into irresistible actions that may be illegal (for example, kleptomania). The demonstration of irresistible impulse may be used as grounds for establishing innocence by reason of insanity.

joinder. Legal term for the merging of two complaints or suits.

joint liability. Legal term for the state of being legally responsible for another's actions, such as in a partnership.

journeyman. In a craft union, a person who has completed his apprenticeship.

juvenile. The period of life including puberty and adolescence.

katasexual. See p. 31.

kibbutz. A child-rearing institution used in Israel, in which communal grouping and housing, under the supervision of substitute parents, carry out the functions of the child's own parents.

kinship. Blood relationship of individuals of common ancestry.

kleptomania. See p. 37.

lay therapist. A nonprofessional psychotherapist (such as one without the training and credentials of a psychiatrist, clinical psychologist, social worker, or psychoanalyst).

lesbian. See p. 32.

lethal catatonia. See p. 32.

liaison. Consultation between psychiatrists and other practitioners; especially where a regular consultation service is in effect.

libel. Legal term meaning any publication or statement that exposes someone to public contempt or ridicule, whether accurate or not.

lie detection test. See p. 32.

lie detector. See p. 32.

lien. Legal term for judgment that a person is entitled to receive payment for a debt. Often the lien is attached to property so that transfer of ownership carries with it the debt in question.

life chart. A patient's chronological life history gathered to assist the therapist in understanding the patient. The organized recording of such data was instituted by Adolph Meyer and is still suitable for use in psychiatry.

line organization. The channel of command in an organization, in contrast to staff organization.

liquidation (of assets). The process of dividing the assets of an organization in order to pay off debts and obligations; often preparatory to dissolution of the organization.

logistics. The activities and organization associated with the collection and distribution of material, supplies, products, manpower, and other resources.

London School. Name given to the psychological laboratory at the University College of London under the directorship of Charles Spearman during the first quarter of the twentieth century. It became a widely known center of training.

lunacy. See p. 32.

lunatic. See p. 132.

lust murder. See p. 32.

mactation. See p. 32.

malfeasance. Legal term for practices that are illegal or contrary to one's expected duties; especially as applied to a public official.

malingering. See p. 32.

mandamus (writ). Legal term for a document of a court directing a person to do something that is specified in the writ.

manslaughter. Legal term for the killing of another person through a negligent action.

manual training. Training in the use of tools and craftwork.

mens rea. Legal term meaning guilty mind or wrongful intent.

mental hospital. A hospital specializing in the care and treatment of the mentally ill.

mental hygiene. Originally, it was a term meaning good health as applied to psychiatric status. It now connotes preventive public education movements for psychiatric issues.

mental incompetence. Generally means that the person is unable to perform certain legal acts (such as sign contracts) and that he does not understand the nature or purpose of the transaction. There are no closely defined or universally applicable criteria to determine competency.

mental status. The total mental, emotional, and behavioral state of a person. Such determinations are made by psychiatrists through clinical evaluation, psychological tests, and interviews with family and community agencies.

milieu. The environment.

military psychiatry. Psychiatry used in the armed services; essentially a form of occupational and social psychiatry in which preventive measures are stressed.

misdemeanor. Legal term meaning a minor crime.

McNaughten Rule. In criminal law, in order to use the plea of insanity as a defense, it must be proved that at the time the crime was committed the accused person must have been of such a mental state as to be unaware of the nature and quality of his action or unaware that it was wrong.

module. A component of a system that can be added to or subtracted from the total to make it more or less complex.

naturopath. A pseudomedical practitioner who relies chiefly on exercise and diet for his prescriptions.

negligence. Legal term for the failure to exercise reasonable care in one's activities, thus endangering others.

nepotism. Favoring one's relatives in the allocation of jobs.

neurology. A specialized branch of medicine involved in the study and treatment of diseases and injuries to the brain, spinal cord, and peripheral nerves. Many of the organically oriented psychiatrists have placed much stress on neurology. Freud himself was originally a neurologist.

neuropsychiatry. A medical specialty in which both neurological and psychological conditions are treated. More commonly now, a specialist is either a neurologist or a psychiatrist.

neuropsychology. The study of the central nervous system in order to shed light on psychological phenomena. Ebbinghaus stated that one of neuropsychology's great contributions was the realization that the ancient search for the seat of the soul was pointless.

night hospital. A treatment situation in which the patient works or is home during the day, but returns to the hospital during the evening for inpatient therapy and to spend the night. This is usually part of a transition from complete inpatient status to complete discharge from the hospital.

nolle pros. Legal term meaning that a formal statement has been made dropping the charges against a person.

nomenclature. The formal classification system used in naming the elements of interest in a science, such as the diagnoses in medicine or the names of anatomical parts.

non compos mentis. A legal term meaning not mentally competent.

non suit. Legal term meaning an adjudication to the effect that the plaintiff's case is not good enough to require the defendant to proceed with his case.

nonsupport. Failure to provide for the subsistence of someone for whom one has responsibility (such as a wife or children).

non vult. Legal term used to indicate that the defendant is unwilling to stand trial in his defense because of the strength of the prosecution's case. As a plea, it is tantamount to a plea of guilty.

nursery school. A preschool setting for day care of children.

nymphomania. See p. 34.

obscenity. See p. 132.

occupational psychiatry. Study and treatment of

mental problems of workers, the work environment, and employee-employer relationships.

occupational therapy. A hospital treatment modality designed to retrain physically or mentally ill patients in skills and activities important to normal functioning. Seldom involves actual job training, but rather uses crafts, hobbies, and various tasks of progressive difficulty to help patients develop generally sound *habits* of socialization and productivity.

occupation neurosis. See p. 35.

old age benefits. Insurance premiums paid to retired persons, especially those coming under the provisions of Social Security.

one-way mirror. A glass panel between two rooms. The glass is specially tinted so that when one of the two rooms is darkened the glass reflects light back into the lighted room and therefore takes on the appearance of a mirror.

ontoanalysis. Daseinanalysis.

open-door. Open hospital.

open hospital. A hospital setting in which minimal or no locked doors are used; usually associated with general or community hospitals; it requires that the patient be admitted on a voluntary status.

opiumism. See p. 35.

ordinary life insurance. Life insurance in which the individual pays premiums throughout his life.

orgy. See p. 132.

orthopsychiatry. Psychiatric study and treatment of children; preventive psychiatry. It is synonymous with mental hygiene.

outpatient. A person being treated during regular visits to the therapist without being admitted to a hospital. The distinction between outpatient and inpatient is being blurred now by the flexibility offered by day hospital and night hospital programs.

paid-up insurance. A type of life insurance in which the individual pays premiums only for a specified number of years.

paraphilia. See p. 36.

parens patriae. Legal term for the right of a court or state to act as guardian for someone (such as a child) who is unable to look after his own interests.

paresis. See p. 36.

parole. Legal term for the shortening of a prison sentence with the provision that activity outside of prison will be supervised by an official or responsible person.

partial hospitalization. A form of inpatient psychi-

atric treatment in which the person is allowed extensive activities outside the hospital.

patient government. The inclusion of patients in the administration of a psychiatric ward. This is usually done formally with the election of representatives and other officials from the patient group.

pauper's oath. Legal term for a sworn statement that a person is unable to afford the costs of litigation.

Pedagogical Seminary. The first journal of child psychology, founded by Stanley Hall in 1891 and renamed *Journal of Genetic Psychology* in 1927.

pederasty. See p. 37.

pedicatio. See p. 37.

perversio horribilis. See p. 37.

perversion. See p. 37.

pervert. See p. 37.

phylogenetics. The study of the racial history of an organism.

placement. The process, in social work, of locating a person in a new job, a foster home, or a treatment situation.

plaintiff. The legal term referring to the person in a civil suit who is making a claim on another person.

pornography. See p. 132.

post-K2 syndrome. See p. 38.

postmortem. After death; sometimes used to mean autopsy.

posttraumatic syndrome. See p. 38.

predeviate. See p. 38.

preliminary examination. Legal term for a hearing preceding a trial to determine if there is enough evidence to warrant a trial.

presumptive puberty. The assumption that boys over the age of 14 and girls over 12 are old enough to have children.

pretraumatic personality. See p. 39.

preventive psychiatry. A function of community psychiatry most often associated with the name of Gerald Caplan, who has brought some of the principles of public health into psychiatry. In this, the psychiatrist attempts to reduce the incidence of psychiatric disorders as well as to help remove the disabilities already in existence in psychiatric patients.

prima facie (evidence). Legal term for evidence that has self-evident implications.

prison psychosis. See p. 39.

private agency. An agency, such as a social welfare agency, that is administered and financed by non-governmental sources, except in the case when private agencies become recipients of certain grants from the government.

privilege. The statutory right of a patient to prevent his physician from giving testimony using information obtained in the course of treatment by the physician.

privileged communication. Refers to the confidential nature of communications between patient and psychiatrist. In many states this confidentiality is protected by law so that the psychotherapist cannot be legally compelled to reveal, even in court, information he has obtained during therapy. The law is changing and exceptions to the rule are now being made.

prognosis. The prediction of the outcome of a disease.

progress notes. Notations made weekly by the physicians, nurses, and therapists in the patient's hospital chart, but may be made at any time when something of importance happens concerning the patient.

prosthesis. In medicine, a device, such as an artificial leg, that assists a disabled person to make fuller use of his body.

prostitution. Engagement in promiscuous sexual activity for pay.

psychiatric aide. The title given in some hospitals to a person working in mental hospital wards under supervision from a registered nurse, helping to treat patients. Generally, the person is trained by the institution for which he works and does not have the broad formal training that a registered nurse or licensed practical nurse would have.

psychiatric hospitals. Mental hospitals.

psychiatric interview. A meeting of the psychiatrist and patient for evaluation and treatment. Early in the course of therapy these sessions are often more for data gathering, with the therapist actively seeking information, but proceeding to intensive therapy with little verbal participation from the therapist.

psychiatric nurse. A registered nurse specializing in the care and treatment of the mentally ill. Ideally, will have special training and experience in management of psychiatric patients. Sometimes, only nurses with advanced degrees in psychiatric nursing. The nurse may work in a variety of therapeutic settings (community mental clinic, acute and chronic inpatient units, outpatient clinics, day hospitals, and research units). May have administrative responsibility over ward with program planning, supervising milieu therapy, recreational and group psychotherapy.

psychiatric patient. A person under psychiatric care as an inpatient or outpatient.

psychiatric social worker. A person specially trained to work in psychiatric hospitals and clinics and in social service agencies to help deliver care to the mentally ill. They may work as part of a treatment team and, as such, deal mainly with families; however, many are trained to give individual and group psychotherapy.

psychiatric team. A group of persons with various levels of training who are dedicated to treating mental patients. It usually includes a psychiatrist, a psychologist, a social worker, a nurse, and a nurse's aide; but in a real milieu program, all hospital employees and patients are included to one degree or another. It is often a misused term loosely applied to any collection of persons working on a psychiatric ward, who may not be interested in working together.

psychiatrist. A specialized physician trained to treat the mentally ill.

psychiatry. The study and treatment of people having disorders of the mind.

psychical research. Parapsychology; studies of extrasensory perception.

psychoanalyst. A psychiatrist who takes additional training in psychoanalysis. Nonphysician therapists are no longer accepted in most psychoanalytic institutes.

psychobiology. Psychiatry taught at Johns Hopkins University under Adolf Meyer; originally similar to functional psychology in that emphasis was placed on the adaptational nature of behavior, and psychiatric syndromes were seen as failure in adaptation.

psychodrama. Groups of patients in supervised dramatic settings in which inner conflicts and psychological problems are verbalized and are acted out, with other performers acting as important persons in the patient's life.

psychology. The study of thinking and behavior in animals and man, based chiefly on statistical techniques.

psychopathia sexualis. See p. 40.

psychopathology. Abnormal psychological functions (such as delusions, hallucinations, illusions); broadly, any mental or emotional state that requires therapy.

psychopharmacology. The study of or use of drugs having an effect on the central nervous system.

psychophysics. The study of vision, hearing, smell,

touch, and proprioception in relation to psychology.

psychosomatic medicine. Awareness of and search for relationships between emotions and bodily symptoms.

psychotechnology. Practical applications of psychology (such as industrial psychology).

public agency. An agency that is administered by the government and supported by tax money, such as a social welfare agency, as opposed to a private agency.

public domain. Belonging to the public at large. An expired copyright, for instance, becomes part of the public domain.

putative father. A man reputed to be the father of a child.

pyromania. See p. 40.

quality control. The process employed in a factory, for instance, to maintain output of products according to a set of standards. This includes inspection at various stages of the manufacturing process and rejection of substandard units.

quarantine. A period of forced isolation from the community; usually caused by a disease being present in a household, a ship, a building, or even a country.

questionnaire. A formalized series of questions designed to collect information from populations.

quitclaim. A document giving up the rights to certain property.

rape. Legal term for a criminal sexual attack upon a woman under any one of the four circumstances: (1) if she is below the legal age of consent, (2) if it is by force and against her will, (3) if she is subject to duress that renders her fearful of noncompliance, or (4) if it is done through deceit or trickery.

recidivist. A repeated offender.

recognizance. Legal term for an obligation to do something, such as reappear in court.

registered nurse (R.N.). A nurse who has successfully passed a 2- and 3-year training course and licensure examination and thus is eligible for a state license.

reprieve. Legal term for a temporary postponement of sentence.

research, psychiatric. Scientific attempts to find new data on causes, effects, treatment, and management of psychiatric patients and problems.

residential treatment. Specialized treatment centers for children; ranging in type from special schools for mildly disturbed children, to state hospital units for the care of chronically and severely mentally ill children.

res ipsa loquitur. Legal term meaning "the thing speaks for itself." The assumption used by the plaintiff is that any damages incurred as a result of the defendant's actions were, necessarily, indicative of negligence on the part of the latter.

restraints. Devices or measures (such as camisoles, packs) used to control violent or destructive behavior.

retrograde amnesia. See p. 41.

right to treatment. Legal definition of the obligation of a facility to provide adequate treatment for individuals for whom that facility has assumed responsibility for providing treatment.

rooming-in. Housing the mother and her newborn child in the same hospital room to allow greater physical contact and the formation of earlier emotional bonds between the two.

sadism. See p. 41.

sadomasochism. See p. 41.

sane. Of sound mind.

sanitarian. A public health worker trained in sanitation engineering.

sanity. Soundness of mind.

sapphism. See p. 41.

school psychiatry. Practice of psychiatry in a school setting. This may range from consultation by the psychiatrist on specific and general problems in a public school, to the development of special treatment boarding schools, or to practicing as a student health psychiatrist in a college or university.

sexual deviate. Pervert.

sexual deviation. A pattern of sexual activity carried out to satisfy sexual needs other than those gratified by normal coitus. This activity is impulsive and inflexible, with the individual being unable to resist the impulse or to change his behavior. Examples are exhibitionism, fetishism, frottage, masochism, necrosadism, pedophilia, pornographomania, voyeurism, and zoophilia.

shell shock. See p. 42.

sign. See p. 42.

slander. Legal term for spoken libel.

social hygiene. A type of social work concerned with prostitution or venereal disease problems, drug dependency, and so on.

social psychiatry. A term applied to a psychiatric movement that departs from the traditional face-to-face relationship of physician to patient and is instead concerned with sociological backgrounds of people's problems.

social psychology. The application of psychological methods of study to social groups; often indistinguishable from sociology.

sodomy. A sexual perversion (penis to anus; sometimes, mouth to genitals); broadly, includes intercourse with animals or corpses.

space medicine. A new subspecialty of medicine that deals with the problems of very rapid flight at extremely high altitudes. Such variables as decompression, acceleration, hypoxia, weightlessness, cosmic radiation, extreme variations in temperature, and isolation are some of the problems in this area.

space psychiatry. The study and treatment of special problems in and of psychological reactions to space flights.

staff organization. Allocation of responsibility according to levels of expertise instead of authority; distinguished from line organization.

statute of limitations. Legal term for a number of specified years following the commission of a crime after which a person cannot be prosecuted for the crime.

subpoena. Legal term for a written court order requiring that a person appear in court.

subpoena duces tecum. Legal term referring to a subpoena requiring a witness to produce certain records in court. Medical testimony, particularly, may be subpoenaed this way.

suicide. Taking one's own life; a frequently used method of resolving psychological problems, either by actually commiting the act or by simulating an attempt.

suicide risk. The likelihood that a person will commit suicide. A severely depressed person is more likely to commit suicide than a normal person, so that it may be said that the suicide risk is increased in severe depression.

surrogate. Substitute (such as parental surrogates, people who are not real parents, but who may serve as such).

Synanon. A self-help group of drug addicts in which praise, exhortation, and group acceptance or rejection are used to help motivate the individual to conquer his drug dependency.

technological unemployment. Reduction in the number of workers needed by an industry as a result of mechanization.

telecommunication. Transfer of information across long distances.

terror neurosis. See p. 43.

testamentary capacity. The mental ability to make a valid will.

testator. Legal term for a person making his will.

tort. Legal term for negligence arising in the discharge of duty and not in violation of a contract. Malpractice suits are usually tort actions.

tort-feasor. Legal term for one who commits a tort.

total disability. A legal determination supported by medical evidence that an injury or disease renders a person totally unable to work.

transvestite. See p. 44.

transvestism. See p. 44.

trauma. See p. 44.

traumatic. See p. 44.

traumatic encephalopathy. See p. 44.

traumatic neurosis. See p. 44.

traumatic neurosis, subacute phase. See p. 44.

triage. The process of selecting patients for treatment; especially during a major disaster where classification of patients into groups of those needing immediate attention and those less severely affected is mandatory.

truancy. Absence from school or work without permission; shirking or neglecting one's duties.

twins. A pair of individuals produced in one pregnancy and birth. Identical twins are produced from a single ovum and sperm. Fraternal twins are produced from separate ova, each fertilized by a different sperm.

undue influence. Legal term referring to the circumstances under which a will might have been drawn up, indicating that the testator was influenced by another to make decisions against his wishes.

uranism. See p. 45.

uxoricide. Murder by a husband of his wife.

visiting nurse. A registered nurse who makes regular treatment visits to homes of mental patients as part of an aftercare program.

visiting teacher. An instructor working on a private basis or as part of the public school system, who goes to the homebound patient; also a term sometimes used for a social worker who works with school children and their families and with principals and teachers to effect changes in home and school conditions for children who are having difficulty in school.

vocational rehabilitation. A service often administered by a state division of vocational rehabilitation that determines eligibility and arranges for disabled workers to obtain occupational retraining or prosthetic appliances.

voyeur. See p. 45.

voyeurism. See p. 45.

waiver. Legal term for the voluntary relinquishment of certain rights. A defendant might, for instance, waive his right to a jury.

walk-in clinic. A psychiatric clinic organized to give immediate care to disturbed persons. Such persons may come directly to the clinic or be referred from a hospital emergency room, without being placed on a waiting list. Such clinics are usually part of a community psychiatry program.

ward rounds. The daily or weekly meeting of all the patients on the ward by the psychiatrist and his staff. This is usually carried out in an organized fashion, and its purpose is to take care of medical and practical problems of the patients rather than for psychotherapy.

war neurosis. See p. 45.

wills, psychiatric aspects of. In order to carry out the writing and signing of a will, a person must be mentally competent; he must understand the nature and effect of this transaction; and he must know the limits of his bounty. Psychiatrists are often asked to help determine mental competence.

work capacity. Generally taken as the ability to carry out gainful employment. This can be impaired even where function for other activities is minimally affected.

workmen's compensation. Payment for time lost from work caused by injuries sustained at work; usually required by state law and facilitated through workmen's compensation insurance obtained by the employer.

writ of certiorari. Legal term for a court order from a higher court requiring a lower court to send the proceedings of a trial for review.

zooerastia. See p. 46.

zoolagnia. See p. 46.

zoosadism. See p. 46.

CHAPTER 5

Related sciences

GENERAL MEDICAL TERMINOLOGY

To a considerable extent, practitioners in mental health and the behavioral sciences use terms found in the various medical specialties, and a number of specific terms tend to be used repeatedly. Some of the ways in which general medical terms have a rather special application to mental health terms include:

1. Biochemistry and physiology. In discussions about emotional reactions, stress reactions, and sensory phenomena, as well as in behavioral research on these subjects, an understanding of basic physiological and biochemical processes is important. Subjects dealing with homeostasis, for instance, concern whole-body responses to stress in which optimal equilibriums are maintained. Thus, they also involve emotional reactions and situations. Therefore, this leads to information about the function of the adrenal glands, of the cardiovascular system, and so on. In addition, many of the external manifestations, seen either clinically or in research studies, of psychological problems are in the form of physiological changes (such as changes in blood pressure).

2. Psychosomatic conditions. There are conditions found in human beings that are often thought to be a combination of psychological and physical abnormalities. A peptic ulcer is one example. In these cases, then, the interaction of purely medical phenomena and psychological phenomena becomes a subject of interest.

3. Differential diagnosis. In many cases, the choice of appropriate diagnosis of a given condition lies between that of a serious physical disability and a psychological problem. Real versus imagined heart attacks, for instance, are frequent examples.

4. Treatment. References can be found in the literature to old types of treatment that employed methods common to nonpsychiatric branches of medicine. For a brief period of time following World War II, for instance, prefrontal lobotomies were surgically performed on many seriously disturbed mental patients. Although the technique is no longer used, the man who originated the procedure (Egas Moniz) actually received the Nobel prize for it. Insulin treatment for schizophrenia (originated by Manfred Sakel), which was popular for a while, employed complex medical techniques.

5. Neuroanatomy-neuropathology. The anatomy and pathology of the central nervous system is of fundamental interest to some of the mental health professionals, especially those closely related to medicine. The questions of interest involve both the issues of the neurological aspects of mental health cases and the psychological consequences of neurological deficits. Since any damage (injury or disease) to the central nervous system is likely to have consequences in either sensory or thinking functions, the opposite possibility also arises; namely, the possibility that any sensory or thinking disturbance might be related to damage to the central nervous system. The terms neurology, neuroanatomy, neurophysiology,

neuropathology, and neuropharmacology refer, respectively, to the diseases of, the structure of, the function of, the manifestations of damage to, and the drug effects on the nervous system. Neurosurgery is the subspecialty of surgery involving treatment of nervous system injuries and diseases.

GENERAL SCIENCE TERMINOLOGY

Some terms from the basic sciences find their way into the mental health literature and are used with a fairly high frequency. The reason for including them in this glossary is to indicate their meaning in the context of the mental health professions. To a major extent, the relevant terminology comes from the biological fields, especially from that of genetics. Terms pertaining to general scientific methodology, linguistics, and the philosophy of science are also found in common use.

STATISTICAL AND COMPUTER TERMINOLOGY

As early as the beginning of the nineteenth century, the literature of the mental health field contained frequent discussions of statistical data. Only in very recent years, however, has there developed an entirely new language for statistics, in which very precise definitions, usually enjoying widespread acceptance, have developed. Especially since research in the field has flourished during the past 20 years, the mental health literature has become replete with these statistical terms. In most cases, the terms are used outside as well as inside the field of mental health, but those having to do with, for instance, "sample populations" are most directly relevant to the human behavioral sciences. Superimposed on this language, and usually associated with it very closely, there has developed more recently another glossary of terms from the field of computer technology. These terms, too, have acquired very precise definitions and are fairly well standardized. Statistics and computer technology are heavily immersed in mathematics, and mathematical terms are likely to be found in conjunction with them.

GLOSSARY

abdominal epilepsy. See p. 16.

abiotrophy. Loss of function, growth, or vitality of tissue or cells, especially early in the development of the organism.

ablation. Destruction or removal of all or part of an organ.

abortifacient. See p. 76.

abscissa. In analytic geometry, the horizontal coordinate of a point (X).

acanthesthesia. A paresthesia involving the experience of sensations of pinpricks.

access method. Computer term; the method used to link the computer program with the data in order to make the transfer into or out of memory.

acenesthesia. Inability to feel or perceive one's body.

acetylcholine. An acetyl ester of choline found in many tissues of the body; its most important location is at certain synaptic junctions in the peripheral and central nervous system, where it is thought to have a role in the transmission of impulses across these synapses.

achromatopsia. Total color blindness; inability to discriminate between all colors; perception of color stimuli as a colorless gray; achromatism.

acmesthesia. Ability to perceive sharp points by touch, but without experiencing the pain usually associated with such perception.

acoustic spectrum. The range of human hearing; 16,000 to 20,000 cycles per second; the range of sound wave frequency perceptible to the human ear.

Addison's disease. Chronic insufficiency of adrenal corticosteroid compounds. This condition sometimes has associated nonspecific psychiatric symptoms.

address. Computer term; the code used to identify a memory location in order to store it or retrieve it.

adiposogenital dystrophy. Also called Fröhlich's syndrome; characterized by obesity and hypogonadism in young males. True Fröhlich's syndrome is caused by a pituitary tumor that extends into the hypothalamus. Pseudo-Fröhlich's syndrome usually, but not always, represents a mislabeling of pubertal boys who are obese and slow in development but are otherwise normal.

adrenergic. Pertaining to the sympathetic nervous system; nerves or organs activated by epinephrine norepinephrine.

adrenochrome. An oxidative metabolic product of

epinephrine that is thought to have psychotoxic properties and that is possibly related to the abnormal symptoms of schizophrenia.

adrenocorticotropic hormone (ACTH). A hormone secreted by basophilic cells of the anterior pituitary gland, which stimulates secretion of adrenal corticosteroid compounds; except for aldosterone, it is the regulator of the production and secretion of all the hormones of the adrenal cortex.

adrenogenital syndrome. Masculinization of young girls and women and precocious puberty in young males, caused by overproduction of androgens by the adrenal cortex. Psychiatric problems are many, especially in girls mistakenly reared as boys, and usually are secondary to the physical changes brought about.

aesthesiometer (also esthesiometer). An instrument for measuring tactile sensitivity.

afferent. Moving or carrying toward the center. In the central nervous system, the nerves carrying impulses from peripheral endings to central centers.

agenesis. Total or partial failure of tissue development.

agenetic. Absence of body parts.

agerasia. Youthful appearance, vigorous health in old age.

agranulocytosis. Reduction or absence of circulating granulocytes; a blood dyscrasia seen by psychiatrists as a rare complication of psychotropic drug therapy.

agrypnocoma. Coma vigil.

ahypnia. Pronounced insomnia.

algorithm. Computer and mathematical term; a uniform procedure for solving a problem.

allele. Either of a pair of opposing genes that transmit alternative mendelian characteristics.

allocation. Computer term. To ensure against erasure or loss of data previously collected, it is necessary to specify the location in memory where information is stored; this process is one of allocation.

alopecia. The loss of hair; can be general or partial (alopecia areato) and can be related to nonspecific emotional factors.

alphanumeric. Computer term; all the characters appearing on the input keyboard of a computer, including integers, alphabet, and other signs, that are used to record input.

alpha rhythm. See p. 18.

altitude sickness. A condition caused by limited oxygen supply at high altitudes. Persons may exhibit anxiety, among other symptoms, but no other consistent psychiatric problems have been found associated with this condition.

Alzheimer's disease. See p. 18.

amaurotic familial idiocy. See p. 18.

amenorrhea. The cessation of menstruation; beyond the expected time of the menses.

Amerind. An American Indian.

aminoacidemia. Excess amounts of certain amino acids in the urine; usually associated with varying degrees of mental deficiency.

amusia. Inability to comprehend or reproduce musical tones.

amyostasia. Tremor. See p. 44.

analog. Computer term; making calculations analogously, as with a slide rule, where quantities are related to distance on the rule; solves mathematical problems by using physical analogues of numerical variables. Precision is limited in this method.

anencephaly. A developmental anomaly in which the fetus has no brain and seldom lives after birth.

anthropometry. Measurement of bodily dimensions.

aphemia. See p. 20.

apoplexy. Apoplectic stroke; usually taken to mean the sudden onset of paralysis and unconsciousness secondary to cerebrovascular accident such as hemorrhage or blockage of an artery.

arithmetic mean. Statistical term for the sum of all the data divided by the number of items.

array. Statistical term for the arrangement of a set of data in the order of their magnitude.

artificial language. Computer term; communications with the computer memory carried out through the use of an artificial language (for example, FORTRAN that is necessarily rigidly precise, but that can be quite arbitrary otherwise.

ascending reticular activating system. A diffuse midbrain structure postulated to be the major portion of the wakefulness system; possibly more physiologically than anatomically distinct as an entity.

astasia. Unsteadiness and motor incoordination while maintaining a standing position.

asthma. A condition of the respiratory system characterized by recurrent episodes of severely labored breathing, wheezing, and coughing. It is thought to have strong-psychological factors as a cause in many cases.

athetosis. See p. 20.

athyreosis. Absence of a functioning thyroid gland; usually a congenital anomaly.

atonic seizures. See p. 20.

attributable risk. The rate of the disorder in exposed individuals that can be attributed to the exposure, derived from subtracting the rate (usually incidence or mortality) of the disorder of the nonexposed population from the corresponding rate of the exposed population.

auditory seizures. See p. 20.

automatic data processing (ADP). Computer term: general term for data processing systems, including the older accounting machines and new electronic data processing devices.

autonomic nervous system. That part of the nervous system directing involuntary organ activity, including the digestive, respiratory, and cardiovascular systems.

autopsy. The medical examination of a dead body.

ballismus. See p. 21.

basal ganglia. A group of nuclei (clusters of nerve cells) deep inside the brain tissue. These ganglia include the globus pallidus, caudate nucleus, amygdala, claustrum, and the internal capsule. They have rich neuronal connections between the cerebral cortex and other brain structures. Injury to these structures causes pronounced neurological symptoms.

basal ganglia disorder. A condition brought on by disease of or injury to the basal ganglia (for example, Huntington's chorea, Wilson's disease, Parkinson's disease, and drug-induced disorders.)

BASIC. Computer term; one of the several computer languages; Beginner's All-purpose Symbolic Instruction Code. This is one of the simplest to learn.

benign. Not severe, mild; not able to cause death; as opposed to malignant.

beriberi. A generalized systemic disease caused by thiamin (vitamin B$_1$) deficiency. Mental symptoms may be mild to severe, including serious brain damage.

beta rhythm. See p. 21.

binary code. Computer term; a numbering system using only two integers, 0 and 1. The arabic numbers 0, 1, 2, 3, 4 are represented as 0, 1, 10, 11, 100.

Binswanger's disease. See p. 21.

biogenetics. The study of biochemical and biophysical aspects of the hereditary process.

biogenic. Produced by a living organism.

biometry. The measuring of life processes.

bionics. A new branch of science or technology, which employs biologic processes for hardware systems. Study of bat sonar, for instance, assisted in the development of sonar hardware.

biosphere. The total of internal and external environment in which one's biological processes take place.

biostatistics. Vital statistics.

biotransformation. Alteration of compounds mediated by enzymes in the body. Malfunctioning in these processes are thought to cause abnormal molecules to be formed that in turn could cause or contribute to mental illness.

biotype. All persons who are genotypic equals.

birth injury. Injury to the child that occurs during the birth process.

bit. Computer term; a single, irreducible unit of information. In the binary system, a bit is either 0 or 1.

black-box problem. The deduction of the processes within a closed and unobservable system by altering the input into the system and observing the corresponding output.

block diagram. A method of describing a system in which components are depicted as squares, circles, triangles, and so on; lines connecting them indicate relationships and time.

blood-brain barrier. A theoretical structure or mechanism that allows some but not all substances to enter the brain from the blood. The site or manner of this phenomenon is not known.

blood dyscrasia. Alteration of components, especially the cells, of the blood; a rare side effect of some psychotropic drug administration.

brachycephaly. Abnormal breadth of the forehead; associated with mental retardation.

brain. That part of the nervous system included within the skull.

brain cells. Nerve cells or neurons that make up the greatest part of the brain tissue.

brain hemorrhage. Bleeding into or upon brain tissue from a broken artery or vein.

brain lesions. The site of a permanent change in brain tissue secondary to alteration of function or loss of neurons of their parts.

brainstem. That portion of the brain including motor and sensory tracts and cranial nerve nuclei, but excluding the cerebellum, the cerebrum, and white matter connecting them. It includes the pons and medulla oblongata.

brain tumors. Space-occupying new growth anywhere within or upon brain tissue.

brain wave. See p. 21.

branch. Computer term; in a computer program, a

branch is a point where a given decision directs the sequence into various pathways.

Broca's aphasia. See p. 21.

bromidrosis. See p. 21.

bromoderma. See p. 22.

bufotenin. A derivative of the normal neurochemical serotonin; has been found to induce abnormal psychological states.

calculator. A device or machine that can perform mathematical tasks.

carbon-monoxide poisoning. Accidental or deliberate exposure to enough carbon monoxide (an odorless, colorless, tasteless gas produced by incomplete combustion of heating gases, coal, wood, and so on and contained in automobile exhaust fumes) to produce symptoms. These symptoms range from mild drowsiness, dizziness, and headache to coma and death. Severe poisoning may result in damage to brain tissue, with lasting mental and neurological symptoms and signs.

castration. Removal of the sex glands (gonads).

catabolism. That part of metabolism during which food material is broken down into smaller and less complex forms.

cataplexy. See p. 22.

central processing unit. Computer term; the part of the computer that holds the circuitry that executes the function of the program.

cerebral anoxia. Reduction of the oxygen supply to the brain; produces irreversible damage to brain tissue and may result in death when severe or prolonged.

cerebral palsy. A condition affecting muscular coordination that is caused by brain damage of varying degrees; caused by events before or after birth (such as injury, infection, hereditary factors, or anoxia).

cerebrovascular accident. A blocking of or bleeding from the blood vessels of the brain; nearly always causes pronounced neurological symptoms and signs, coma, and sometimes death.

chiropodist. See p. 101.

cholinergic. A term denoting nerves that discharge acetylcholine from the synaptic endings. These include all autonomic preganglionic fibers, all postganglionic parasympathetic fibers, and certain postganglionic sympathetic fibers.

chorea. See p. 22.

chromosomes. Threadlike particles in the nucleus of cells that carry the genes.

chronic subdural hematoma. See p. 22.

clitoris. Part of the female external genitalia analogous to the penis in the male; a main organ for sexual stimulation.

cluster headaches. See p. 23.

COBOL. A computer language (common business-oriented language).

code. Symbols used to convey messages usually carried by another order or type of symbol.

coding. Computer term for the process of converting a program design into the actual machine language suitable for data processing.

cohort. Grouping according to characteristics (for example, age, race, eye color) evident prior to the appearance of the disorder being studied.

command. Computer term for a control signal or an instruction to the computer.

communication link. Computer term for the means of connecting the various and remotely located parts of a complex computer system into a working unit. The link might be, for example, commercial telephone lines.

community language. In J. H. Woodger's concept of divisions of language, that which relates information about groups of people.

compiler. Computer term for an intermediary program used to translate one language into another.

computer. A machine or series of machines designed to do mathematical computations. Although the ancient adding machine, the slide rule, and the abacus are examples of computers, the term is usually reserved today for highly complex and rapid electronic data-processing machines.

computer program. A detailed and systematic plan for solving a problem that is capable of being solved or processed by a computer. The problem must be translated into a language for which the computer is equipped to respond.

computer system. Large modern computers are generally composed of a number of different components, each serving a particular purpose (such as memory). When linked together, they become a system.

concussion. See p. 23.

control character. Computer term for a single character (as on a typewriter key) that signals the computer to control some action, such as to start or stop a sequence.

control group. Statistical term for a population studied to compare it with some other experimental group.

conversion routine. Computer term for a program that can change the data presentation from one form to another, such as from binary to decimal.

correlation coefficient. Statistical term for the numerical measure of the degree to which two series of variables correlate with each other. A perfect correlation gives a value of 1.0.

correlation (linear). Statistical term for the manner in which two variables relate to each other. If the correlation is linear, then when the two variables are plotted against each other, the points appear along a straight line.

cortex, cerebral. The outer layer of brain tissue; often called gray matter.

cortical. Relating to the cortex or outer layer of gray matter of the brain.

craniostenosis. A congenital malformation of the skull associated with mental deficiency.

cretinism. See p. 24.

cross-sectional. Measurements of causes and effects made, usually retrospectively, at the same point in time.

crowd. An aggregate of persons with no particular interaction; social group.

crude (death, birth, mortality) rates. The total number of deaths, births, or cases of specified illnesses divided by the population.

cryptogenic. Of unknown cause.

cryptorchism. Failure of one or both testes to develop or descend.

Cushing's syndrome. A condition caused by excessive secretion of growth hormone.

cybernetics. Norbert Wiener's term to describe the general subject of communications, both human and mechanical. He equated the feedback and control mechanisms of computer operations to human thinking. In this, language and concepts of the physical sciences, especially from the computer field (such as input, output, feedback, servo, black box, impedence, and noise) are used to describe human behavior. It is a series of concepts, formulated by Norbert Wiener at Massachusetts Institute of Technology, concerning the human system of communication. A particular stress is placed on the importance of feedback; that is, information returned in response to a transmitted message that aids the person in learning how to make his next step. Information theory is a modern formulation of this.

cycle. Computer term for the time interval required to complete a sequence.

data. Information, signal, input.

data processing. Computer term for any operation that manipulates information or data.

data processor. Computer term for a device that mathematically stores, retrieves, or manipulates information.

data reduction. Computer term for the process of converting raw data as collected to an orderly and systematic form suitable for processing.

decerebrate rigidity. See p. 24.

decision (computer). Computer term for a statement that specifies which of various alternative actions the computer is to follow.

deck. Computer terminology for the stack of computer punched cards on which is punched a program or set of data.

delerium tremens. See p. 24.

delta rhythm. See p. 24.

demand characteristics. Effects of an investigator on a research subject, which may influence the performance or reaction of the subject and therefore influence the results; strong feelings or expectations are perceived by the subject and cause him to behave according to those perceptions.

demyelinating disease. See p. 24.

deoxyribonucleic acid. A complex chemical occurring in cell nuclei. It is the molecular basis of heredity and, as such, is an integral part of the gene.

dependent variable, independent variable. In statistics, the difference between two variables, one of which, the dependent, has a value determined by the value of the other, the independent.

dermatitis. An inflammation or irritation of the skin.

deterministic. A philosophical term applied to a phenomena wherein a given set of circumstances invariably produces a certain result (as in arithmetic); thinking in which constant and rigid consequences are expected to result from any given series of events. A deterministic view of nature is often equated with teleological viewpoints that assume a purpose to natural events.

detumescence. Loss of swelling; often used to denote the loss of penile erection or of engorgement of the female genitals by draining of blood from the veins of the genitalia.

diagnostic (computer). Computer term for a process of identifying malfunctions in a program or memory.

diffuse sclerosis. Severe and progressive demyelination and deterioration of the brain; Schilder's disease.

digital computer. The type of computer, different from the analog type, that employs arithmetic functions on data.

discordance. Dissimilarity in a pair of twins regarding the presence or absence of a disease or trait.

disk. Computer term for one of the memory storage methods, one of which uses magnetic tapes.

dispersion. Statistical term for the spread of values in a set of data. A measure of dispersion is the standard deviation.

dominant. A gene that produces a phenotype, whether homozygous or heterozygous.

dopamine. See p. 26.

double-blind. A method used in drug research in which neither the patient nor the rater knows whether the patient is taking a drug or a placebo for that drug.

downtime. Computer term for the period of time the computer is inoperative for repairs.

dromolepsy. See p. 25.

duplex. Computer term for the simultaneous transmission of two messages on the same communication line, such as incoming and outgoing calls on the same line at the same time.

dysesthesia. See p. 25.

dysfunction. Medical term for an impairment of function.

dyskinesia. See p. 25.

dysmenorrhea. Painful menstruation.

dyspareunia. See p. 25.

dyspnea. Difficult or labored breathing; shortness of breath.

dysrhythmic abdominal pain. See p. 25.

dystonia. See p. 26.

eclectic. A combination or mixing of differing theoretical points of view.

ecology. The environment in which an individual or group (plant or animal) survives; the study of environmental factors in the survival of organisms.

ecphoria. Re-emergence of a memory trace or engram.

ecphorize. Revival of a memory trace or engram.

ectype. Any type widely deviant from the norm.

electroencephalogram. See p. 26.

electronic data processing. Modern complex computer equipment systems.

emprosthotonus. Pronounced spasmodic forward flexion of the body; opposite of opisthotonus.

encephalitis. Infection or inflammation of the brain.

encephalitis lethargica. See p. 26.

encephalomalacia. Softening and atrophy of the brain.

encephalopathy. A diseased condition of the brain.

endemic. A disease recurring in a given area; sometimes used to refer to local behaviors, such as "car theft is endemic in the area."

endocrine gland. A gland within the body that secretes its hormone directly into the blood or lymph stream. Examples are the thyroid, adrenal glands, pancreatic beta cells, and the gonads; as opposed to exocrine glands.

endocrinopathy. A condition of disease or malfunction of an endocrine gland or glands.

endogenous. Arising from within the body.

endoplasmic reticulum. A network of interval membranes and channels within the nerve cell.

entropy. Roughly speaking, measure of disorder; a lack of organization within a system.

epicureanism. A philosophy founded on the desirability of seeking the good life in earthly pleasures.

epidemic. A wide and relatively rapid spread of a disease; sometimes used analogously to refer to the spread of behaviors, such as "an epidemic of stealing."

epidural hematoma. Blood clot between the dura mater and inner table of the skull; nearly always caused by arterial bleeding, and rapidly fatal if untreated.

epilepsy. See p. 26.

epileptic status. See p. 26.

epinephrine. See p. 83.

ergotropic dominance. Dominance of sympathetic nervous system or ergotropic activity.

ethnic. Pertaining to human races.

ethnology. The study of human races.

ethology. Study of the behavior of animals in their natural environment; the study of the relationships between the environment and the physiology of animals.

etiology. The study of causes.

eunuch. A man castrated prior to attaining puberty.

eunuchoidism. Partial absence of hormone production by the sex glands.

exocrine gland. A gland within the body that secretes into some structure (such as the gastrointestinal tract) other than the blood or lymph streams; as opposed to endocrine gland.

extrapyramidal system. The nuclei, nerve cells, and tracts, but not including the pyramidal tracts, that exert effects on the skeletal muscles of the body.

false transmitter. A substance that when released by the nerve impulse from the nerve ending causes little or no stimulation of the receptor site.

feedback. A return message to a sender telling him of the effect of his original message on the recipient person or mechanism. This is a term borrowed from the communications language of Norbert Wiener.

filtering, sensory. The process of selectively admitting stimuli to the central nervous system.

fixed point. Computer term referring to a way of treating decimal points, meaning that a fixed number of integers follows the decimal point.

floating point. Computer term referring to a way of treating decimal points, indicating that varying numbers of integers may follow the point.

flow chart. A term used in many types of scientific and engineering analysis, including computer programming. It is a diagrammatic way of illustrating the occurrence of and interrelationships among different events in a system.

FORTRAN. A computer language, or rather a series of languages, each one identified by a number (for example, FORTRAN 4). It is convenient for programs in which sub-routines are written.

frequency distribution. Statistical term for a set of numerical data arranged according to magnitude.

Fröhlich's syndrome. Adiposogenital dystrophy.

function (in statistics). A mathematical expression that specifies the relationship between variables. The function acquires a value when values are assigned to the variables.

functional diagram. In a systems analysis that employs a flow chart to illustrate the occurrence of events and their relations to each other, each component is indicated as the function of that part of the system, rather than as the function of its structure.

galactosemia. An inherited defect of sugar (galactose) metabolism that nearly always leads to mental retardation if not detected and treated early.

gamma-aminobutyric acid. A biogenic amine found in the brain, thought to be a transmitter substance.

gamma rhythm. See p. 28.

Gaussian curve. In statistics, the normal distribution curve.

gene. The hereditary unit. It occupies a fixed location on the chromosome.

genealogy. The study of ancestral history.

general paresis. See p. 29.

generation (first, second, third, and so on). Computer terminology for the stage of sophistication of a given computer, the first generation having been the original, most primitive (sometimes called the "model T").

genetic. Inherited; capable of being transmitted from parent to offspring through the genes.

genetics. The science or the study of heredity.

genital. Pertaining to the reproductive organs.

genotype. The inheritable attributes of an organism that are not necessarily observable; as opposed to phenotype.

geometric mean. Statistical term for the Nth root of the products of N items in a set of data.

ghetto. See p. 131.

gonads. The sex glands; in the male, the testicles, and in the female, the ovaries.

grand mal epilepsy. See p. 28.

granulocytopenia. Reduced number of circulating granulocytic white blood cells; a rare complication of psychiatric drug treatment.

gyrectomy. Surgical removal of a gyrus of the brain that is used as a treatment of certain types of mental illness and convulsive disorders.

gyrus. A fold or convolution of the cerebral cortex.

hallucinogen. See p. 84.

harmonic progression. Statistical term for the reciprocals of a series of arithmetic means.

hematoma. A clot of blood occurring within body tissues.

hemiballismus. See p. 29.

hemichorea. See p. 29.

hemicrania. Headache on one side of the head; migraine. Also, partial congenital maldevelopment of the brain.

hemiplegia. Paralysis of only one side of the body.

hemispherectomy. See p. 84.

heredity. The sum total of traits and characteristics passed on to a person from his parents.

heredodegenerative. A disease acquired by heredity and characterized by progressive loss or malfunction of cells, tissues, or organs (for example, Huntington's chorea.)

hermaphrodite. Strictly speaking, the term means the presence of both sex glands in one body, but more generally refers to the condition in which the gonads of one sex and the external genitalia of the opposite sex occur simultaneously. In psychiatry, the term may refer to a psychological state of bisexuality.

heroin. See p. 84.

hertz (Hz). Cycles per second.

heuristic. Trying a number of different approaches to find a solution; favoring discovery.

histogram. A graph or chart in which a series of values are represented as flat-topped bars.

holistic. An approach to the study of man that considers all the processes within the person (such as the physical, chemical, and spiritual) and without the person (such as the milieu) that affect that person; a consideration of the entire man in all aspects of his being.

homeostasis. Cannon's concept of physiologic mechanisms that maintain desirable equilibrium in body functions; used analogously to describe the principle of balance in one's manner of living, with the implication that psychological difficulties can result from upsetting the equilibrium.

hormone. Secretion of an endocrine gland (for example, thyroxin, insulin).

Huntington's chorea. See p. 29.

Hurler's disease. See p. 29.

hydrocephalus. See p. 29.

hyperhidrosis. See p. 29.

hyperkinesis. See p. 29.

hypertension. High blood pressure.

hyperthyroidism. An increased amount of circulating thyroid hormone; associated with physical and mental symptoms.

hypertonic. Increase in muscle tension; also, increased osmotic pressure of a solution.

hypnotics. See p. 85.

hypocalcemia. Lower than normal amounts of circulating calcium in the blood; a state that may be associated with convulsions or tetany.

hypoglycemia. Lower than normal amounts of glucose in the blood; can be associated with mental and physical symptoms (such as weariness, profuse sweating, tremor, confusion, and coma).

hypogonadism. Production of less than the normal amount of sex hormone.

hypoplasia. Inadequate development of a body part or tissue.

hypotension. Low blood pressure.

hypothyroidism. Insufficient production of thyroid hormone; often associated with depressive symptoms and even with psychosis when severe.

hypotonic. Usually or abnormally low tone or tension of the muscles; also refers to low osmotic pressure of a solution.

hypsarrhythmia. See p. 30.

iatrogenic. See p. 85.

idiopathic. A condition in which the cause has been undetermined.

IF statement. Computer term; in FORTRAN 4 language, a statement that can be either true or false, and whichever it is will determine the next step in the sequence (for example, greater than or less than zero).

illuminating-gas poisoning. Anoxia brought about by breathing the gas used for cooking or heating; can precipitate various mental symptoms and, when severe, may result in coma or death. It is a common method of suicide.

incidence. The number of new cases of a condition that develop in a population within a given time.

infant mortality. Death rate for infants, usually given as the number of deaths occurring in the first year of life per thousand live births.

infertility. The inability to conceive or bear a child.

information retrieval (or storage). The process of removing or placing information in a memory bank. The card catalog of a library, together with the book-coding system, serves in this capacity. Electronic data processing does this on a computer.

input. The information delivered into a system. This might be sensory signals coming into the human brain or data fed into a computer.

instinct. In biology, purposeful action that does not require learning or experience and that is, therefore, presumably innate. In psychoanalytic theory, great emphasis is placed on the importance of instinct as a motivation for behavior, and different theorists have claimed different instincts as being of paramount importance.

isozymes. Inherited variations of normal body enzymes. Some of these may play a part in causing certain mental illnesses.

iteration. Repetition.

jacksonian epilepsy. See p. 31.

Jakob-Creutzfeldt's disease. See p. 31.

Jarisch-Herxheimer reactions. An inflammatory reaction of skin, viscera, and even the nervous system that occurs during the treatment of syphilis. It is thought to be caused by the toxic effect of breakdown products of the syphilis spirochete.

kernicterus. Bilirubin encephalopathy; a condition in which abnormal amounts of bilirubin accumulate in the brain of the fetus or newborn child because of an overly rapid breakdown of hemoglobin in the child. It is often associated with residual mental deficiency.

keypunch. Computer term for a machine that punches holes in cards (such as IBM cards) used in data processing.

kinetic. Pertaining to movement.

Krabbe's disease. See p. 31.

kurtosis. Statistical term for the degree of sharpness of the peak of a distribution curve or the degree of closeness of the data showing the highest frequency.

kuru. See p. 31.

Laennec's cirrhosis. A severe disease of the liver characterized by eventual shrinking and hardening of liver tissue, loss of function of the liver cells, and severe general systemic signs and symptoms secondary to the liver changes. Approximately one half of the cases of this disease occurs in chronic alcoholics.

Lamarckian hypothesis. The concept that acquired characteristics can be genetically transmitted to offspring.

lead encephalitis. A brain disorder caused by poisoning with the heavy metal lead; may be acute or chronic. If severe, it may be irreversible.

lesion. Any injury, wound, or morbid change in body tissue.

lethal gene. A genetic mutation that causes the death of the organism carrying it.

limbic system. A portion of the brain that mediates visceral functions and that is concerned with feelings and emotion rather than thinking.

limit. Statistical term for the first or last value in a frequency series.

linguistics. The study of language.

lipochondrodystrophy. Gargoylism. (See p. 28.)

lissencephaly. See p. 32.

lithium. See p. 86.

location (computer). Computer term for a place in which data can be stored. It is necessary to identify the location by some code.

lues. See p. 32.

leutic. See p. 32.

lysergic acid diethylamide (LSD). See p. 86.

macrocephaly. Abnormal enlargement of the head; may be associated with mental deficiency.

malignant. Able to cause death; as opposed to benign.

Marchiafava's disease. See p. 32.

marijuana. See p. 86.

mean. The sum of all the values divided by the number of values.

mean deviation. Standard deviation.

median. The point in a set of values that divides the set's distribution into two parts so that an equal number of values lies above and below the point; a measure of central tendency.

Meniere's disease. See p. 33.

meninges. The membranous coverings of the brain and spinal cord. The outermost covering is the dura mater; the middle is the arachnoid mater; and the innermost is the pia mater.

meningitis. Infection or inflammation of the covering of the brain and spinal cord.

meningovascular lues. See p. 33.

mercurial encephalopathy. An organic brain condition brought about by intoxication with the heavy metal mercury.

mescaline. See p. 87.

messenger RNA. A ribonucleic acid that transfers genetic information from the cell nucleus to the cytoplasm.

metabolic disturbance. Certain vitamin deficiency states (such as pellagra), endocrine disorders (such as diabetes and hyperthyroidism) and accumulation of body wastes (such as uremia). These are sometimes associated with psychiatric conditions.

metabolism. All the chemical and physical processes that occur when the organism ingests, breaks down, and transforms food material into energy and discharges waste matter.

metalanguage. Gestures, tone of voice, and arrangement of words that convey additional information about what is being communicated (for example, tone of voice that indicates anger or humor).

methadone. See p. 87.

methionine. See p. 87.

methodology. Scientific study of the way in which procedures are carried out.

microcephaly. Abnormally small head size; associated with mental deficiency.

migraine. See p. 33.

miosis. Sustained contraction of the pupil.

mitochondria. A discrete complex of enzymes within the cell.

mode. Statistical term for the one or more peaks of a high degree of frequency within a population.

monamine oxidase (MAO). An enzyme within the cells, especially certain nerve cells, that metabolizes and activates certain transmitter substances (for example, monamines).

morphine. See p. 87.

mucous colitis. See p. 34.

multipara. A woman who has had more than one child.

multiple sclerosis. A degenerative disease of the nervous system in which loss or hardening of the sheath of the nerves occurs throughout the body at multiple sites causing motor, sensory, and emotional disorders; generally leads to disability and death. Etiology is unknown.

myelinoclastic. Destruction of normally formed myelin; also called demyelination.

myelitis. Inflammation or infection of the spinal cord.

myelopathy. Any disease of the spinal cord.

myopia. Nearsightedness.

myxedema. Severe hypothyroidism; usually a chronic state in which there is almost total absence of circulating thyroid hormone. The clinical picture often closely resembles severe depression.

nalorphine. See p. 87.

nanism. See p. 34.

narcolepsy. See p. 34.

narcotic. See p. 87.

necropsy. Autopsy.

neoatavism. Recurrence in a descendent of traits of an immediate ancestor.

neocortex. Generally means the nonolfactory portion of the frontal lobes of the cerebrum. It is sometimes used loosely to mean the cortex of the frontal lobes.

neoplasm. Literally, new growth: usually a tumorous growth, whether benign, such as a wart, or malignant, such as cancer.

nerve impulse. The combination of events begun by stimulation of a nerve cell that is of sufficient strength to cause that cell to stimulate another nerve cell.

neuralgia. See p. 34.

neuraxia. The brain and spinal cord.

neuritis. Inflammation or infection of nerves.

neurochemical. A chemical associated with acting upon or elaborated by a nerve cell.

neurochemistry. The study, use, or modification of the chemical activity of the nerves.

neurodermatitis. See p. 34.

neurofibromatosis. Tumorous growths on the nerves that are associated with mental deficiency; also called Recklinghausen's disease.

neurohumor. A diffusable substance occurring at nerve endings that can act as a transmitter substance or modify the conditions under which the transmitter substance acts.

neuron. The nerve cell.

neuropathy. Any disease of the nervous system.

neurophysiological. Pertaining to the activity of nerve cells.

neurotransmitter. A chemical that carries the nerve impulse from one nerve cell to another, usually across the synaptic cleft.

nitrous oxide. See p. 88.

noise. Any unwanted signal.

nonlinear trends. A statistical term for a plotted growth curve that does not follow a straight line.

noradrenaline. See p. 88.

norepinephrine. See p. 88.

norm. A comparison of the raw score obtained by an individual on a test to average scores obtained by others in his group on the same test.

normal distribution. Statistical term for a frequency distribution that is symmetrical, with low frequencies at both extremes and the highest frequency in the middle. When plotted on a graph, the curve is a bell curve because of its shape.

nosography. Description of disease.

nosology. The study of or classification of disease.

null hypothesis. The assumption that an experimental effect does not exist, that any difference between two samples is purely accidental.

numerical control. In automated mechanical operations, the process of controlling the sequenceing of tasks on a machine by means of punched cards or tape.

nystagmus. See p. 34.

obesity. The condition of being overweight.

octopamine. An amine that functions as a false transmitter.

olfactory seizure. See p. 35.

oligophrenia. See p. 35.

open systems. A concept used in systems theory to mean, simply stated, that a system (that is, a cell or an organism) can at any time receive input (such as food or information), react internally to this input (that is, metabolize it, translate it), and elaborate an output (such as energy, motion, or messages).

ophthalmology. A medical specialty dealing with the care and treatment of the eyes.

opiates. See p. 89.

opium. See p. 89.

ordinate. In analytic geometry, the vertical coordinate of a point (Y).

osteopathy. A medical practice founded on the theory that all diseases are caused by pressure on the nerves coming from the spine.

otolaryngology. A medical specialty that deals with the care and treatment of ear, nose, and throat diseases.

otology. A medical specialty devoted to diseases of hearing.

output. In scientific or engineering language, the end result of a process, the beginning of which is the input. In the case of the human being, input is the stimulus and output is the response.

ova. Eggs.

ovary. The female sex gland.

paralysis agitans. See p. 36.

paralytic ileus. See p. 36.

parameter. A limit, such as an upper or lower limit or boundary, or coefficient that is sufficient to identify a curve in a family of curves. In computer terminology, a number or quantity assigned as a constant to control or influence a process.

paraplegia. Paralysis of the lower half of the body, including both legs.

paresis. See p. 36.

Parkinson's disease. See p. 36.

paroxysmal. Having the quality of occurring suddenly and at intervals.

parthenogenesis. Reproduction from an ovum not fertilized by a sperm.

parturition. The birth process.

pathoclisis. O. Vogt's term for the phenomenon of only a part of an organism undergoing a pathologic change when the entire organism is exposed to a toxic agent.

pathognomonic. Characteristic to the degree of being reliable evidence for the existence of some condition (such as a disease).

pattern recognition. A manner of comparing an image with a remembered pattern similar to the image. Complex visual memories are patterns, the retrieval of which might be accomplished by matching with some currently perceived pattern. Certain types of mechanical devices can do this through the matching of photographs, for instance.

pediatrics. A medical specialty that deals with diseases of children and adolescents.

penicillin. See p. 90.

penis. The male external sex organ.

pepsin. Pepsinogen.

pepsinogen. A substance secreted by the chief cells of the gastric mucosa. Acid in the stomach converts pepsinogen to pepsin, an enzyme that starts digestion of many proteins. I. A. Mirsky found increased urinary pepsinogen levels to be highly predictive of development of peptic ulcer, pointing to a possible genetic predisposition to a psychosomatic illness.

peptic ulcer. A circumscribed effect, usually chronic, occurring in the wall of the stomach or duodenum. Peptic ulcers are said to occur only in the presence of acid and pepsin.

percentile. Statistical term meaning that when a member of a population is X percentile, X% of the total population have lower values.

periarteritis nodosa. A collagen disease affecting blood vessels and connective tissue, including those of the brain. It is sometimes associated with nonspecific psychiatric symptoms.

period prevalence. The total number of cases of a disease that have existed at some period during a specified time; the sum of incidence and point prevalence.

permanent storage. Computer term for stored information that is rapidly retrievable and nonerasable.

pernicious anemia. A deficiency of circulatory red blood cells caused by vitamin B_{12} deficiency. It is no longer pernicious because of early treatment. The severe psychotic states associated with it are now rarely seen because of effective treatment with vitamin B_{12}.

petit mal epilepsy. See p. 37.

peyote. See p. 90.

peyotism. A religion, practiced mainly by the Mescalero Indians of the North American Southwest, the followers of which believe that God put some of His Holy Spirit into the peyote.

peyotl. See p. 90.

phallus. Penis.

phantom limb phenomenon. Experiencing the vivid existence of an amputated limb. The experience is usually one of pain and appears to come from the lost limb.

pharmacogenetics. Study of the influence of genetically controlled variations within the individual that help determine the manner in which his body will handle the drug and the reactions he will have to the drug.

phenothiazines. See p. 90.

phenotype. The total of all the observable genetic attributes.

phenylketonuria. An inborn error in the metabolism of the amino acid phenylalanine that is caused by an inherited deficiency in the enzyme phenylalanine hydroxylase; associated with mental retardation.

photophobia. Literally means fear of light, but is generally used to mean hypersensitivity of the eyes to light.

phototoxicity. Production of a harmful effect (for example, dermatitis or sunburn) by light.

Pick's disease. See p. 38.

pneumoencephalography. See p. 38.

point of central tendency. Statistical phrase for the tendency of a frequency distribution to rise or cluster in one area.

point prevalence. Disease frequency occurring at a specified point in time.

polyandry. Having more than one husband.

polycythemia. Excess numbers of circulating red cells in the blood.

polyneuritis. Inflammation and infection of many peripheral nerves.

population genetics. The study of hereditary traits and distribution of genes in normal and abnormal populations.

porencephaly. A congenital defect of the brain characterized by the presence of cysts or cavities in the cortex, some of which may communicate between the ventricles and subarachnoid space; may be associated with mental deficiency.

porphyria. A disorder of metabolism in which

breakdown products of hemoglobin, porphobilino-gen, and delta-aminolevulinic acid, accumulate and bring about severe gastrointestinal, neurological, and psychiatric symptoms.

practice effects. Improvement in performance (especially test performance) resulting from repeated trials of the task or test.

pressor agent. See p. 91.

prevalence. The number of cases present in a population at a given time.

primipara. A woman who has had, or is about to have, her first child.

printout. Computer term for an output device that produces a printed copy of the information.

process of control. The application of statistical methods to quality control. This includes, for instance, the inspection of representative samples of products instead of every single item.

prototype. The first and earliest example in any series.

pruritis. See p. 39.

psilocybin. See p. 91.

psychedelic drugs. See p. 91.

psychic seizures. See p. 39.

psychomotor epilepsy. See p. 40.

punched card. Computer term for a paper card about 3 × 7 inches on which is printed 80 columns of digits from 0 to 12. By punching holes at certain locations, a card or a deck of cards can be used to activate a computer. Any information or instructions intended to be fed into the system is coded on these cards.

punched tape. Computer term for a modification of the punched card method of coding information. A roll of narrow paper tape is punched with a succession of holes that serve as a code and that can be made to activate components of the computer. The old-fashioned player piano role was a similar example.

pyknolepsy. See p. 40.

Q-sort. A personality profile test in which a standard set of responses are sorted on the basis of how well they describe the subject matter.

quadriplegia. Paralysis of both arms and legs.

quicktran. A computer language used in timesharing systems.

rabies. An acute infectious disease of the central nervous system caused by a filterable virus transmitted to man by the bite of a rabid animal. After a variable incubation period, there occurs the characteristic restlessness, hyperesthesia, convulsions, laryngeal spasms, paralysis, and death. Attempts to swallow liquids cause severe pain lead-ing to a violent rejection of liquids; hence the name hydrophobia.

radioactive iodine uptake. A test of thyroid gland function: higher than normal range of uptake indicates an overactive gland; a lower than normal uptake indicates an underactive gland.

random access. Computer term for a data storage component that searches for the stored information according to a random time sequence.

random sample. Subjects selected in such a manner that each member of the group has an equal chance of being chosen.

range. Statistical term for the amount or extent of dispersion of spread of a set of data.

rank correlation. A way of illustrating how the members of a population in a frequency distribution correlate with each other by merely ranking them according to some measurable value.

rapid-eye-movement sleep. Sleep during which the eyes show rapid, apparently purposeless movement, a phenomenon accompanied by characteristic EEG changes. It is a phase of normal sleep, elucidated by Aserinsky and Kleitman. Subsequent research has shown that dreaming occurs during this time, so that it is also called dreaming sleep. There are other physiological changes, such as increased heart rate and respiration, noted during this phase. It makes up approximately 50% of an infant's sleep cycle. Its occurrence decreases with age but never disappears from normal sleep.

rauwolfia alkaloids. See p. 92.

Raynaud's disease. See p. 40.

real time. Computer term for actual current time of day or for the actual time required to complete an action.

receptor site. In neurophysiology, the site on the nerve membrane at which a drug or transmitter substance interacts with the nerve cell.

recessive. A gene that when paired with its dominant allele does not produce a phenotype.

recursive. Computer term for a process or sequence that repeats itself on completion of one cycle.

reflex. Automatic or involuntary activity.

registration. Computer term for the alignment or positioning of coordinates, such as the positioning of the punched holes in a card.

REM sleep. Rapid-eye-movement sleep.

restless legs syndrome. See p. 41.

rest tremor. See p. 41.

reticular activating system. A diffuse network of nerve cells scattered through the gray matter of the midbrain; a system rich in connections with the cerebral cortex, the spinal cord, hypothalamus, and limbic system. It apparently influences nearly all other areas of the brain, exerting inhibition of some areas and facilitation of others.

retrograde amnesia. See p. 41.

rheumatic diseases. A group of diseases that are characterized by inflammation of the joints, periosteum, and connective tissue and that have strong psychological factors in their causes. They are generally considered to be psychosomatic.

Rh factor. A factor in the blood that causes incompatibility between certain blood types. Such incompatibility may occur between the mother and the fetus, causing a reaction (such as kernicterus) in the infant that may lead to mental deficiency.

rhinitis, vasomotor. An inflammation of the nasal passages usually caused by allergic factors, but that often has strong emotional factors in its cause.

rhinoplasty. Alteration of the shape of the nose by surgery.

rhinorrhea. Flow of mucus from the nose.

rhizotomy. Cutting of nerve roots by an incision into the spinal cord; usually made to relieve intractable pain.

rhythmicality. Assessment of occurrence of the sleep-wake cycle, hunger, elimination, and appetite in order to measure development of children.

rosacea. Increased vascularity with papule formation over the blush area of the skin of the face and the upper chest; thought to have emotional factors in its cause and clinical changes.

rubella. A febrile disease caused by a virus. If the pregnant woman contracts this disease during the first trimester, mental deficiency in the child may result.

scopolamine. See p. 94.

Schilder's disease. See p. 41.

sclerosis, tuberous. See p. 42.

scotoma. See p. 42.

seborrhea. Excessive secretion of sebum (a fatty exudate) by sebaceous glands of the skin. It may be accompanied by scaling, itching, and burning, and it is associated with emotional factors.

secondary storage. Computer term for auxiliary storage facilities in addition to the primary storage facility.

semeiotic. See p. 42.

seminal fluid. The viscous liquid ejaculated by the male at orgasm. It contains the sperm and is made of secretions from the prostate, seminal vesicles, and Cowpers' glands.

sequential access. Computer term for the sequence in which data is stored in an orderly fashion, rather than a random fashion.

serotonin. See p. 94.

servomechanism. Engineering term for a device or a system that monitors itself; that is, information is generated from and about its operation. This information is feedback used to control subsequent operations.

set. A stable attitude or method of thinking or thought process; also referred to as an internal referent system.

shaman. A priest-doctor of primitive tribes who is believed by the tribe to have magical abilities to cure disease; sometimes derogatorily used for psychiatrist.

sham-death reflex. Motor rigidity occurring in animals (for example, the opossum) in response to danger.

signal. An event, word, posture, or sign that carries or conveys information from point to point; also, computer terminology for an event that does this within the computer system.

simulation. A mode, replica, or representation of an object or system.

singultus. Hiccough.

skewed distribution. Statistical term for a frequency distribution that is asymmetrical, with the highest frequency toward one end instead of in the middle.

sleep paralysis. See p. 69.

sodium amytal. See p. 95.

sodium pentothal. See p. 95.

sodium permanganate. See p. 95.

sodium phenobarbital. See p. 95.

software. Computer term for the program as distinguished from the computer apparatus, which is referred to as hardware.

soma. The body.

somatic. Pertaining to the body.

somnambulism. See p. 69.

soporific. See p. 95.

spastic colon. Alternating diarrhea and constipation, abdominal distress; an abnormal condition of the large intestine. It is thought to have strong mental and emotional factors as causes.

split brain. A condition in which the two cerebral hemispheres are disconnected by severing the corpus callosum. This has been done in man only rarely and then only as a therapeutic measure after all other methods have failed. It is used in animal experiments to gain knowledge of how the cerebral hemispheres function.

spontaneous hypoglycemic states. A rapid fall in blood glucose levels. This state is often associated with psychiatric symptoms such as altered states of consciousness, dizziness, anxiety, autonomic symptoms, and various bodily symptoms. These are usually of short duration and sometimes follow food intake. The underlying cause of the neurological and psychological symptoms is altered brain metabolism caused by reduced blood glucose.

standard deviation. A measure of dispersion in a distribution. It is equal to the square root of the sum of squares of the deviations from the arithmetic mean, divided by the number of items in the population.

standard error of estimate. The standard deviation of the differences between true values and estimated values.

standardized (death, birth, mortality) rates. The crude rates modified to allow for age distribution, immigration, and so on. For instance, the rate, when standardized, might be given for adults only or for men only.

statement. Computer term for a simply and indivisible specification for an action, such as IF statements.

sterilization. Rendering a person incapable of reproduction; usually accomplished by vasectomy or tubal ligation, but such procedures as castration and hysterectomy are occasionally used.

stimulant. See p. 95.

stratification. In brain function and mental processes, a hierarchic order or layering occurring by superimposition of higher portions of brain elements that successfully assume dominant function.

streptomycin. See p. 95.

stress. An overload that the organism cannot handle; may be caused by inadequacies in the organism, extreme environmental input, or both.

stressors. Any agent, situation, thought, person, or stimulus able to produce stress.

stress polycythemia. A relative increase in circulating red blood cells brought on by emotional factors. In this, the total red cell mass is normal while plasma volume is below normal. It is also called stress erythrocytosis and emotional polycythemia. It is distinguished from polycythemia vera in being benign and having laboratory findings different from the malignant disease.

stroke. Cerebrovascular accident.

subcortical integration. The linking by the brainstem, reticular activating system, limbic system, and other lower brain centers, of physiological and external activities through visceral, hormonal, and metabolic functions, through motor and postural activity, and through facilitatory and inhibitory mechanisms.

subdural hematoma. A blood clot occurring between the dura mater and arachnoid from venous bleeding; usually occurs secondary to head trauma.

subroutine. Computer term for a body of computer instructions contained within or amended to the principal programs.

succinimides. See p. 95.

succinylcholine. See p. 95.

sympathin. See p. 96.

symptom. A manifestation or indication of a disease not necessarily specific for any particular disease. A headache is an example.

synapse. The point of contact of one nerve with another.

synaptic cleft. The minute space between two nerves at the synapse. The nerve impulse is carried across this space by a neurotransmitter substance.

syntax. Computer term for the rules of the language used. Necessarily, these rules must be inflexible, as they are in mathematics.

system. A set of functionally related components organized to perform some useful purpose.

systems research. Scientific endeavor encompassing biology, psychology, behavioral and social science, technology, and other sciences.

systems theory. A theory based on elements of biological, mathematical, psychological, and socioeconomic theories in which the system is the person. The input is a stimulus, and the output is a response by the person.

tabes. A late complication of syphilitic infection of the central nervous system; a chronic, progressive condition eventuating often in paralysis and even death.

taxis. A term used in behavioral science to denote the tendency of an organism to orient to an object.

temporal lobe epilepsy. Seizures caused by lesions of the temporal lobe. The symptoms may be highly varied and include psychotic and antisocial behavior. The diagnosis depends upon demonstrating focal pathological discharges from the temporal lobe area.

tension headache. See p. 43.

teonauacatl mushroom. See p. 96.

terminal. Computer term for a component of a computer system where input data can be entered or output data retrieved. Terminals might be located a long distance from the principal apparatus, connected to the main center by means of telephone lines.

testicle. The male sex gland.

testosterone. The main male sex hormone.

tetanus. An infectious disease caused by the bacterial agent, *Clostridium tetani;* a condition characterized by localized or generalized muscle spasms caused by a toxin produced by the bacteria. It may be associated with delirium. Synonym: lockjaw.

tetraplegia. Quadriplegia.

thalamic syndrome. A decrease in ability to perceive sensations on the opposite side of the body; usually secondary to a cerebrovascular accident.

thalamotomy. Incision of the thalamus to sever the nerve fibers that run from the thalamus to the cerebral cortex; used as a treatment of severe and intractable mental illness. It is rarely used now.

thalamus. One of the large ganglia in the midportion of the brain. It is richly supplied with nerve interconnections with other parts of the brain and nervous system.

thanatomania. Voodo death.

thermagnosia. See p. 70.

thiamin. See p. 96.

thyroid gland. One of the endocrine glands. It is located in the anterior part of the neck and partly surrounds the trachea. The chief function of the gland is to secrete hormones that control metabolism by increasing the rate of cellular oxidation. Excessive decrease or increase in amounts of these hormones can cause clinical symptoms of psychiatric disease.

thyroid hormones. Hormones secreted by the thyroid gland and the mechanism by which the gland exerts its chief effects. The main component of these is thyroxine, but others include triiodothyronine and occasionally diiodothyronine.

thyrotoxicosis. Pronounced excess of circulating thyroid hormone in the blood; a condition characterized by restlessness, hyperactivity, sleeplessness, weight loss, and agitation, often to a degree that closely resembles mania.

time-sharing. Computer term for a modern development by which many distant locations can share a common computer facility, each one connected by telephone lines to its own terminal.

tinnitus. See p. 44.

tissue needs. The requirements of the body; the need for food, air, and water.

tonaphasia. See p. 44.

topagnosia. See p. 44.

topalgia. See p. 44.

torsion spasm. See p. 44.

torticollis. See p. 44.

totem. An animal or other object that serves as an emblem of a family or clan; a representative or reminder to the family or clan of its origins and ancestors.

toxic delirium. See p. 44.

toxic psychosis. See p. 44.

traits. The appearance, pattern of activity, or any other internal or external characteristic of an organism; used especially where these are genetically determined.

transducer. A link in a communications channel; a unit that passes information from one point to another, usually through the use of power from another source. One example is a telephone. In communications theory a person can serve such a function.

transmitter substance. Neurotransmitter.

tremor. See p. 44.

trimethadione. See p. 97.

trophotropic dominance. Dominance of parasympathetic or trophotropic activity.

truth table. In Boolean mathematics, a way of solving problems using a matrix in which many combinations can be answered as true or false, by elimination, which yields a solution.

tryptamine. An intermediate metabolite of tryptophan; a precursor of serotonin.

tryptophan. A naturally occurring amino acid; a metabolic precursor of serotonin.

tuberculous meningitis. Infection of the coverings of the brain and spinal cord by the tubercle bacillus.

tuberous sclerosis. An inherited condition of the central nervous system characterized by multiple gliotic nodules throughout the CNS; associated with mental retardation.

typhoid fever. A systemic infectious disease caused by ingestion of *Salmonella typhosa*. It is usually severe and may be associated with exhaustion delirium.

tyramine. See p. 97.

ulcerative colitis. A severe disease of the colon characterized by remissions and relapses and even a fatal outcome. There is an inflammatory reaction of the colon mucosa and submucosa, without a specific infectious agent being involved. Clinically, there is a passage of blood and pus alone or with the stool during the inflammatory phases. It is thought to have psychological factors in its cause.

uncus. A small outcropping of cerebral cortical tissue on the median or upper margins of the temporal lobe.

underload. In communications theory, a condition where the increment or decrement of a stimulus is so small that no change can be perceived.

unit-trait. A genetic trait transmitted by a single gene not associated with other unit-traits.

uremia. Abnormally high levels of urea in the blood; usually caused by a decrease in kidney function, and usually carries a grave prognosis.

urethra. The tubular passageway from the urinary bladder to the outside of the body.

urticaria. See p. 45.

vaginismus. See p. 45.

validity. The degree of accuracy that a test is able to indicate; the quality or attribute that the test measures.

vanillylmandelic acid. See p. 98.

variable. A component of a problem statement that is capable of being assigned more than one value.

vasectomy. A sterilization procedure for men; severing and ligating the vas deferens (seminal ducts).

vegetative dystonia. Effort syndrome. (See p. 26.)

vegetative nervous system. See autonomic nervous system.

venereal disease. A disease contracted through sexual intercourse.

ventriculogram. See p. 45.

vertigo. See p. 45.

verumontanum. An elevation on the floor of the urethra where the seminal vesicles enter.

virilism. See p. 45.

visceral brain. McLean's term for the limbic system.

visceral system. That portion of the brain, including the insula, claustrum, uncinate fasciculus, and amygdala, that deals with taste, thirst, hunger, colic, and other alimentary conditions.

vital statistics. Data on births, deaths, and incidence of various diseases in relation to a known population. In the United States, this data is regularly collected by local and state departments of health and is then consolidated for the nation by the United States Public Health Service.

vitamin B$_{12}$. See p. 45.

voodoo death. Death in a person who believes he is the victim of a black magic spell that has been cast upon him. Exact mechanism or cause of such deaths has not been found.

vulvismus. See p. 45.

vulvitis. Inflammation or irritation of the labia of the female external genitalia.

Wetterleuchten. Myoclonia and twitches of the facial muscles; a condition sometimes associated with syphilitic infections of the brain.

white matter. The nerve tracts of the central nervous system.

Wilson's disease. An inherited disease characterized by degeneration of the liver and lenticular nucleus of the brain. It is associated with mental deficiency.

xanthines. See p. 98.

xanthoma. Localized deposits of cholesterol.

X chromosome. One of the sex chromosomes.

x-rays. Ultrashort wavelength emissions generated in a special vacuum tube, useful because of their ability to penetrate solid objects. They are used in diagnostic procedures to determine existence of abnormal conditions such as tumors and broken bones within the body.

XX chromosomes. The pairing of sex chromosomes that produces a female.

XY chromosomes. The pairing of sex chromosomes that produces a male.

XYY. An abnormality of sex chromosomes called a trisomy. It has been associated with certain mental abnormalities.

Y chromosome. The sex chromosome, carried by the sperm, that determines that the sex will be male.

yohimbine. See p. 98.

zygote. The fertilized ovum; a single cell formed by the union of the sperm and egg.

Abbreviations, slang, and colloquial English terms

As in most professions, a substantial vocabulary of specialized slang and abbreviated terminology is present in the daily usage of workers in the areas of mental health and the behavioral sciences. These terms are encountered more frequently in spoken rather than written language and, as such, tend to be subject to more rapid change in sense and application than words that achieve standardization and longevity through appearance in the professional literature. The prominence of abbreviation and other modes of expressing technical terminology in other than conventional fashion is largely a response to the unusual length and complexity of many standard medical terms. Adrenocorticotropic hormone, which affects the cortex of the adrenal gland, is, for example, understandably referred to simply as ACTH. Additionally, many lay terms for psychiatric phenomena are necessarily employed by the professional in establishing communication with an individual who has some sense of what is meant by "a nervous breakdown," but to whom "depressive episode" and "psychosis" mean little.

For both the purpose of simplifying complex terms derived from Latin and Greek and also for the purpose of portraying one's familiarity with the language of the field, a certain amount of professional slang has developed. The meaning of slang terms is likely to change rapidly with passing fashions, so that glossaries tend to become quickly obsolete. In many places, the use of slang is regarded within any specialized field as a kind of index of how current the individual is in regard to the trends. It is typical, thus, for the novice to seek to establish his status of "being on the inside of what is going on" by overusing and often misusing slang. The short half-life of professional slang is probably caused by the tendency for slang to "leak" out of the profession into public usage and then cease being useful as an index of one's "insider" status. In addition to the professional slang that develops in each profession, the mental health field also makes frequent use of slang originating from other cultures. This is likely to happen because of the frequent use of a client's own verbal expressions in clinical descriptions. Thus, a case study of an individual from the "hippie" subculture might be presented with colorful slang from that culture. The slang in common, but transient, use in the drug subcultures is especially likely to turn up in the literature or case discussions.

Not infrequently, everyday English terms have been given specialized meanings in the mental health fields. Conscious and unconscious are typical examples of words having both general meanings in the colloquial language and special meanings in the technical language. The prevalence of this disparity often raises the questions in the mind of a novice as to whether or not a given common English term also has a special and different technical meaning. Some note needs to be made, therefore, in a comprehensive glossary of those common terms that, though used in the professions, still retain their colloquial meaning.

ABBREVIATIONS

ADP	Automatic data processing
ACTH	Adrenocorticotropic hormone
A.G.C.T.	Army General Classification Test
ALGOL	A computer language introduced in 1958
CNS	Central nervous system
DNA	Deoxyribonucleic acid
ECT	Electroconvulsive therapy
EDP	Electronic data processing
EEG	Electroencephalogram
ESP	Extrasensory perception
EST	Electroshock treatment
GABA	Gamma-aminobutyric acid
ICT	Insulin coma therapy; insulin treatment
I.Q.	Intelligence quotient; a term devised by Alfred Binet for the ratio between a child's mental age, as determined by psychological tests, and his chronological age
LP	Lumbar puncture
LSD	Lysergic acid diethylamide
MAO	Monamine oxidase
M.M.P.I.	Minnesota Multiphasic Personality Inventory
M.A.	Mental age
NREM sleep	Non–rapid-eye-movement sleep
OT	Occupational therapy
REM sleep	Rapid-eye-movement sleep
RAI uptake	Radioactive iodine uptake
s-r psychology	Behavioral or stimulus-response psychology
TAT	Thematic Apperception Test
ucs	Unconscious
VMA	Vanillylmandelic acid
W.A.I.S.	Wechsler Adult Intelligence Scale
W.I.S.C.	Wechsler Intelligence Scale for Children

SLANG AND COLLOQUIAL ENGLISH

almoner. One who distributes charitable gifts.

amulet. An object worn to ward off evil spirits.

astrology. The practice of divining the future through study of heavenly bodies.

backward. Mental hospital ward housing severely and chronically disturbed patients. Sometimes used pejoratively (slang).

binge. Prolonged drinking spree.

blackout. A common term for fainting or loss of consciousness, but can refer to a period of time for which the person has no memory; associated with alcoholism, epilepsy, hysterical states. Synonym: blank spells, absence.

blank spells. Blackout, absence.

bug. An unpleasant paresthesia associated with cocaine withdrawal symptoms.

bugger. Anal intercourse, sometimes, any homosexual intercourse.

coke. Cocaine.

crash. Depression, especially following withdrawal of stimulant medication. Spending the night together, especially sleeping together.

debug. Computer term (slang) for the process of correcting oversights and errors in a program or in the data.

fainting. Syncope; temporary, acute loss of consciousness; a common finding in young hysterical girls that usually has no organic basis.

falling sickness. Epilepsy.

fit. Seizure, convulsion.

gang. A group; generally used to denote a group organized for some malevolent behavior.

ghetto. The poorer or slum section of a city. Rural ghettoes refers to substandard living conditions in rural areas.

GIGO. Computer term (slang) meaning "garbage in, garbage out," referring to the fact that the quality of output cannot exceed the quality of input.

hangover. A dysphoria following ingestion of alcohol and other sedative drugs; usually occurs "the morning after."

hardware. Computer slang for equipment, machinery, and instruments in the computer. Software applies to plans, programs, ideas, and paper.

the heat. Police; law enforcement agencies.

highway hypnosis. A trancelike state in which the individual loses track of time and place but often stays in sufficient contact with the environment to continue to drive, often drives past his destination, may become immobile at the wheel, may hallucinate false conditions of the road, and because of these, may be involved in an accident. This state is thought to be responsible for many accidents.

hog. Heroine addict who progressively increases dose.

horrors. Pronounced dysphoria occurring in delirium tremens.

inebriate. An habitual drunkard; an alcoholic.

kallikaks. A family observed to show mental deficiency and various types of antisocial behavior over many generations; now used almost as a synonym for a socially or mentally degenerate family.

lunatic. A term used to denote a mentally ill person; now usually taken in a derogatory sense.

mainline. Intravenous injection (slang).

mickey mouse. An inferior or trivial plan, idea, or device (slang).

mob. An agitated crowd.

nervous breakdown. Nonspecific term for any type or degree of mental illness.

nirvana. A blissful and relatively unaware state.

obscenity. Anything seen or heard that is invidiously or commonly taken to be offensive; especially as in regard to sexual connotations.

occult. Of hidden meaning; irrational; magic, soothsaying.

occultism. The practice of so-called magic.

orgy. Pleasurable excesses carried on by a group.

orthodox psychoanalysis. A term used in psychiatry to refer to a type of psychoanalysis that closely follows Freud's theories (slang).

ostracism. The intentional exclusion from group or social activities or membership.

oversensitivity. The increased awareness of subtle stimuli, especially hidden meanings, slights, or nonverbal cues that occur in every conversation. It is a pronounced trait in many persons with mental illnesses.

overprotection. Certain childrearing practices in which the parent is to be permissive, overindulgent, and restrictive of the activities of the child. Such practices are thought to lead to personality and behavioral problems in the person reared in such a manner (for example, dependency, passive dependency).

pad. One's bedroom or living quarters. Also, a place to indulge in drugs of abuse.

pornography. Art, movies, writing, or acting that is for the primary purpose of being sexually stimulating through the use of obscene, salacious themes.

proselytizing. The recruitment of others to one's habits or beliefs; usually in reference to alcoholics and drug users who tend to induce others to follow their patterns.

psychopath. Psychopathic personality. (See p 40.)

punch drunk. Posttraumatic psychosis, diffuse.

pusher. One who sells illicit drugs.

quack. A fraudulent practitioner; usually a person who makes special claims and uses special bu valueless techniques to defraud the ill.

queen. A male homosexual (argot).

queer. A common name (or argot) for a homosexual especially the male homosexual.

racism. A doctrine that promotes the dominance or superiority of one race over another.

reefer. A marijuana cigarette.

revolving door. A pattern of early admission speedy discharge, and readmission for certain patients.

rum fits. Seizures following ingestion of alcohol; no the same as delirium tremens.

salvation. Something that saves or delivers a person from danger or difficulty; especially where there is religious meaning. Guilt-ridden patients may be concerned with needs for salvation, and psychotic patients will often incorporate this as a theme of their delusional system.

sex glands. The gonads; in the male, the testes; in the female, the ovaries.

sixty-nine. Simultaneous fellatio and cunnilingus, sometimes, simultaneous mutual fellatio.

snow. Cocaine (slang).

snow bird. Cocaine addict.

soixante-neuf. Sixty-nine.

sorcery. The use of or belief in magic, especially black magic or evil.

spell. A trance or other effect brought about in a person by himself or another person, especially through the use of sorcery, black magic, or witchcraft.

spiritualism. The belief in or practice of magic, especially that which deals with divining aid from or with having communication with a deceased person.

taboo. A social prohibition.

taint. Affected by an undesirable inherited trait.

teasing. Tantalizing; provoking desire without intending to satisfy any need thereby aroused; may be used to provide sadistic-masochistic gratification, but is often seen in normal interpersonal relations.

temperament. One's total moods and reactions to various situations and circumstances. This is strongly influenced by the state of physical and mental health at the time.

thaumaturgy. Use of magic or performance of miracles.

tiredness. A state of weariness; the subjective feeling of fatigue, exhaustion, or being worn out. It is a common complaint of persons with a mental or emotional disturbance.

vagina dentata. A folklore concept that some women have a vagina with teeth; the hurtful female genital.

virgin. A person who has never had sexual intercourse.

visionism. Voyeurism. (See p. 45.)

visions. A commonly used or lay term for visual hallucinations.

water head. A lay term for hydrocephalus. (See p. 29.)

wet dream. The passage of seminal fluid, usually accompanied by a pleasant, erotic dream. A normal occurrence especially likely to occur in young men after prolonged sexual abstinence.

witchcraft. The use of or belief in magic; the occult.

wryneck. Torticollis. (See p. 44.)

yen. In the argot of narcotic addicts, denotes a strong desire for the drug that develops during withdrawal.

yen sleep. In the argot of the narcotic addict, denotes the sleep that comes during withdrawal from the drug.

yoga. A mental discipline that stresses achieving control of one's physical and mental faculties through exercises, concentration, and devotions. It has found some following among psychiatrists and psychologists as a treatment mode.

yoga exercises. Elaborate breathing and postural exercises that enable the person to relax and gain some control over autonomic nervous system function.

Historical biographies

This section presents brief biographies of many of the people whose writings or other types of influence had a significant impact on the entire field of mental health. For the most part, contemporary people are not included, since their names can be found in the current literature. The historically important people are listed, however, because their work is often referred to in the current literature, but additional information about them might otherwise be very difficult to find.

The various people who had an influence on the evolution and development of the field of mental health and the behavioral sciences came from a diversity of fields, including philosophy, literature, and religion. Their contributions have not been invariably positive; in many cases, they were more destructive than constructive. However, even the so-called pseudosciences, such as mesmerism and phrenology, played an important part in this development.

The field of human behavior, human thinking, or human nature is intimately bound up with nearly everything that man does or has done. The thinkers and writers of the past who studied these issues or tried to modify the activities in which these issues were relevant included those in such areas as education, politics, and business management. In more recent times, even such fields as advertising and salesmanship can properly be regarded as examples of applied psychology and, as such, have something to teach. The philosophers of the past were especially concerned with studies of human motivation and thinking, and though these studies were not usually done in a scientific way, they nevertheless laid the groundwork on which the science of psychology was ultimately founded. For instance, William James, the first truly well-known ''psychologist'' in the United States, was trained in physiology but held a position in the department of philosophy at Harvard.

Many of the earliest examples of medical interest in the psychiatric problems of people came from physicians' humanitarian, rather than their professional, involvement. These interests, however, established the precedents that eventually brought the responsibility for the care of psychiatric problems under the province of medical people. During the Inquisition, for instance, the cruel way in which the alleged witches were treated prompted a Dr. Weyer in Germany to investigate some of the people accused of witchcraft. His descriptions of what he found became the earliest clinical studies of typical mental health problems—those that today are classified usually as either hysteria or schizophrenia. Similarly, during the eighteenth century, the Royal Academy of Medicine in England conducted inspections of institutions (such as Bethlehem Asylum) in order to recommend improvements in living conditions for the inmates. The horrible conditions then prevailing in the few institutions of this sort prompted the Quakers in York, England, to establish a model retreat (known as the York Retreat) that would serve as a more desirable example for others to follow. A merchant

134

named William Tuke was the leader in this movement, and several of his descendents became prominent English psychiatrists (for example, Daniel Hack Tuke).

Concepts of human behavior were, for a long time, intimately related to religious theories, so that the idea of the soul and of the mind were used interchangeably. Often in the past, the prime direction followed in trying to induce people showing aberrant behavior to conform to more normal ways was through a kind of religious or moral conversion. Penitentiaries, for instance, were originally meant to be places where prisoners would repent their sins and achieve acceptable social status through a religious commitment. "Moral treatment" prevailed throughout the nineteenth century as an equivalent to what today is called psychotherapy. The long-standing debate, still unresolved, on the question of the role of heredity in causing psychiatric problems has been a derivative of the Christian theology that presupposes an original (inherited) sin, in opposition to counter theories that see man as inherently good.

It is most important to realize that the terminology that has come into use in the mental health professions during the present era is relatively new in origin and especially new in the definitions used. Terminology used before the present century was different, more limited in its vocabulary, and less precise in its definition. Much of the terminology has changed over the years for euphemistic purposes; that is, a previously common term had fallen into some sort of disrepute, leading to the invention of a new term meaning the same thing but sounding more elegant. For example, at different times in history, people with very serious psychiatric problems have been referred to as mad, as lunatics, as non compos mentis, as psychotic, and today as mentally ill. Similarly, the institutions in which they were placed were called, at different times, madhouses, lunatic asylums, sanitariums, retreats, psychopathic hospitals, and today either mental hospitals or psychiatric hospitals. People who, today, are referred to as mentally retarded were previously called mentally deficient, morons, imbeciles, or idiots. There also

exists differences in the use of euphemisms from one country to another, so that what is called psychiatry in the United States is called psychological medicine in England; and in France it is referred to as the study of alienation. In general, there is a tendency for the general public usage of these terms to lag behind the adoption of new euphemisms in the professions themselves. In the popular literature, consequently, the older styles persist. These remarks are relevant to the question of historical personages, because not infrequently these people are known for contributions that were presented in what is now obsolete terminology. Their contributions, however, might not be as obsolete as their terminology is.

Abraham, Karl (1877-1925). A German psychiatrist who became a loyal follower of Freud in the psychoanalytic movement. He was especially known for his application of Freud's concept of the anal character to an analytic theory of depression. The obsessive-compulsive personality, theorized as an outgrowth of the anal character, was described by Abraham as being especially prone to depression.

Adler, Alfred (1870-1937). A Viennese psychiatrist who joined Freud's psychoanalytic movement early in the 1900s but broke away before World War I to found his own movement, which he called individual psychology. He placed less stress than Freud on the sexual forces in character formation and more emphasis on the self-preservation instincts. He saw man as motivated to lifelong struggle for power, initially to overcome his childhood sense of inferiority. People develop their own life styles as they fail or succeed to compensate or overcompensate for their original sense of inferiority. A common form this struggle might take is to seek power over other people. Adler's school of thought attracted a substantial following in Europe and in the United States.

Alexander, Franz (1891-1964). One of many Hungarians who joined Freud's psychoanalytic movement in Europe and who then came to the United States prior to World War II. Although he remained fairly faithful to the freudian doctrines, he expanded them considerably. He emphasized transference as the central problem of psychoanalytic therapy and offered a solution to the irrationality of the relationship between therapist and patient through corrective emotional experiences. Alexander founded the Chicago Psychoanalytic Institute and was its director for 25 years. Just before his death he moved to Los Angeles where he became a leading figure in psychoanalytic circles.

Anaxagoras (ca. 500 B.C.). A Greek philosopher who was influenced more by biological and medical knowledge than by the prevailing mysticism of his times. He saw knowledge as the product of experience and described its acquisition as the finest goal of life. He insisted, however, on the need to apply knowledge to practical problems. The mind is an element itself that is pure and homogenous, imparting orderliness to existence. The site of the mind was the lateral ventricles of the brain.

Angell, James Rowland (1869-1949). A pioneer in academic psychology in the United States, after having studied under Ebbinghaus and Helmholtz in Germany. He joined Dewey at Michigan, went with him to the University of Chicago, and played a major role in the formulation of functional psychology. John Watson, the founder of the behavioral school was a student of his. Functional psychology was developed from concepts of biological evolution, in which human psychology is viewed as a peculiarly human adaptational device.

Aristotle (384-322 B.C.). In addition to his many other influential contributions, this Greek philosopher also examined the phenomenon of the human mind. He saw human existence as composed of a hierarchy of processes, with simple, vegetative functions at the bottom and intellectual activities at the top. In spite of allegations by others that he was highly teleological in his thinking, he ascribed purpose to man alone, and saw this as something created by man. He emphasized attention in the learning process and postulated concepts of memory as based on association. The importance of motivation toward a goal was seen as the essence of understanding human behavior.

Augustine, Saint (354-430). An early philosopher of the Catholic Church who provided a coldly logical rationale for Christianity. He tended to take a traditional and conservative view in opposition to liberal movements of his time. He presented in his *Confessions* an explanation of memory.

Bacon, Francis (1561-1626). As much a statesman as a philosopher, this Englishman is best known today for his concept of the scientific method as a pioneering contribution to scientific development.

Above all, he emphasized the necessity of finding knowledge through experimentation rather than intellectual speculation. He emphasized the ways in which the senses can yield faulty information. The need to withhold conclusions until all possible information is collected became his axiom of scientific thinking.

Bain, Alexander (1818-1903). This English psychologist was perhaps the first to make psychology a lifelong career. His pioneering textbooks (*Senses and the Intellect,* 1853; and *Emotions and the Will,* 1859) established the precedents followed by later textbook writers. Bain emphasized the importance of habit formation in the learning process and placed considerable importance on instinct as the substructure for psychology.

Bartlett, Frederic (1886-1969). A contemporary English psychologist, the first to receive a knighthood for his psychological work. He has taught at Cambridge and for many years has been editor of the *British Journal of Psychology.* He stresses the importance of skill as the outstanding quality of thinking. Study of these human skills is more informative than artificial laboratory studies.

Battie, William (1703-1776). An English physician who probably deserves the title of the first full-time psychiatrist. As a member of the Board of Governors of Bethlehem Asylum he fought a losing battle to bring about reforms in the treatment of patients. He then founded a new hospital, St. Luke's, where he was able to install his own progressive measures and to introduce, for the first time, medical students to the teaching of psychiatry. His *Treatise on Madness* (1757) is one of the earliest publications that can be looked upon as a textbook of psychiatry.

Beard, George (1839-1883). An American physician noted for his introduction of the diagnostic entity neurasthenia—known elsewhere as "the American disease." He described the condition as a vague but rich assortment of complaints, which he attributed to some sort of nervous exhaustion. Commonplace concepts of nervous breakdown are derived from this popular diagnosis, which remained in fashion as late as World War II.

Beers, Clifford (1876-1943). An American layman who, after several admissions as a patient in private and state mental hospitals, sought to bring about a reform of the inhuman practices he found there. His book *The Mind that Found Itself* was a popular account of his hospital experiences. With the help of William James and William Osler he founded and was executive secretary of the National Committee of Mental Hygiene. After his death this organization underwent considerable strengthening and expansion to become the present National Association for Mental Health, a society of laymen and professionals seeking to improve the care of mental patients.

Bentham, Jeremy (1748-1832). This English philosopher and sociologist was the founder of the school of thought known as utilitarianism. He offered an ethical framework for social reform based on the concept of the "greatest good for the greatest number." After interesting himself in prison reform, he extended his efforts, with little success, to reforms in the care of mental patients. He advanced the principle of human motivation known as the pleasure-pain principle; that is, the drive of human beings to seek pleasure and avoid pain.

Berkeley, George (1685-1753). An English-Irish prelate of the Church of England who stressed perception as the sole test of reality: "To be is to be perceived." Man only knows his own mental world and the real world exists only as he sees it (*An Essay Towards a New Theory of Vision,* 1709).

Bernheim, Hippolyte (1837-1919). A French physician who studied hypnotism and hysteria with Charcot but developed an opposing view. Freud's view was probably influenced considerably by Bernheim. Instead of the physiological changes that Charcot postulated, Bernheim described hysteria as merely a state of heightened suggestibility and maintained that hypnotism was effective simply as a mode of counter-suggestion. He called his mode of treating hysterics suggestion therapy.

Binet, Alfred (1857-1911). With Simon in France, Binet developed the first graded series of tests that became standardized as tests to measure intelligence quotients. He based his standard on the ratio between mental age, determined by testing, and chronological age. The test was standardized for adults in the United States Army during World War I, and has come to be known as the Stanford Binet test. Fundamental to these efforts was the assumption that the individual's capacity for learning remains relatively fixed at the same level throughout life.

Bleuler, Eugen (1857-1939). This Swiss psychiatrist was considerably influenced by Freud's theories and sought to apply them to the study of psychoses. He developed the concept of schizophrenia to replace Kraepelin's concept of dementia praecox. By the term he meant a splitting off of the

emotions from thinking. He saw the condition as primarily psychological and as the end result of a patient's striving for contradictory goals, thus accounting for the irrationality of his ideas. In spite of his psychological explanations, however, his writings frequently mention heredity and metabolic factors as also important.

Boerhaave, Herman (1668-1738). A Dutch physician well known in his time throughout Europe for his medical teaching in nearly all aspects of medicine. His lectures were widely published in many languages. He emphasized the importance of good hospital records and complete histories on his patients. He lectured, as well, on "madness" but took rather conventional views on the subject, ascribing mental difficulties to disorders of the blood flow through the brain.

Braid, James (ca. 1795-1860). An English physician who studied hypnotism with a new and objective spirit that finally settled much of the controversy surrounding Mesmer's work. He offered physiological and psychological explanations of the phenomenon that were credible, at least, to physicians.

Brentano, Franz (1838-1917). A Viennese philosopher who taught at the University of Vienna during the period when the city was the center of European cultural and intellectual refinement. He opposed Wundt's structuralism in experimental psychology and advocated the empirical approach to the study of human behavior. He stressed the difference between the act, or what the individual actually does in the process of perceiving and understanding, and the content, or the actual reality of the experience.

Brigham, Amariah (1798-1849). One of the original founders of the present American Psychiatric Association (1843) and the first editor of the association's journal. He advocated, as have the subsequent editors of the journal, an organic causation of mental disorders. He also adopted the conventional, moralistic notion that contemporary emotional problems were related to affluent living and intellectual excitement. He came to be the superintendent of the state hospital at Utica, New York.

Brill, Abraham (1874-1948). A Hungarian psychiatrist, trained in Switzerland, who was largely responsible for introducing Freud's theories into the United States. He translated Freud's early works into English and was one of the handful of founders of the New York Psychoanalytic Institute.

Brown, Thomas (1778-1820). Professor of Moral

Philosophy at the University of Edinburgh, Brown founded what came to be known as the "Scottish" or "common-sense" school of psychology. This was largely an outgrowth of Locke's ideas, based on empiricism. Brown contributed to concepts of association as an important factor in learning. He devised the secondary law of association, which defines the ways by which learning is facilitated when it is associated with an experience charged with excitement or repetition.

Burton, Robert (1576-1639). An English clergyman who published a classic literary description of depression under the title *Anatomy of Melancholy* in 1621. With elaborate allegorical allusions, he painted a vivid, and not too inaccurate, picture of clinical depression.

Buytendijk, F. J. J. (1887-　　). A Dutch physician who was Professor of Physiology at Groningen and took up the study of existentialism in later life. He popularized the concept of the encounter in reference to his notions of the importance of communication in human relationships. He stressed the importance of experiences characterized by suffering and pain as essential to the deep understanding of human behavior.

Cabanis, Pierre (1757-1802). A French physician who was much involved in the changes and reforms instituted after the Revolution. He offered an explanation for certain pathological states brought about as a result of emotional factors. He was influenced by the moral treatment advocated by the Tukes at the York Retreat and brought to France by Pinel. His medical explanations tended to give a new respectability to the study of psychological influences. These efforts might be considered early attempts to establish a basis for psychosomatic medicine.

Cannon, Walter (1871-1945). The American physiologist who established the importance of homeostasis in the study of all body processes. His *Bodily Changes in Pain, Hunger, Fear and Rage* (1915) presented the phenomenon of emotions in a new physiological light.

Carr, Harvey (1873-1954). Carr succeeded Angell as Professor of Psychology at the University of Chicago and also assumed leadership of the functional school. He emphasized the empirical method of studying psychology, in contrast to the laboratory method. Attention and perception are the essential ingredients of learning, and mental activity is the process of adapting and organizing past experiences into conduct habits.

Cattell, J. McKeen (1860-1944). The first professor of psychology in the United States, first at the University of Pennsylvania and then at Columbia. He studied with Wundt in Germany, then with Thorndike and Woodward in the United States. He was the first to place heavy emphasis on the use of statistics in psychology, and he sought quantitative means of expression in human behavior.

Celsus, Aulus Cornelius (ca. 50 A.D.). A Latin encyclopedist whose extensive writings also included medicine. He divided all illness into acute and chronic forms. The psychiatric conditions of mania and melancholia were included under the latter. He advocated the use of torture in treating mental conditions, suggesting it as a kind of shock treatment.

Charcot, Jean (1825-1893). A prominent French neurologist at Saltpetriere whose students included Bernheim, Janet, and Freud. He rejuvenated Mesmer's techniques in the treatment of hysteria and subscribed to the theory that both hysteria and hypnosis were physiological rather than psychological phenomena. He believed that hysteria was, ultimately, a disorder of the ovaries.

Cheyne, George (1671-1743). A highly respected and fashionable London physician who wrote extensively on many medical subjects. He popularized the term "the English malady" by which he meant what later became known as hysteria in women. He blamed the condition on high living and indolence. He felt the English were unusually prone to develop this condition.

Combe, Andrew (1797-1847). A Scottish psychiatrist who, with his brother George, did a great deal to introduce and popularize the phrenology of Spurzheim into the British Isles. When much of the superficial ritualism of his approach to the management of psychiatric patients is set aside, what is left is rather straightforward psychotherapy. He founded a journal of phrenology.

Comte, Auguste (1798-1857). A French philosopher who founded the school of thought known as positivism. His philosophy was sociologically oriented and had as its goal a type of widespread social reform characterized by people living together in peace and harmony. He felt that the human mind was directed toward the search for truth and that mysticism would be replaced by science.

Confucius (K'ung-futzu) (ca. 550 B.C.). A Chinese philosopher who rose from humble origins to become a great political leader. He saw a universal moral order in human affairs, which good men aspired to and which is capable of a kind of codification that can serve as an idealized standard of conduct. Patience, serenity, and tolerance are virtues to set up as goals.

Conolly, John (1794-1866). An English psychiatrist who was on the original faculty of the University of London. He wrote a widely used textbook of psychiatry. He was best known for his advocacy of nonrestraint in the management of psychiatric patients, believing that moral treatment makes the use of physical restraints unnecessary. The discussion and controversy that arose over this policy had a direct influence on the psychiatrists of the United States organizing the first national medical society (1843), which was the forerunner of the present American Psychiatric Association. (The American Medical Association was organized five years later.)

Copernicus, Nicolas (1473-1543). This Polish monk and astronomer discovered the true nature of the rotation of the planets about the sun. His works were published after his death for fear of Church reprisals. The effect this had on the thinking of European man was enormous, for it displaced man from the center of the universe and established scientific methods as a new competitor with religion for man's beliefs. Religion ceased from being the central theme of philosophy and of the study of man from this point on.

Crichton, (Sir) Alexander (1763-1856). A prominent teacher in the medical school at Westminster Hospital in London. Although he had no special experience in psychiatry, he made pronouncements about the management of psychiatric patients that had great influence. He followed the concepts of Locke, Hartley, and Reid. Among other things, he advocated self-analysis, by which he meant the necessity of understanding the human thinking process through examination of one's own.

Cullen, William (1710-1790). In an era when Edinburgh was the outstanding medical training center, Cullen was one of the University's leading teachers. He developed an elaborate classification scheme for psychiatric conditions (following the precedents of botanical classification). He invented the terms paranoia and neurosis. He blamed many diseases on disorders of the nervous system.

Darwin, Charles (1809-1882). In addition to his *Origin of Species* with its first promulgation of the theory of evolution (1859), Darwin also published *Descent of Man* in which he emphasized human

evolution. He saw human civilization as a process of evolution, arising from man's drive to socialize and organize his activity.

Darwin, Erasmus (1731-1802). Grandfather of Charles Darwin, poet, botanist, and philosopher. He classified all known diseases, including numerous trivial psychological phenomena, according to the prevailing botanical system of nomenclature. Concerning madness, he stated that every type will show a peculiar idea of desire or aversion that is perceptually excited in the mind with all its connections. Thus, each type leads either to muscular activity or inactivity, depending upon whether desire or repulsion dominates the patient.

Democritus (ca. 460-370 B.C.). The "laughing philosopher" of Greece who developed the concept of atomism, thereby perhaps the first to conceive of ultimate indivisible particles of matter. Both material things and the intellect are composed of similar atoms, and mental processes are made up of motions of these particles.

Descartes, Rene (1596-1650). French philosopher and mathematician. His "cogito ergo sum" (I think, therefore I am) became a fundamental Renaissance doctrine. He felt no need for experimentation to develop psychological knowledge. He expounded a fantastic theory of central nervous system function in which the peripheral nerves were described as hollow tubes through which spinal fluid was pumped to inflate the muscles. The ventricles of the brain and their fluid contents were the sites of memory and the pineal gland regulated the process of remembering in mechanical fashion.

Dewey, John (1859-1952). An educator and philosopher who is known as the founder of progressive education. He taught several places but ended up at Columbia Teachers College. He attacked the behavioralists of his time as being mechanistic and saw the intrinsic human qualities in psychology as creations of man. The concept of truth itself is an invention of man's. In education, he advocated the need for students getting their own experiences and not being confined to listening to the experiences of others.

Dickens, Charles (1812-1870). The English novelist noted for his social commentaries. He made a visit to the United States, which he described in a book, *The American Notes* (1844). He visited the Boston Lunatic Asylum where there was currently an emphasis on moral treatment and nonrestraint in the management of patients. He praised what he saw there. He was also impressed by the morale and good treatment of women factory workers in New England.

Dix, Dorothea Lynde (1802-1887). A schoolteacher from Boston, Miss Dix began, in middle life, to make a crusade of reforming the care of mental patients. She appeared in the Federal Congress and in various state legislatures to advocate the abolition of the town-country form of care of mental patients in favor of state hospitals. Probably over 25 different state mental hospitals owe their origin to her lobbying efforts.

Dugdale, Richard (1841-1883). A self-styled social investigator who published the popular book on the Jukes Family. He described an extensive family network of social dropouts that, he alleged, inherited their antisocial dispositions from a particular ancestor. The eugenics movement was getting under way at the time, and the sort of dramatic propaganda promoted by Dugdale did a great deal to increase its popularity. The sterilization laws of the early twentieth century were a direct outgrowth of this movement.

Durkheim, Emile (1858-1917). A French sociologist known as the founder of sociological methodology. He relied heavily on ethnographic data and statistics to strengthen his conclusions. An advocate of the collectivist school, he saw society as the sum total of the individual minds of its members. He was especially interested in the moral factors affecting labor distribution. Suicide was seen as a significant indicator of sociological trends, being indicative of the state of religious and political integration of a society.

Ebbinghaus, Herman (1850-1909). A German psychologist who, like Wundt but unlike Brentano, placed primary emphasis on laboratory experimentation as the source of psychological data. His study of learning and memory led to his formulation of the curve of retention, which sought to define the history of memory. He developed sentence completion tests and nonsense syllable tests to study memory.

Eddy, Mary Baker (1821-1910). As an outgrowth of the nineteenth century pseudosciences, her founding of the Christian Science movement has had no equal. She herself was prompted to develop her concepts of mind over matter after a mesmerist "cured" her of an hysterical paralysis.

Emerson, Ralph Waldo (1803-1882). Writer and philosopher from Harvard and founder of a philosophical principle he called transcendentalism. His essays portrayed his concepts of human nature, which were founded on a simplistic somewhat back-to-nature approach to the "good life." With Thoreau and others, a unique type of American intellectualism grew up in nineteenth century New England.

Empedocles (495-435 B.C.). The Greek founder of the Sicilian school of medicine, but also a poet, philosopher, and political reformer. He postulated an elementary form of biological evolution wherein only the fittest survive to perpetuate the race. Thinking is a function of the blood circulation, taking its essence from the pneuma (oxygen?), which it gets from the lungs and is conveyed to all parts of the body to perform action as a result of the action of the heart. Heat is an undesirable result that tends to accumulate in the body with age and eventually causes death.

Epicetus of Hierapolis (ca. 100 A.D.). A Greek Stoic philosopher who taught in Rome, then in Epirus following expulsion of all philosophers from the capital. He described the goal of happiness and serenity as coming from intellectual attainments, through a sense of freedom. All troubles are to be seen as trivial and external, while true satisfaction comes from internalized wisdom that is immune from external forces.

Esquirol, Jean Etienne (1772-1840). The successor to Pinel and France's second pioneer psychiatrist. He was especially influential through his extensive teaching of psychiatry to medical students; students from many countries came to France to study with him. His textbook became a model widely followed by other writers. He emphasized moral treatment in the management of patients.

Falret, J., and Lasegue, C. H. (nineteenth century). Two French psychiatrists who were the first to describe the clinical phenomenon they called folie à deux. Still a term in good repute, it refers to the occurrence of very similar states of psychosis in two closely related people: husband and wife, two siblings, or parent and child.

Fechner, G. T. (1801-1887). An early German experimental psychologist-physiologist. He is known as the founder of psychophysics. He expected to be able to explain all mental phenomena from the findings of sensory physics. Fechner's law states that the strength of a sensation is proportional to the log of the stimulus.

Freud, Anna (1895-   ). Sigmund Freud's daughter who studiously took up where she believed her father left off—in the study of ego psychology, especially in children. She has spent most of her career as the foremost child psychoanalyst of England and a rival of Melanie Klein there. Her rather precise listing of the defense mechanisms that she sees as the fundamental attribute of characteriological traits is well known.

Freud, Sigmund (1856-1939). A Viennese neurologist who studied under Charcot, then developed his own theories of neurosis on the basis of his experience in treating hysterics with hypnosis. His psychoanalytic theory of neurosis and treatment technique became the center of a widespread movement that reached into many fields of thought, largely as an intellectual reaction against Victorian social practices. He first saw the process of treatment as one of catharsis. As he found that the psychological problems of his patients were more complex than he first thought, he developed the concept of the unconscious. This led to the oedipal theory of neurosis. Therapy became the resolution of the transference problem. Many of his students broke away to found rival schools of thought.

Gall, Franz (1758-1828). A German neuroanatomist who developed a theory of behavior that came to be known as phrenology. His student, Spurzheim, was mostly responsible for developing the theory into a widespread movement and pseudoscience. The theory was based on the concept that each type of mental activity takes place in a certain part of the brain and that that part might then become either large or small depending on how well-developed the faculty is. These varying-sized parts of the brain are represented by hills and valleys on the external skull, which can be studied in order to assess the individual's personality.

Galton, (Sir) Francis (1822-1911). A cousin of Charles Darwin who used this relationship as authority to develop a pseudoscience of genetics. He was principally interested in hereditary genius and did much to popularize the new eugenics movement. He was perhaps the first to use the questionnaire method for surveying psychological questions.

Goddard, Henry (1866-1957). A psychologist and director of the Training School for Feeble-Minded Children at Vineland, New Jersey (1906-1918). He conducted a study that he reported in a highly popular book, *The Kallikak Family,* which purported to substantiate the hereditary nature of mental retardation. This book, with a similar one on the Jukes family, provided justification for widely held theories on the hereditary nature of mental and social problems. Although subsequently shown to be filled with many scientific inaccuracies and unwarranted assumptions, these theories continue to prevail in many circles.

Gray, John (1825-1886). Superintendent of the state mental hospital at Utica, New York, and long-time editor of the official journal of the present American Psychiatric Association. In a period when a hot dispute raged among psychiatrists over the issue of organic versus psychological causes of mental disorder, Gray used his influence as editor to favor the organic theory. During his editorship there were few, if any, favorable articles on the psychological side of the controversy. Ultimately, by the turn of the twentieth century, all state mental hospitals acquired a reputation as havens of the organic theory and of the use of organic treatment measures.

Griesinger, Wilhelm (1817-1868). Probably the first full-time psychiatrist in Germany, and author of a textbook that served as a model followed by subsequent writers. He strongly endorsed the theory of organic cause of mental disorder, unlike Esquirol in France. He saw depression as the early sign of psychosis. He tended to minimize, contradictorily, the difference between normal and psychotic people, believing there was a little madness in everyone.

Haeckel, Ernst Heinrich (1834-1919). A German biologist who was Professor of Comparative Anatomy at Jena and who was noted for his introduction of Darwin's concepts of evolution into Germany. He attempted to apply the evolutionary doctrine to religion, to philosophy, and to psychological concepts. He made much of the ancient controversy of the body–soul dichotomy and applied rather old and unbiological theological concepts to the discussion.

Hall, Stanley (1844-1924). A psychologist who pioneered in the study of children and established the first journal in the field (*Pedagogical Seminary,* 1891). He also established the first laboratory in psychology at Johns Hopkins University, then became the first president of Clark University. He is also noted for having induced Freud to make his only trip to the United States to give a series of lectures (1909). He refined the questionnaire method of making psychological investigations. His concept of childhood development was that of a process of civilizing an essentially savage being, with adolescence described as a state midway between the uncivilized and civilized.

Hartley, David (1705-1757). An English physician who published *Observations on Man* (1749). This work provided the foundation for the association school of thought in psychology. He described mental activity as vibratory action. This was used to account for the transmission of neural impulses, in place of the prevailing notion of animal spirits moving through hollow tubes. He accounted for memory on the basis of events with pleasurable or unpleasurable emotions.

Haslam, John (1764-1844). An apothecary to Bethlehem Asylum in London who defended the cruel methods used there to manage mental patients. His defense countered the attempts being made at the time to bring about reform. Few improvements were made at Bethlehem for another hundred years. Meanwhile, other hospitals were opened where more humane methods were employed, a notable example being the Retreat at York, launched by the Quakers under the leadership of William Tuke. William Battie also founded another hospital, St. Luke's, after he failed, as a member of the Board of Governors, to improve conditions at Bethlehem.

Heidenhain, Rudolf (1835-1897). A respected physiologist and Professor of Physiology at the University of Breslau. He reactivated interest in Anton Mesmer's animal magnetism and sought to explain the phenomenon of hypnotism on physiological grounds. His farfetched theories were based on central nervous system physiology.

Herbart, Johann Friedrich (1776-1841). A German philosopher who launched the study of educational psychology. He founded his science on metaphysics and mathematics rather than on physiology.

Hippocrates (ca. 460-370 B.C.). A Greek physician who is given the credit for establishing an ethical and professional base for medical practice. He wrote extensively on anatomy and injuries. He sought, particularly, to demystify medicine, an example of these efforts being his attack on prevailing concepts of epilepsy as the sacred disease.

Hobbes, Thomas (1588-1679). An English philosopher who was much involved in the politics of his time. He supported the Stuarts against Cromwell and was in exile with them in France. He described man as essentially a savage and bestial animal who becomes forced by circumstances into collaborative efforts for mutual protection. His psychology became the prototype of Locke's. He justified political tyranny as long as rulers serve the people, but also justified revolution when they failed to serve the people.

Horney, Karen (1885-1952). A Hungarian psychiatrist who started in Germany as a loyal follower of the freudian doctrine, but then came to the United States. She broke away from the New York Psychoanalytic Institute when she found that conventional, or orthodox, psychoanalysis produced little therapeutic results. She then became the leader of a group known as the Horney school; which advocated a theory of behavior founded on the interaction of the individual with his culture, instead of the freudian emphasis on instinctual drives. She classified people according to whether they tend to move toward, away from, or against others. She wrote a number of popular books, such as *Neurotic Personality of Our Time*.

Howard, John (1726-1790). The English prison reformer. After succeeding to the post of Sheriff of Bedfordshire, Howard began a series of inspections of the prisons of England and Ireland, then later the continent. The appalling conditions he found prompted him to publish a book, *The State of the Prisons* (1777), meant for the attention of the British Parliament, that described the conditions he found in each one of the prisons. He accompanied the descriptions with a list of recommendations for reform. These were widely admired and discussed, but seldom implemented. He died in Russia after contracting "jail fever" during one of his inspection tours.

Huarte, Juan (1530-1589). A Spanish physician who wrote what might be considered the first modern book on psychology, *Probe of the Mind*. He was perhaps the first to suggest the use of vocational testing in planning the careers of young people. His book was widely translated.

Hull, Clark (1884-1952). An American psychologist who contributed widely to the subjects of aptitude testing, statistics, hypnosis, and reinforcement. In the behavioral tradition, he saw learning as a continuum of the stimulus-response experience.

Hume, David (1711-1776). A Scottish philosopher who brought a healthy skepticism to bear on the views of Locke and Berkeley. Man only knows that of which he is conscious, and his ideas are often imperfect copies of his sensations. He devised laws of association of ideas in which resemblance or coexistence or cause and effect relationships bring about combinations of ideas into more complex ones (*An Enquiry Concerning Human Understanding*, 1748).

Jackson, Hughling (1834-1911). A British neurologist noted for his criticisms of the prevailing psychiatric practices. To a considerable extent his attacks were well meaning and constructive.

Jaensch, Eric (1883-1940). A German psychologist who developed categories of personality on the basis of the introvert-extrovert mix of characteristics. He also studied imagery and particularly eidetic imagery.

James, William (1842-1910). The founder of psychology at Harvard University, who began his career as a physician and then became a philosopher. His textbook *Principles of Psychology* was widely used in the United States. He was not an experimentalist, but brought experimental psychologists to Harvard University from Germany. He understood mental functions in terms of their survival value.

Janet, Pierre (1859-1947). A leading French psychiatrist whose career and contributions closely paralleled Freud's, in spite of the fact that the two considered themselves in marked opposition to each other. Like Freud, Janet studied the use of hypnotism in treating hysteria under Charcot and then went on to develop his own theories. He placed primary emphasis on l'idee fixé, or obsessive ideas, and a life energy that tend to build up states of tension demanding release. He conceived of a subconscious in which dissociated thinking takes place to yield psychological problems. He saw most neurotic states as either hysteria or psychasthenia, the latter being indistinguishable from obsessive-compulsive neurosis. The hysteric hides conflicts from consciousness while the other faces them indecisively.

Johnson, Samuel (1696-1772). An American clergyman (not the British lexicographer) and president of King's (later Columbia) College. He wrote a textbook on psychology, which he called pneumatology, that covered philosophy, ethics, pedagogy, and child development.

Jones, Ernest (1879-1958). An English psychiatrist who was largely responsible for introducing Freud's concepts into England and for translating many of Freud's writings into English. He was also responsible for moving Freud to England during the Nazi regime in Austria. He expanded some of Freud's ideas, adding the concept of repetition compulsion, by which he meant the tendency of neurotics to repeat the same mistakes in life (for example, the same kind of unhappy marriages). He and Freud were heavily influenced toward a pessimistic view of human behavior after what

they considered the uncivilized behavior of Europe during World War I.

Jung, Carl (1875-1961). An early follower of Freud who, like Adler, broke away from the classical psychoanalytic school to establish his own opposing school in Switzerland. He postulated a fundamental racial unconsciousness consisting of an inherited repository of racial memories shared by other people in the culture. This is made manifest in the form of fantasies, dreams, and myths. His teachings became increasingly more mystical as time went on, and his appeal tended to be directed more toward writers and artists than to fellow psychiatrists. The American writer, Philip Wylie, was one of these.

Kallmann, Franz (1891-1965). Trained in Germany, Kallmann spent the latter part of his life in the United States. He made a lifelong study of the incidence of schizophrenia in twins in the New York state hospital system. He used his findings to substantiate the hereditary theory of schizophrenia.

Katz, David (1884-1953). A student of G. E. Muller, Katz established a psychological laboratory at the University of Gottingen where he pursued the work on color vision started by Ewald Hering. He also studied other sensory modes, including hunger and the proprioceptive sense.

Kirkbride, Thomas (1809-1883). One of the 13 original founders of the American Psychiatric Association and superintendent of the Pennsylvania Hospital (Philadelphia). He published a book describing in detail how to design and manage mental hospitals, as a result of which between 25 and 30 kirkbride hospitals have been built.

Koffka, Kurt (1886-1941). With Wertheimer and Kohler, Koffka founded the gestalt school at the University of Berlin and then moved to the United States.

Kohler, Wolfgang (1887-1967). Founded the gestalt school of psychology with Wertheimer and Koffka at the University of Berlin, then later moved to the United States.

Kraepelin, Emil (1856-1926). A prominent psychiatrist of Germany who wrote a textbook that passed through 8 editions. He was the first to collect a group of previously separate diagnostic categories together under the one dementia praecox, later termed schizophrenia by Bleuler. He also grouped two previous independent categories together under manic-depressive psychosis. Known for clinical descriptions and classification schemes, but advocating the organic viewpoint on causation, his type of psychiatry has been often referred to as synonymous with descriptive and obsolete forms.

Kramer, Heinrich, and Sprenger, James (fifteenth century). Two monks who provided the rationale for the execution of witches during the Inquisition in a publication that also provided means of testing whether or not someone was a witch.

Kretschmer, Ernst (1888-1964). A German physician who studied body types and developed a theory that psychiatric syndromes were associated with particular configurations. Schizophrenia, for instance, was said to be associated with the asthenic body type, and manic-depressive psychosis was associated with the pyknic type.

Kulpe, Oswald (1862-1915). A German psychologist who studied the thinking process itself, unlike the other German experimentalists. He founded the Wurzburg school, famous for its studies on imageless thought.

Leibnitz, Gottfried Wilhelm (1646-1716). The German philosopher and mathematician who, with Newton, invented the calculus. He subscribed to a concept that has been known as psychological parallelism, referring to a dual and harmonious but independent pair of mechanisms, one making up the soul and the other the body. The harmony governing their mutual operation is a preexisting one established by God *(New Essays on Human Understanding).*

Lewin, Kurt (1890-1947). Left the University of Berlin to come to the United States and more or less followed the gestalt school of thought. He explored the question of personality measurement and developed the concept of life space. His field theory begins with the individual's concept of reality, which is based on his relations to his environment and the space he occupies in it.

Locke, John (1632-1704). An English philosopher who founded what came to be known as the empirical school in psychology as well as philosophy. Opposing Descartes' view on the innateness of ideas, he postulated that the child is born with a "clean slate" on which all subsequently acquired knowledge comes from experience. This concept places a special emphasis on the importance of sensation as the source of knowledge. Ideas are generalizations formed from accumulated perceptions *(Essay Concerning Human Understanding,* 1890).

Lombroso, Cesare (1835-1909). An Italian psychiatrist who came to be known as the father of criminal anthropology. He explained criminal behavior on the basis of degeneration and identified stigmata obstensibly as being of constitutional origin and recognizable in anatomical or physiognomical features. His theories were used to support the popular antipsychological eugenics movement of the turn of the nineteenth century. Some of his publications include *The Delinquent Man, The Female Offender, The Legal Psychiatric Evaluation,* and *The Man of Genius.*

Lotze, Hermann (1824-1881). A German philosopher and physician who became Professor of Philosophy at Gottingen in 1844, at a remarkably young age. He sought to establish a physiological basis for psychology, especially through the study of the role of the senses in learning and memory. He wrote a textbook in medical psychology that was widely imitated by later writers.

Luca, Costa Ben (twelfth century). An Arab physician from Syria who studied and taught at the University of Toledo in Spain. He translated many Arabic treatises into Latin, making them available to Western European scholars. He advanced a mechanistic theory of the human thinking process that was widely accepted and that later was echoed by the theories of Descartes.

McDougall, William (1871-1938). The American psychologist who became the leader of the behavioral school. He studied at Oxford University and at Cambridge University, then replaced William James at Harvard University. He emphasized the importance of goal seeking in behavior (hormic psychology) and postulated seven instincts that control behavior and that have corresponding emotional reactions. The school of thought he founded became increasingly mechanistic, more concerned with animal than with human behavior, and tended to be discredited as advances were made in the opposing schools that placed less stress on instinct and more on learning. In later life, McDougall became quite mystical, which further discredited his work.

McNaughten, Daniel (ca. 1840). A Scotsman who mistakenly murdered the secretary of Sir Robert Peel, head of the London police, in response to a delusion that blamed Peel for his personal difficulties. At his trial, the court recognized his obvious psychotic state and referred the matter to the House of Lords. From this came the McNaughten Rule, which has provided courts of England and the United States with a test used in the insanity defense ever since 1843. According to the test, a person can be held innocent by reason of insanity if it can be shown that he did not know the nature of his act or could not tell right from wrong.

Maimonides, Moses (1135-1204). Born in Spain, this rabbinical scholar became a physician who practiced and taught in the Arab cultural centers in the Middle East. His writings, *Guide for the Perplexed,* sought to clarify many common religious and superstitious mysteries of the times. His *Diseases of the Soul* offered his explanations for what might be called mental health.

Maudsley, Henry (1835-1918). A highly respected late nineteenth-century English psychiatrist who left his fortune to found the present Maudsley Bethlehem Hospital. He was influenced by the popular evolutionary theories and saw psychotic states as failures in adaptation, "the result and evidence of discord between the man and his surroundings." He stressed the role of responsibility in the development of character, and failures in this area were equated with clinical psychiatric problems.

Mesmer, Anton (1734-1815). An Austrian physician who was made unwelcome in Austria and established a lively and controversial center in Paris. He used animal magnetism (hypnotism) to bring about dramatic changes in people who later were termed hysterics. He attributed the changes to energy coming from the cosmos. Throughout the nineteenth century, studies of his methods were widely debated, leading eventually to the careful work of Braid, Charcot, Freud, and Janet.

Meyer, Adolf (1866-1950). A Swiss pathologist who became the first head of the Department of Psychiatry at Johns Hopkins University. Although his students in emulating him have tended to follow the organic approach to treatment, Meyer himself belonged to a much more functional school of thought. He saw mental conditions as failures in adaptation. His students were taught to take elaborate life histories of their patients.

Mill, John Stuart (1806-1873). An English philosopher and economist who applied his father's (James) concepts of association to a mechanistic view of behavior. Learning proceeds from sensations to simple ideas and from simple ideas to complex ideas. He used naive notions of mental chemistry to explain mental mechanics.

Mitchel, Weir (1830-1914). A leader in nineteenth-century American neurological circles who made a fortune operating a private psychiatric hospital that catered to the whims of the neurotic rich. He advo-

cated long periods of rest (the rest cure) and offered explanations of psychiatric problems on the grounds of overwork and nervous exhaustion. Much of today's folklore about nervous breakdowns and so on stems from his concepts. In 1871 he published *Wear and Tear,* which helped popularize his theory.

Monro, John (1715-1791). An English physician and the first of five generations of psychiatrists in his family who dominated English psychiatry for years. William Battie attacked his advocacy of the methods of treatment used at Bethlehem Hospital. A major point of controversy was Monro's refusal to permit medical students to study in the hospital.

de Montaigne, Michel (1533-1592). Formerly a magistrate and mayor of Bordeaux, France, de Montaigne retired to write his well-known *Essays.* Among many other subjects, he discoursed on mental health, advocating moderation in all things and blaming human troubles on behavioral excesses.

Morison, (Sir) Alexander (1779-1866). The first teacher to introduce a series of lectures in psychiatry to medical students at the University of Edinburgh. His experience, however, was limited to that of a hospital inspector. He became captivated by the pseudoscience of physiognomy of the insane, which grew out of phrenology.

Muller, Georg (1850-1934). A German psychologist at the University of Gottingen. He experimented with memory, vision, and psychophysics and attracted many students. He developed and systematized psychophysical methodology.

Muller, Johannes (1801-1858). A German physiologist who developed the concept of the specific energy of nerves. This refers to the idea that awareness of a particular sensory stimulus is caused by the signal conducted by a particular nerve, not by the nature of the stimulus itself.

Munsterberg, Otto (1863-1916). Born and educated in Germany and brought to the United States by William James to teach experimental psychology at Harvard University. He became interested in the application of psychology to law and industrial relations. He was often criticized for his popular writings. He was also a physician and practiced psychotherapy in addition to his academic work.

Neitzsche, Friedrich (1844-1900). A German philosopher who taught at Basel. Although close to the more romantic philosophy of Wagner and Shopenhauer, he maintained a classic orientation. He became especially known for his advocacy of the rule of the weak by the strong, and this became a central theme of Nazi ideology. He died in a psychotic state.

Paracelsus, or Theophrastus von Mohenheim (1493-1541). A physician who sought to upset the obsolete notions in medicine that had been passed down from Galen. In his *Diseases that Deprive Man of His Reason* he sought a natural instead of a superstitious explanation for psychotic behavior. He ascribed much of psychosis to heredity. Mere imagination, on the other hand, might be at the root of other types.

Pargeter, William (1760-1810). One of the first physicians to specialize in psychiatry (England), his writings were widely quoted. In the tradition of William Battie and Samuel Tuke, he advocated the need to draw a distinction between the management and the medical treatment of psychiatric patients. He laid the groundwork for a systematic psychotherapy by emphasizing the need to instill in the patient a sense of trust and confidence in the physician. He attacked the drastic measures then in common use in mental hospitals.

Pavlov, Ivan (1849-1936). The first Russian to be granted a Nobel Prize, Pavlov studied the physiology of animals and developed the original concepts of the conditioned reflex. This became the basis for widespread theories of learning that look upon the process as a match between stimulus and response, with little attention to the nature of the intervening thinking process.

Pinel, Phillippe (1745-1826). The famous French reformer known for his bringing a new and humane type of care to the management of mental patients. He was influenced by the Tukes and the York Retreat as well as the eighteenth-century rationalists (Voltaire, Diderot, and so on). His concept of the cause of mental disorders was based on organic lesions, but his treatment approach was along the lines of moral treatment.

Plato (429-348 B.C.). The Greek philosopher who influenced science, religion, and philosophy for the next thousand or more years. He taught at the "Academy" for fifty years and left many writings. His famous doctrine of the dualism of mind and body became the subject for debate for centuries. The soul has three major components (reason, courage, desire), each located in a different part of the body and occurring in a variety of different ratios as far as dominance is concerned, thus accounting for the differences in personalities. He saw sensation as a major source of misinformation; therefore he stressed the importance of introspec-

tion and logical reasoning. All knowledge has been laid down in the human mind at birth and only waits to be discovered, not implanted.

Preyer, Wilhelm (1842-1897). This German psychologist of dubious qualifications is remembered for a diary he kept that described the details of development of his son. This became a prototype for the more sophisticated developmental studies of Sesell and Janet.

Prince, Morton (1854-1929). A leading psychiatrist at Harvard University at the turn of the century and founder of the Harvard Psychological Clinic. He may or may not have been influenced by Freud, but many of his writings parallel the latter's theories, especially in the matter of stressing the importance of an unconscious.

Pritchard, James (1786-1848). An English psychiatrist noted for his theories of criminal behavior. He postulated that a kind of moral insanity by which he meant that some people might be quite rational except in moral matters and that this leads to criminal behavior. The term psychopath came from his concepts.

Ray, Isaac (1807-1891). One of the 13 original founders of the American Psychiatric Association and superintendent of the state mental hospital in Maine. He published a book, *Mental Hygiene* (1863), which in turn has been largely replaced by drug treatment by those treatment centers that advocate organic methods.

Schopenhauer, Arthur (1788-1860). A German philosopher known for the pessimistic theme of his writings. He probably influenced Freud. He presented a concept of conflict as a fundamental fact of life, the resolutions of which lead to various difficulties, compromises, and sacrifices.

Scot, Reginald (ca. 1538-1599). A magistrate in Scotland who contributed to the literature on witchcraft during the period of the Inquisition, thus adding a Protestant support for the basic validity of witchcraft. He attacked the prevailing practice of torturing alleged witches, and the criticism that this aroused led, among other things, to a support of the practice by King James I.

Seguin, Edouard (1812-1880). A French physician who spent most of his career in New York state institutions for the retarded. His textbook on idiocy became a classic. He advocated the physiological method of treatment, which was noteworthy mostly for its optimism.

Skinner, Burrhus F. (1904-   ). A Harvard University psychologist who has developed concepts of learning and teaching based on conditioned reflex psychology. Essentially oriented to the stimulus and the response, rather than to the internal thinking process, and getting most of its information from laboratory animals, the skinnerian concepts have provided a rationale for much of current psychological experimentation. Critics of the method, however, see little justification for extrapolating findings to the human being.

Smith, Adam (1723-1790). A pioneer English economist who developed theories of industrial economy on his concepts of human behavior. He stressed the need, in industry, of a subdivision of responsibility and labor. His *Wealth of Nations* strongly influenced subsequent economic theorizing.

Soranus of Ephesus, and Aurelianus, Caelius (ca. 500 A.D.). Soranus was a physician of Alexander who wrote extensively on medical subjects, and Aurelianus was another physician who translated his works from Greek into Latin, adding some of his own contributions. He discussed madness, dividing it into several types, including mania and melancholia. The former, for instance, he described as a defect in reasoning.

Spencer, Herbert (1820-1903). An English philosopher who had a substantial influence on the development of psychology. His *Principles of Psychology* appeared in 1855 and was used as a foundation for William James' efforts in the same direction. He developed a kind of evolutionary theory of adaptation before Darwin's theory was published.

de Spinoza, Benedictus (1632-1677). A Jewish philosopher in Holland who earned his living as a lens grinder. His teachings were based on a kind of mental health concept with the goal of peace of mind in the presence of turbulence and controversy. He advocated the use of the creative powers of thinking as a means of finding inner satisfactions. The present concept of being philosophical—that is, calm in the presence of conflict—is an outgrowth of his teachings.

Spranger, Eduard (1882-1963). A philosopher at the University of Berlin who developed concepts of character based on 6 basic human goals: theoretical, esthetic, economic, religious, social, and managerial.

Spurzheim, Johann (1776-1832). A German physician who was largely responsible for popularizing the pseudoscience of phrenology, although Franz Gall originated the early concepts. In spite of the flimsiness of the theory and the irrelevance of the technique, the practice of attaching individualized

significance to each person's character had a great impact on the birth of systematic psychotherapy. It has been said that no other single school of thought in psychology has enjoyed as wide a following as did phrenology.

Stekel, Wilhelm (1860-1940). A German psychiatrist who was once a loyal follower of Freud but who broke away from the orthodox psychoanalytic position. He surpassed Freud in finding universal symbolism, all having sexual meanings.

Stern, Wilhelm (1871-1938). A German psychologist who attempted to bridge the chasm then existing between laboratory psychology and introspection psychology. His personalistic psychology emphasized the person in which the thinking or behavior is being studied.

Stewart, Dugald (1753-1828). A Scottish philosopher at the University of Edinburgh who was a leader in the prevailing controversy over the issue of physiological versus psychological explanations of psychosis. He sided with the psychological view and had a marked influence on psychiatric thinking of his time. He referred to emotions as contagious communications.

Stuart, James (James I of England, 1566-1625). The controversy raging over the validity of witchcraft prompted the king to add his influence in support of the idea of witchcraft. He wrote *Demonologie, in Forme of a Dialogue,* which sought to discredit the notions of Reginald Scot and Johann Weyer, who explained the behavior of alleged witches on psychological grounds.

Stumpf, Carl (1848-1936). An experimental psychologist who taught and worked at several German universities. He opposed the trend of psychology of his time, especially as represented by Wundt and Ebbinghaus. He studied language and music and became a founder of the functional school. This added a new perspective to the limitations imposed by phenomenological studies.

Sullivan, Harry Stack (1892-1949). An American psychoanalyst who was trained by Freud but founded a countermovement in the United States, known as the cultural school. He emphasized the importance of cultural influences in the development of personality and psychiatric problems and saw the mother as a key figure, the agent of culture. He participated more actively in therapy than did the orthodox analysts. The William Alanson White Psychiatric Foundation was founded by his students as a training center in the Baltimore-Washington area.

Sydenham, Thomas (1624-1689). A highly respected English physician who wrote on many medical subjects. He influenced and was influenced by his friend John Locke, the philosopher and founder of empirical psychology. He established the medical principle that hysteria was a diagnostic term applied to conditions in which the patient offered complaints simulating other conditions, but in which no evidence of disease existed. He attributed the state to a disturbance of the mind. Heretofore, only grossly pathological psychological states were included in the category of psychiatric disturbances.

Terman, Lewis (1877-1956). An American psychologist who sought to relate the intelligence levels of people to their behavior and social outcome. He taught at Clark University when it was the center of psychological ferment, under the leadership of Stanley Hall.

Thorndike, Edward (1876-1949). A student of William James at Harvard University and an early pioneer in the psychology of education. He was strongly influenced by Wundt's concepts of association in learning in animals, leading to an edict widely followed in educational circles that forbade exposing students to any pleasant experience in making errors. Learning is largely a trial-and-error process, in which what is remembered is that which is pleasant.

Tichener, E. B. (1867-1927). An American psychologist who studied under Wundt in Germany and established an experimental laboratory at Cornell University. He defended the structural viewpoint, which stressed the importance of individual experience in learning. The task of psychology is to answer the "what, how, and why" of mental processes. Consciousness has three levels: sensation, images, and emotion.

Tolman, Edward (1886-1959). An American psychologist who departed from the more common stimulus-response type of psychology to combine behavioralism with gestalt concepts. He developed a more holistic view of behavior than the molecular view of the conditioned reflex school by devoting more attention to the inner thinking process.

Tuke, Daniel Hack (1827-1895). A great grandson of William Tuke, a psychiatrist and leader of the progressive elements in nineteenth-century England. His book *Influence of the Mind upon the Body* (1872) was one of the early works on psychosomatic medicine.

Tuke, Samuel (1784-1857). A grandson of William Tuke who, like other descendants of the latter, was active in the operation of the York Retreat, a private psychiatric hospital founded by the Quakers under William Tuke's leadership. In 1813, Samuel published a book on *The Retreat at York,* which described the philosophy of moral treatment and the mode of management of the Retreat. This book was widely followed in other places (such as the Hartford Retreat in Connecticut) as a guide in mental hospital construction and management.

Tuke, William (ca. 1730). A Quaker merchant of York, England, who tried but failed to reform conditions in the York Asylum, and so founded the York Retreat (1792), which became a model of the moral treatment philosophy. Many physicians (including Pinel in France) and hospitals throughout the world were influenced by this model. A number of his descendents became prominent English psychiatrists.

Tylor, E. B. (1832-1917). An English anthropologist who had a great influence on subsequent anthropological studies. He described several primitive cultures and portrayed them as stages in the development of civilization, seeing a kind of inevitability and lawfulness in the evolution.

Vives, Juan Luis (1492-1540). A Renaissance humanist who deserves credit as the forerunner of many modern concepts in psychology. His book *De Anima et Vita* (1538) stressed the importance of understanding human thinking in the fields of education, science, philosophy, and politics. His contribution to knowledge of the association of ideas stimulated much of subsequent psychological investigation.

Voltaire, Francois Marie Arouet de (1694-1778). A French philosopher and leader of eighteenth-century rationalism. He influenced Phillippe Pinel, who became France's leading pioneer in psychiatry. He described a way in which the passions could be both influenced by and, in turn, influence the physiology of the body. This thinking provided a basis for psychosomatic theorizing, launched by Cabanis at the turn of the nineteenth century.

von Feuchtsleben, (Baron) Ernest (1806-1849). An Austrian nobleman who was the first physician in Austria to make psychiatry his career. He wrote a textbook in psychiatry that was imitated by other German writers. He tended to follow the teachings of Pinel and Esquirol, taking a rather soft and humane approach to the management of psychiatric patients. People are motivated, primarily, by pleasure and displeasure, yielding either love or hatred. A major aim of therapy is to offer to the patient a model of affection to assist in changing habitual behaviors founded on hatred.

von Hartmann, Eduard (1843-1906). A German psychiatrist who advanced a viewpoint about the psychological nature of mental disorders that was derived from Shopenhauer's philosophy and that was somewhat parallel to Freud's later psychoanalytic theories. He stressed the dominant influence of instinctual forces (vital energy) needed for survival and saw conscious thinking as primarily used to rationalize behavior rather than to plan it.

von Helmholtz, Hermann (1821-1894). A German physiologist who studied the sense of hearing, vision, and speed of reaction time. He was responsible for establishing the early methods used in experimental psychology, which were really studies in physiology.

von Wolff, Christian (1679-1754). Perhaps the one deserving credit for popularizing the term psychology in his treatises *Psychologia Empirica* and *Psychologia Rationalis.* He was a German philosopher and mathematician, well known in his day.

Watson, John (1878-1958). A psychologist at the University of Chicago who became the principal spokesman for the behavioralist school. His concept of the objective viewpoint in psychology was that of observing external behavior without regard to the inner psychological processes. He obtained his information from animal experiments, but freely extrapolated to human beings.

Weber, E. H. (1795-1878). A physiologist at the University of Leipzig in Germany who first experimented with the sense of touch. He measured the degree of sensitivity of the sense, establishing the methodology used later in sensory psychology.

Wertheimer, Max (1880-1943). A psychologist at the University of Berlin who later came to the United States and who with Koffka and Kohler founded the school of gestalt psychology. The gestalists emphasized the importance of viewing the whole of each mental process, indicating that anything less would miss its significance.

Weyer, Johann (1515-1588). A German physician during the Inquisition who explained the behavior of alleged witches on grounds that would be regarded as psychiatric today. He provided lucid case histories of recognizable psychiatric conditions. His book *Delusion of Witches* attacked the practice of torturing and executing witches and became very controversial throughout Europe. He has been called the first psychiatrist of modern Europe.

White, William Alanson (1870-1937). A superintendent of St. Elizabeth's hospital for mental patients in Washington, D.C. who was perhaps the first mental hospital psychiatrist to subscribe to the freudian school. A training institute for psychoanalysis in the Baltimore-Washington area is named after him and tends to follow the teachings of Harry Stack Sullivan.

Willis, Thomas (1621-1675). A respected English physician known for his contributions to neuroanatomy. His prestige gave him influence in medicine, and he used this to advocate the common practice of torture and cruelty in the management of mental patients. He likened the behavior of the psychotic person to that of animals.

Woodworth, Robert (1869-1962). An American psychologist at Columbia University. He called his type of psychology dynamic psychology. This referred to the study of cause and effect relations in thought and action as the proper field of study for psychology. He sought to divorce himself from behavioralism and came closer to the functional school.

Wundt, Wilhelm (1832-1920). A prominent physiologist turned psychologist who was responsible for training many of the early experimental psychologists at his laboratory at Leipzig. He thought that mental processes could be explained from knowledge gained from studying the senses. He limited the scope of his psychology to immediate experiences. His rather atomistic approach dominated the field of experimental psychology for a long time, and the influence is still apparent in many laboratories.

Yerkes, Robert (1876-1956). An American anthropologist who studied primate behavior, then extrapolated his findings to human beings. He headed a group during World War I to develop a psychological screening test; the Army Alpha Test was the result.

INDEX

150

Ego strength, 59
Egocentric, 58
Egodystonic, 82
Egosyntonic, 82
Eidetic image, 59
Eigenwelt, 82
Ejaculatio deficiens, 26
Ejaculatio praecox, 26
Elaboration, 82
Electra complex, 82
Electroconvulsive therapy, 82
Electroencephalogram, 26
Electronarcosis, 82
Electronic data processing, 119
Electroshock therapy, 82
Electrosleep, 82
Elementism, 82
Ellipsis, 59
Elopement, 82
Emancipated minor, 104
Emasculation, 59
Embezzle, 104
Embololalia, 26
Emergency emotions, 82
Emerson, Ralph Waldo, 140
Emotion, 59
Empathy, 59
Empedocles, 140
Empirical philosophy, 83
Empirical psychology, 83
Emprosthotonus, 119
Enantiopathic, 59
Encephalitis, 119
Encephalitis lethargica, 26
Encephalomalacia, 119
Encephalopathy, 104
Encopresis, 26
Encounter, 59
Encounter group, 83
Endemic, 119
Endocept, 59
Endocrine gland, 119
Endocrinopathy, 119
Endogamy, 59
Endogenous, 119
Endomorph, 83
Endoplasmic reticulum, 119
Endopsychic, 59
End-pleasure, 59
Enfant terrible, 26
Engineering psychology, 104
Engram, 59
Entatic, 59
Enteroception, 59
Entropy, 119
Enuresis, 26
Environmentalism, 83
Eonism, 26
Epicetus of Hierapolis, 140
Epicureanism, 119
Epidemic, 119
Epidural hematoma, 119
Epilepsy, 26
Epileptic status, 26

Epinephrine, 83
Epinosic gain, 26
Epsilon alcoholism, 26
Erethism, 26
Ergasia, 83
Ergasiology, 83
Ergotropic dominance, 119
Ergotropy, 83
Eros, 83
Erotic, 59
Erotogenic zone, 59
Escape from reality, 59
Eschatology, 59
Escrow, 104
Esquirol, Jean Etienne, 140
Essence, 83
Esthesiometer, 115
Esthesotype, 59
Estrangement, 59
Ethnic, 119
Ethnology, 119
Ethology, 119
Etiology, 119
Eunuch, 119
Eunuchoidism, 119
Euphoria, 26
Euthanasia, 104
Euthymia, 59
Eviration, 26
Executive ego function, 59
Exhaustion psychoses, 26
Exhibitionism, 26
Existence, 83
Existential anxiety, 83
Existential crisis, 26
Existential guilt, 83
Existential psychology, 83
Existentialism, 83
Exocrine gland, 119
Exogamy, 59
Expansiveness, 26
Ex parte, 104
Expatriation, 105
Experience psychology, 105
Experimental psychology, 105
Exploitative personality, 26
Externalization, 26
Extinction, 59
Extrapyramidal effects of drugs, 83
Extrapyramidal system, 119
Extrasensory perception, 83
Extrovert, 59

F

Fabrication, 26
Factor analysis, 83
Faculty psychology, 83
Fainting, 131
Falling sickness, 131
Falret, J., 140
False confession, 27
False pregnancy, 27
False-self system, 27
False transmitter, 119

Familial, 59
Family care, 105
Family history, 105
Family stability, 59
Family therapy, 83
Fantasy, 60
Father substitute, 60
Fear, 60
Fechner, G. T., 140
Feeblemindedness, 27
Feedback, 119
Feelings, 60
Field therapy, 73
Fellatio, 27
Felony, 105
Feminine masochism, 27
Festination, 27
Fetish, 60
Fetishism, 27
Field theory, 83
Filtering, sensory, 120
First-signal system, 83
Fit, 131
Fixation, 84
Fixed point, 120
Flagellantism, 27
Flight into health, 27
Flight of ideas, 27
Floating point, 120
Flow chart, 120
Folie à deux, 27
Folk psychology, 84
Food grabbing, 27
Forensic psychiatry, 105
Forgetting, 60
Formication, 27
Fornication, 105
FORTRAN, 120
Foster family, 105
Foster parents, 105
Fraternal twins, 105
Fraud, 105
Free association, 84
Free-floating anxiety, 27
Fregeli illusion, 27
Frequency distribution, 120
Freud, Anna, 140
Freud, Sigmund, 141
Freudian, 84
Fright, 60
Frigidity, 60
Fröhlich's syndrome, 120
Frottage, 27
Frotteur, 27
Frustration, 60
Frustration tolerance, 60
Fugue, 27
Function (in statistics), 120
Functional, 84
Functional diagram, 120
Functional disorder, 60
Functional psychology, 84
Functional psychosis, 27
Fusion, 84

Modality, 87
Mode, 122
Module, 107
Modus operandi, 64
Modus vivendi, 64
Mogilalia, 64
Mogiphonia, 64
Molding, 94
Monamine oxidase (MAO), 122
Mongolism, 33
Monism, 87
Monophasia, 34
Monoplegia, 34
Monosymptomatic schizophrenia, 34
Monro, John, 145
de Montaigne, Michel, 145
Montessori system, 64
Mood, 64
Mood swings, 34
Moral masochism, 34
Moral treatment, 87
Mores, 64
Morison, (Sir) Alexander, 145
Moron, 34
Morphine, 87
Morphinism, 34
Mortido, 87
Motivation, 64
Mourning, 64
Mucous colitis, 34
Muller, Georg, 145
Muller, Johannes, 145
Multipara, 122
Multiple personality, 34
Multiple sclerosis, 122
Munsterberg, Otto, 145
Myelinoclastic, 122
Myelitis, 122
Myelopathy, 122
Myopia, 122
Myxedema, 122

N

Nalorphine, 87
Nancy school, 87
Nanism, 34
Narcissism, 64
Narcissistic neurosis, 34
Narcoanalysis, 87
Narcolepsy, 34
Narcoplexis, 87
Narcosis, 34
Narcosynthesis, 87
Narcotic, 87
Narcotism, 34
Naturopath, 107
Necromimesis, 34
Necrophilism, 34
Necropsy, 123
Necrosadism, 34
Need gratification, 88
Negative feelings, 64
Negative therapeutic reaction, 88

Negativism, 34
Negligence, 107
Nietzsche, Friedrich, 145
Neoatavism, 123
Neobehaviorism, 88
Neocortex, 123
Neofreudianism, 88
Neofreudians, 88
Neography, 34
Neolalia, 34
Neologism, 34
Neomimism, 34
Neomnesis, 64
Neophasia, 34
Neoplasm, 123
Nepenthic, 64
Nepotism, 107
Nerve impulse, 123
Nervous breakdown, 132
Neuralgia, 34
Neurasthenia, 34
Neuraxia, 123
Neuritis, 123
Neurocirculatory asthenia, 34
Neurochemical, 123
Neurochemistry, 123
Neurodermatitis, 34
Neurofibromatosis, 123
Neurohumor, 123
Neuroleptic, 88
Neurology, 107
Neuron, 123
Neuropathy, 123
Neurophysiological, 123
Neuropsychiatry, 107
Neuropsychology, 107
Neurosis, 34
Neurotic, 34
Neurotic traits, 64
Neurotigenic, 64
Neurotransmitter, 123
Neutralization, 88
Neutralizer, 88
Nexus, 64
Nictitation, 34
Night hospital, 107
Night terror, 34
Nightmare, 64
Nihilism, 88
Nihilistic, 34
Nihilistic delusions, 34
Nirvana, 132
Nirvana principle, 88
nitrous oxide, 88
Noctambulation, 34
Nodal behavior, 88
Noesis, 34
Noise, 123
Nolle pros, 107
Nomadism, 34
Nomenclature, 107
Nomothetic psychology, 88
Non compos mentis, 107

Non suit, 107
Non vult, 107
Nonlinear trends, 123
Nonreporting, 88
Nonsupport, 107
Nonverbal communication, 64
Noogenic neurosis, 88
Noopsyche, 88
Noradrenaline, 88
Norepinephrine, 88
Norm, 123
Normal distribution, 123
Normative, 64
Nosography, 123
Nosology, 123
Nostomania, 34
Not me, 88
Noumenon, 88
Null hypothesis, 123
Numerical control, 123
Nursery school, 107
Nyctalopia, 34
Nymphomania, 34
Nystagmus, 34

O

Obesity, 123
Object choice, 88
Object love, 88
Objective anxiety, 88
Objective psychology, 88
Object-sorting test, 35
Oblativity, 64
Obnubilation, 35
Obscenity, 132
Obscurantism, 64
Obsession, 35
Obsessive behavior, 88
Obsessive character, 35
Obsessive-compulsive, 35
Obstruction, 35
Occult, 132
Occultism, 132
Occupation neurosis, 35
Occupational psychiatry, 107
Occupational therapy, 108
Oceanic feelings, 35
Octopamine, 123
Oculogyric crisis, 35
Odontoprisis, 35
Oedipal complex, 88
Oedipal theory, 89
Old age benefits, 108
Olfaction, 64
Olfactory agnosia, 64
Olfactory seizure, 35
Oligophrenia, 35
Omnipotence, 35
Onanism, 35
Oneiorphrenia, 35
Oneiroid, 35
Oneirology, 89
One-trial learning, 64